"The disability benefits system is a result of decades of campc [KU-347-710] *Those benefits are under attack as never before as the Government targets them in its quest to reduce the welfare state. The latest is the plan to abolish the Employment and Support Allowance [ESA] on the grounds that this will encourage disabled people to seek work. Motivation is not the problem but the loss of ESA will impose such financial hardship on many that they will be unable to afford to seek work.*

Government is entitled to ensure that benefits are given to those with a genuine entitlement and to assess people. But the process must be professional and honest. In this book Mo Stewart peels back the layers of deception, and the confused thinking that underpins the destruction of social support for disabled people. She shows how an American insurance company has contributed to this as it sought to expand its market to the UK. Disabled people are expected to undergo medical assessment to claim benefits but the people conducting them seem to know little about disabled people or disability in general.

Inept assessments result in loss of benefits with money withdrawn from disabled people. Some of those assessed as fit for work died just afterwards. Others died later and some committed suicide.

This callous and cruel policy is fully supported by the UK Government, who argue they are concentrating resources at those with the greatest need but provide no evidence. Yet in doing so they are condemning disabled people to greater poverty and more limited lives.

Stewart names names. She shows where and how the policies originated. She destroys all claims that they were based on solid research. And she vividly paints a clear picture of how disabled people are the group chosen to pay for the bankers' greed and stupidity in 2008, as government slashes expenditure.

To understand what is happening and why, this is the book to read and I thank Mo Stewart for writing it."

Sir Bert Massie CBE, DL

Chair, Disability Rights Commission

2000 – 2007

"This compelling book offers an accomplished and vital expose into how welfare reform policies are continually crushing the rights of disabled people in the UK. The book is impressively up to date and concise, no mean feat considering the minefield that has been the changing policy context for disabled people in recent years. Meticulously researched, and always passionately written, Mo tells us what it is like to be on the receiving end of the harsh and cruel regime perpetuated by the government, from a different perspective. As Mo herself clearly states, "this researcher has never claimed to be an academic". The years of detailed research that forms the basis for the book build on Mo's former role as a healthcare professional. This is a huge draw to the book, as it is without the reticence that academic writing is sometimes constrained by, and offers a personal element to the book that is rarely seen.
'Cash Not Care' will make you feel angry, sad and inspired in equal measures. This is a book that needs to be widely read and talked about."

Dr Kayleigh Garthwaite
Research Associate
Centre for Health and Inequalities Research
The University of Durham

"For all those opposed to current welfare reforms, Mo Stewart has provided an invaluable service by joining the dots and revealing the shadowy connections between politicians, American private health insurance lobbyists and the Work Capability Assessment regime. Mo painstakingly goes through the evidence to show that not only are disabled people and their benefits under attack, but that the eventual aim of the Government is to completely dismantle the Welfare State. This is an essential read for those wishing to arm themselves with the arguments and facts to counter the "strivers vs. skivers" rhetoric indulged in by far too many politicians and promoted by a compliant right-wing media. Every Disabled People's Organisation should grab a copy and read it from cover to cover. Not only does it reveal why things have already occurred, it also lays out what further cuts are likely in the near future."

Bill Scott
Director of Policy, Inclusion Scotland
~ a national network of Scottish Disabled People's Organisations

"The research undertaken is thorough and detailed making the conclusions all the more disquieting. Many of the policies, attitudes and ideologies of the UK Government revealed in 'Cash Not Care' will come as a shock to many people, but I feel works of this nature are essential in order to challenge the policies of the government of a supposed social democracy.

The layout of the book is very clear and concise, making it accessible to most readers and the stand alone nature of the chapters make 'Cash Not Care' a readily accessible reference work. Given the nature of the subject matter, 'Cash Not Care' is a prime candidate for a version in Braille and compatibility with screen readers.

To summarise, 'Cash Not Care' is an excellent testament to the culmination of extensive and rigorous research and groundwork and is a must read for anyone engaged in disability studies or research. Given the social interactive nature of disability most people know of, or are close to, a disabled person. Therefore, the issues facing disabled people have repercussions that reach far beyond the individual. Consequently, 'Cash Not Care' is a book that has relevance far beyond the disability community."

George Low
Coordinator of Disability Research Edinburgh
The University of Edinburgh

"Mo Stewart's book offers its reader a compendium of the dreadful attacks on the lives and rights of disabled people in the UK today. But at its heart is one key story that describes in microcosm the moral and intellectual bankruptcy of our current political elite. The book describes how the vested interests of private insurers and the ideological commitment of extreme right-wing politicians have combined to undermine what was an essential component of our social security system - Incapacity Benefit.

It is easy to become dispirited by all of this - but I think Mo Stewart is right to quote Nelson Mandela: "Never underestimate the power of persistence." This book is the fruit of Mo Stewart's own persistence and tenacity. She has had to deal with her own disability while fighting to find the truth and I thoroughly recommend this book to anyone who wants to look beyond Government rhetoric and understand what's really going on."

Dr Simon Duffy
Director, The Centre for Welfare Reform

"When the history of the persecution of disabled people in the name of welfare reform in Britain finally gets written for mainstream audiences, Mo Stewart's evidence will form the starting point. Read it here first."

Catherine Hale, Independent Researcher
Author of : Fulfilling Potential? ESA and the Fate of the Work-Related Activity Group

"I have known Mo Stewart since 2010 when I came across her intelligent research into the welfare state and its destruction. Her tireless support of disability rights and the undermining of the government policy has been a thorn in the Whitehall flesh. 'Cash Not Care' is a major step forward in the fight to protect the most vulnerable in our society from the ravages of "Austerity".

Chris Johnstone
GP, Paisley

"Mo Stewart has played a vital role in raising awareness of how private sector companies have helped to both design and encourage the welfare reforms and cuts that they hope to profit from. Her research has been used by MPs, peers and disabled activists to draw attention to subjects that the mainstream media has repeatedly shied away from. Without that research, we would know far less about the murky figures who have been lurking in the shadows of welfare reform in the UK for the last two decades."

John Pring
Editor, Disability News Service

"Mo Stewart's research on welfare reform, especially the role that private sector companies have played in designing and supporting welfare reforms, has provided invaluable information. This work has led the way in highlighting reforms that have a devastating impact on the lives of disabled people."

Richard Hawkes
Chief Executive Officer, SCOPE 2010 ~ 2015

" Mo's tireless research on welfare reform provides essential evidence for all campaigners. Her determination to disseminate the results means there are no excuses for not knowing the facts behind the reforms."

Pat Onions
Pat's Petition

"Mo Stewart is not someone who gives up. She has been tenacious in carrying out her detailed research into the origins and flaws of the medical tests which various governments have adopted to judge whether people with ill health or a disability are fit to work or not. She has also been relentless in getting her research disseminated to those who need to know."

Dame Anne Begg
Chair, Work and Pensions Select Committee 2010 ~ 2015

"This book is a vitally important addition to the canon on the terrible fallout from austerity cuts and welfare reforms for the disabled people in the UK. If you care at all about politics and if you care about how society and government treats its citizens, then this is a must-read."

Mary O'Hara
Author of 'Austerity Bites'

"Mo Stewart is a researcher who keeps telling it as it is, especially when her work reveals inconvenient truths. Mo's work, over the years, has been invaluable to campaigning groups like ours. Thank you Mo."

Frances Kelly and Rosemary O'Neil
CarerWatch

"Mo Stewart's dedication and advocacy in challenging the unfairness of the disability claims process is of tremendous benefit to the most vulnerable of our society, both in the United Kingdom and United States. Her work has been invaluable by exposing adverse influences that negatively affect the rights of disabled persons to be treated with respect. I highly recommend Mo's work as a skilled researcher as well as her desire to protect those who often cannot defend themselves."

Linda Nee
Licensed Disability Claims Consultant
Maine, USA

"Mo Stewart has been an invaluable source of information for the members of the forum. The detail and precision of her work adds weight to the continuing battle on behalf of the poor and disabled – many of whom simply don't have the strength to fight for themselves."

Anna Annana
WP Examination forum

"This book is a revealing and, frankly, shocking look at the current systems and procedures in place with the Government for assessing peoples' capacity to work, and the effects that the system has on those going through it.

We in the British Psychological Society have grave concerns about the reliability, validity and fitness for purpose of the systems and procedures currently in place and have, for some considerable time, been seeking meetings with the Secretary of State and his Ministers to articulate these concerns, so far without success.

This book makes it abundantly clear that these talks need to take place in order that we can advise and assist the Government with reforming and improving the current system, for the benefit of everybody."

Professor Jamie Hacker Hughes
President, the British Psychological Society

"No-one in the UK has done more than Mo Stewart, with her detailed research, to expose the corrupt links between the private healthcare insurance industry and the British House of Commons. It should be crystal clear to every citizen in the UK that the agenda of cuts and austerity will kill. Mo Stewart is the person who has done more than anyone else in the UK to expose the infiltration of the private healthcare insurance industry into the lifeblood of our welfare state as a toxin."

John McArdle
Creator – Black Triangle Campaign

"Mo Stewart outlines in compelling detail Britain's draconian welfare reforms, and exposes the immense suffering and hardship they inflicted on sick and disabled people. Of particular interest is the role of an American insurance company advising successive governments since the Thatcher era; the toxic rhetoric employed by right-wing media to patronize and berate the poor; and the "sham" Work Capability Assessments."

Samuel Miller
Disabled Academic, Canada
Adviser to UN human rights office re welfare crisis in UK

In loving memory of Alison:
lifelong best friend and
sister of my heart.

RIP

CASH NOT CARE:

the planned demolition of the UK welfare state

CASH NOT CARE:
the planned demolition of the UK welfare state

Published by New Generation Publishing in 2016

Copyright © 2016 Mo Stewart. All rights reserved.

First Edition

The author asserts the moral right under the Copyright, Designs and Patents Act 1988 to be identified as the author of this work.

Mo Stewart is a pseudonym.

British Library Cataloguing in Publication Data
A catalogue record for this book is available from the British Library.

ISBN 978-1-78507-783-8 [paperback]
ISBN 978-1-78507-784-5 [hardback]
ISBN 978-1-78507-785-2 [eBook]

Cover design by Kevin Marman

The purpose of this research is to educate and to inform and every effort has been made to ensure that the content of the book is as accurate as possible. This is an evidence based research text. The majority of the evidence within the text pages was derived from websites and was freely available in the public domain at the time of writing. Links to websites may be subject to change, expire or be redirected without notice.

This book is printed on paper from responsible sources, which is suitable for recycling and is made from fully managed and sustained forest sources.

New Generation Publishing

www.newgenerat ion-publish ing.com

OTHER RELATED TITLES BY MO STEWART

All previous research reports and articles are available via the following websites:

Why Wait Forever – Veterans:
http://www.whywaitforever.com/dwpatosveterans.html

(1)	Atos Healthcare or Disability Denial Factories – summary	June 2010
(2)	Atos Healthcare or Disability Denial Factories – full report	June 2010
(3)	Welfare Reform – Redress For The Disabled - report	Sept 2011
(4)	The Truth Behind Welfare Reforms – summary	Nov 2011
(5)	Atos, Unum and the DWP – summary	Dec 2011
(6)	The Total Failure of the ESA is Confirmed – report	Feb 2012
(7)	Disability Denial Factories working well in the UK – article	June 2012
(8)	Atos, Unum and the DWP – the planned destruction of the Welfare State – article	June 2012
(9)	Welfare Reform Tyranny direct from the USA – article	July 2012
(10)	Disability Denial Factories working well in the UK – update	Sept 2012
(11)	Government use might of American insurance giant to destroy UK safety net – article	Oct 2012
(12)	Backbench Buisness Debate re Atos Healthcare and the WCA - a briefing for MPs	Feb 2013

The Centre for Disability Studies, Leeds University: Mo Stewart
http://disability-studies.leeds.ac.uk/library/author/stewart.mo

(13)	The Hidden Agenda – research summary	March 2013
(14)	From the British Welfare State to another American State	May 2013
(15)	UK Government refuses to accept responsibility for identified Crimes Against Humanity	May 2014
(16)	War and Impairment – the social consequences of disablement *Keynote speech at the launch of the 2014 Disability History Month	Nov 2014
(17)	The influence of the private insurance industry on the UK welfare reforms.	Jan 2015

The research provided via the Centre for Disability Studies at Leeds University was reproduced via ResearchGate, which has a global audience of researchers and academics. As of February 2016, MS research reports have been viewed or downloaded 700 times in eight different countries via ResearchGate.

ResearchGate, Mo Stewart

https://www.researchgate.net/profile/Mo_Stewart/publications

(13)	The Hidden Agenda	March 2013
(14)	From the British Welfare State to another American State	May 2013
(15)	UK Government refuses to accept responsibility for identified Crimes Against Humanity	May 2014
(16)	War and Impairment – the social consequences of disablement *Keynote speech: 2014 launch of Disability History Month	Nov 2014
(17)	The influence of the private insurance industry on the UK welfare reforms.	Jan 2015

Centre For Crime And Justice Studies

http://www.crimeandjustice.org.uk/resources/preventable-harm-government-policy

(18)	Preventable harm is government policy	April 2016

CONTENTS

BIOGRAPHY

Mo Stewart (MS) is a medically retired healthcare professional, a disabled female veteran and, for the last six years, has worked as an independent researcher investigating the history behind the introduction of the Work Capability Assessment (WCA) by the Department for Work and Pensions (DWP), with evidence from the research used during welfare reform debates in the House of Lords and the House of Commons since 2011.

Originally written for the benefit of chronically sick and disabled people who historically don't have a voice, and who must endure the WCA in order to access the DWP long-term sickness benefit needed for their survival, the early research identified the influence of corporate America with the United Kingdom (UK) welfare reforms in the 2010 report: *Atos Healthcare or Disability Denial Factories*.

Since that time, the research has attracted wide interest and academic endorsements over the years. All research reports were routinely shared with Disabled People's Organisations, with academics and with many welfare agencies, including the United Nations, as the Cabinet Office attempted and failed to incentivise MS to stop the research.

Recently accessed evidence, demonstrating that many of the social security policies introduced during the ongoing welfare reforms were not created by the UK government, together with the growing catalogue of the many thousands of associated deaths linked to the WCA, is identified within the text.

ACKNOWLEDGEMENTS

This book was written as I rapidly approached the sixth anniversary of a very long voyage of research discovery by this former healthcare professional and disabled female veteran. (MS)

I had no previous experience when this research began in September 2009, with the first report published online in June 2010. Over time I have benefitted from a lot of help, from both within the United Kingdom (UK) and from supporters in the wider world, and this book would not have been possible without some very special people who I am happy to acknowledge.

The research could not have happened at all had it not been for the kindness of my amazing carers: Tiffany Beckett and Maria Moore and, before them, Val Bliss. Collectively, they all tolerated my endless concerns as I discovered the painful evidence, ordered me to eat when I wasn't interested in food, dragged me out of the study when they decided I was working too hard and tolerated every draft of the various chapters in this book. Between them, they make my life possible and they have my love and very grateful thanks... and cream cakes on a Friday.

Given that I still think of a personal computer as a typewriter with a memory, without technical support the research would not have lasted long. I am very grateful to my friend Guven Dalsar for his vital IT support over the years that has included upgrading the pc twice, accessing and delivering necessary equipment, upgrading software and maintaining a research suite using remote access all for the very reasonable price of a cup of tea whenever he visits. He's a star.

The research would not have been viable without the willing support of my Webmaster, '_Mike Bach_,' who shared his website with me at _www.whywaitforever.com_ to enable the early research reports to be published online from 2010 until 2013 whilst, at the same time, battling with a devastating and terminal diagnosis. _Mike Bach_ was surely a giant amongst men, who lost his battle for life in February 2015, and this book is dedicated to his memory with my love, deepest respect and very grateful thanks.

Valuable donated support from both legal and academic advisers, who must remain anonymous for professional reasons, is readily acknowledged and those amazing professionals know who they are. Thank you so much for your valuable donated time and expertise.

Special thanks to John Pring, disabled Editor of this country's only Disability News Service, who was the one journalist with the courage to expose the reality of the welfare reforms when the entire UK national press refused to identify the influence of a notorious American corporate healthcare insurance giant, with successive UK Governments since 1994, due to a claimed *"fear of possible future litigation by a corporate giant."* John's valuable work is highlighted in *Appendix* 2.

Warmest thanks to the academics, at a variety of UK universities, who have willingly shared their academic research papers, and book manuscripts, welcomed my contact and encouraged my efforts and my heartfelt thanks to Professor Peter Beresford for his continued enthusiastic encouragement of my work over a number of years. Chapter 9 celebrates academic excellence.

My personal thanks to the various politicians and members of the House of Lords, who shared the research and used the evidence in it during various welfare reform debates since 2011.

Special thanks to the team at the Centre for Disability Studies at Leeds University, who have willingly published the research evidence since 2013, and to the team at ResearchGate who have reproduced the research of MS since 2014.

My warmest thanks to all the Disabled Peoples' Organisations (DPO) and Carers' groups, who have identified the research online for their readers, with many reproducing the reports in full on various websites and online blogs. In particular, I am very grateful to John McArdle of the Black Triangle Campaign, who were the first online DPO to share the research and who continue to publish the reports for access by other campaigners.

Warmest thanks to Dr Christopher Johnstone, a Scottish GP, who has accessed relevant published articles from medical journals that are cost prohibitive for this disabled veteran, and my thanks to Bernadette Meaden and the team at Ekklesia and to Dr Simon Duffy, at the Centre for Welfare Reform, who permitted me to write articles for their websites.

Extra special thanks to Mike Sivier, of *Vox Political*. Mike is a freelance journalist and a carer to his disabled wife. He had the courage to publish the detailed research reports online via *Vox Political* to offer the evidence to the wider general public that the government and the national press will not share and, significantly, to permit able bodied readers to have an alternative input to the often dangerous rhetoric of the Cameron government, as happily reported in banner headlines by the tabloid press. Mike's work is highlighted in *Appendix* 3.

My heartfelt thanks are also offered to Dave Lupton, the talented disabled creator of *Crippen* cartoons, for his valuable support to the disabled community and for his generous donation of some of his wonderful cartoon drawings for my use. Special thanks to Dave for the exclusive cartoon designed especially for the book. Warm thanks also to Kevin Marman for his distinctive artwork in Chapter 9 and for his help with the front cover design.

Deep gratitude is owed to my dear friend Merry Cross for her amazing skills as a proof reader, who willingly helped with the earlier draft of the book, and to a modest and talented man who copy-edited the entire manuscript but who wishes to remain annonymous.

Thank you all so very much for very valuable help over such a long time. These people all put the word '*Great*' into Great Britain.

I also have a personal duty to thank supporters from overseas.

Samuel Miller lives in Canada. Samuel is a profoundly disabled man, frequently provides evidence to the United Nations (UN), including research reports by MS, and the UN are now investigating the UK government for possible breaches of the Human Rights of chronically sick and disabled UK citizens. Samuel has been a constant source of support to the disabled community in the UK. In 2014 he created and published an updated mortality total of our chronically sick and disabled people, as reported by the UK national press, who had all died following the Work Capability Assessment as conducted on behalf of the government by a totally unaccountable corporate giant. A link to Samuel's disturbing mortality totals is included in *Appendix* 6.

I must also offer my grateful thanks to Linda Nee, an American consultant who supports claimants in America attempting to claim from their income protection insurance policies from various healthcare insurance companies. Linda has periodically published a variety of my articles on her online blog, as she keeps her readers informed as to the struggle in the UK due to the influence of the second largest healthcare insurance company in the world with successive UK governments' welfare reforms.

Finally, my very grateful thanks to the publishers, editors, academics, activists, independent journalists, national charities and national press syndications who granted permission to allow me to reproduce extracts of third party published work in the book.

Mo Stewart
March 2016

DEDICATION

Commonly known online as 'Mike Bach', this book is dedicated to the memory of my dear friend and original Webmaster, who was a giant amongst men. Mike's concern for others, and unlimited support for my efforts, inspired me to continue the research even during many dark times when there seemed little point.

Mike was the first person to offer help when I began this research a little over six years ago. He immediately offered to share his website at *Why Wait Forever*, to allow my reports to be published online, whilst his own research was also exposing the many failings of the Work Capability Assessment and the influence of foreign corporate business with the UK government. That was in 2009 when Mike had been diagnosed with a life threatening condition. Mike's own research is very significant, especially his Memorandum on Disability Insurance.

WHY WAIT FOREVER: www.whywaitforever.com/dwpatos.html [1]   (Mike's website)
WHY WAIT FOREVER: www.whywaitforever.com/dwpatosveterans [2]   (Mo's website)

By 2011 Mike advised me that both corporate giants involved with the Work Capability Assessment design and application **were monitoring our website up to 50 times per day**, and this continued until the website was no longer updated. In March 2013 Mike stopped updating the *Why Wait Forever* website due to failing health and the more recent research reports of MS are published by the Centre for Disability Studies at Leeds University and by ResearchGate. Almost two years since he stopped updating the website Mike lost his battle for life in February 2015. Mike was an inspiration and a light in my life who will never be forgotten and he is missed by many.

My research is now well known by chronically sick and disabled people in the UK and by carers, academics and other professionals who often make contact; and the research evidence is regularly used during welfare reform debates in the House of Lords and the House of Commons. I would never have been able to pursue the research for so long had it not been for the kindness and encouragement of Mike, and this book is dedicated to his memory with my love, deepest respect and very grateful thanks.

Rest in Peace Mike

SOURCES OF EXTRACTS

Various publishers, newspaper syndications, editors, national charities, academics, activists, the Ekklesia thinktank and the *Private Eye* magazine all generously gave permission for extracts from their previously published work to be included here. Many thanks to all.

Referenced throughout the book:

- THE SCIENTIFIC AND CONCEPTUAL BASIS OF INCAPACITY BENEFITS 2005 ISBN: 0 11 703584 X
  Gordon Waddell CBE, DSc, MD, FRCS
  and Mansel Aylward CB, MD, FFPM, FFOM, FRCP
  ***UnumProvident Centre for Psychosocial and Disability Research, Cardiff University*
- IS WORK GOOD FOR HEALTH AND WELL-BEING 2006 ISBN: 0 11 703694 3 Gordon Waddell, CBE DSc MD FRCS
  Centre for Psychosocial and Disability Research, Cardiff University, UK
  Kim Burton, PhD DO EurErg
  Centre for Health and Social Care Research, University of Huddersfield, UK

Chapter 2

2:1   The truth about spending on disability benefits, Ekklesia, May 2015

Chapter 3

3:1   Margaret Thatcher's plan to dismantle the welfare state, The Guardian, 2012
3:2   Atos Healthcare or Disability Denial Factories? Mo Stewart 2010
3:3   An independent review of the Work Capability Assessment, year 1. Harrington 2010
3:4   Work Capability Assessment descriptors. ME Assoc 2011
3:5   The impact of Thatcherism on health and well-being in Britain. Alex Scott-Samuel, Clare Bambra, Chik Collins, David J Hunter, Gerry McCartney, Kat Smith, International Journal of Health Services, Volume 44, Number 1, Pages 53-71 2014
3:6   Margaret Thatcher left a dark legacy that has still not disappeared. The Guardian 2003
3:7   Thatcher's reckless acolytes don't know when to stop. The Guardian 2013

Chapter 4

4:1   The influence of the private insurance industry on the UK welfare reforms. Mo Stewart, 2015
4:2   Unum bragged about 'driving government thinking' on incapacity benefit reform Disability News Service, 2013
4:3   E pluribus Unum, The Guardian, 2008
4:4   The Freud Report 2007
4:5   An independent assessment of the arguments for proposed Incapacity Benefit reform Alison Ravetz, Centre for Disability Studies, Leeds University, March 2006
4:6   Insurer Unum Group reverses 42% of previous denied claims. Insurance Bad Faith, attourney pages 2005
4:7   A Tale of Two Models, Debbie Jolly, Centre for Disability Studies, Leeds University, March 2012
4:8   Angela Kennedy responds to Professor Sir Mansel Aylward, Black Triangle Campaign, September 2012
4:9   A response to Professor Aylward's statement, Gill Thorburn, September 2012
4:10 Work tests concern disability organisations, Business Day, New Zealand, 2013

Appendix 3 - Extracts from Vox Political (VP) edited by Mike Sivier

1. Here's why Labour needs to go a lot further to win back our trust, VP, 2013
2. UK government refuses to accept responsibility for identified crimes against Humanity. VP, 2014
3. 'It's cheaper to help people to die rather than support them to live.' VP, 2014

Appendix 4 - Extracts from Private Eye

1. Mutual Benefits, Private Eye, 2011
2. Disabled veterans tossed aside, Private Eye, 2011
3. Unum Ad Nauseam, Private Eye, 2011
4. Fit-For-Work-Tests, Private Eye, 2012
5. Paul Foot on the insurance company Unum and cuts to disability benefit. Private Eye, 2015

Appendix 5 - Extracts from Bernadette Meaden (BM) of the Ekklesia thinktank

1. Suicides and the WCA: How much more evidence does the government want? BM, Ekklesia, 2015
2. Malingering, illness deception and disability benefit reforms. BM, Ekklesia, 2015
3. The truth about spending on disability benefits – it's halved. BM, Ekklesia, 2015
4. People with disabilities, the DWP and the struggle ahead. BM, Ekklesia, 2015
5. Far from rethinking sanctions, IDS plans to extend them. BM, Ekklesia, 2015

LIST OF BOXES, TABLES AND ILLUSTRATIONS

Tables

Illustrations

FOREWORD

Peter Beresford OBE
Emeritus Professor of Social Policy at Brunel University, London and
Co-Chair of Shaping Our Lives ~ the disabled people's and service users'
organisation and network.

This book is a significant achievement and source of knowledge in its own right. But it is also a key statement about the position of disabled people in our society in the early twenty first century.

For years disabled people and their movement have struggled to challenge the discrimination, exclusion and oppression that they have faced. As a result they have brought about major change in society, its understandings of disabled people, disabled people's understandings of themselves and the opportunities and access to the mainstream available to many disabled people – including an increasingly wide range of disabled people.

But the challenging of longstanding stereotypes about the inevitable dependency and incapacity of disabled people has had unexpected political and policy consequences. It has resulted – across major political parties – in the crudest and most hostile of reactions to disabled people – for ideological purposes. Often using disabled people's own rhetoric – their determination to be treated equally, to be seen as having abilities and potential – it has attacked them for their 'failure' to have jobs, their need to turn to welfare benefits.

No matter the barriers the labour market continues to put in the way of disabled people's employment. No matter the failure over years of government policy to offer adequate information, support, training and access to the labour market for disabled people. No matter that some people with impairments, long term conditions and illnesses just cannot maintain conventional employment. No matter that years of appalling housing policy particularly mean that many people have no chance of earning enough to have a home through earnings because of the outlandish rise in house prices and are therefore kept in a trap. No matter that western demographics have and continue to change apace, meaning that there will be more and more disabled people and very old people more likely to be frail in our society and that it isn't possible to change this just by draconian attempts to redefine and reduce who is disabled.

So there are massive conflicts and contradictions in the present position of disabled people in a society like the UK. For many, what has most symbolised this has been their presentation as heroic in the 2012 London Paralympic Games and their political and media stigmatization since as scroungers in their daily lives.

This book is desperately important because it connects the impossibly conflicted understandings of disability and disabled people that continue to operate in our society. First, it sets out in detail the evidence showing the failure, dishonesty, cruelty and arbitrariness of government welfare reform in relation to disabled people. Sadly these are policies that tarnish all three major political parties. Second, it shows how disabled people like Mo have risen to the enormous challenge of helping us understand what has been happening through their own determination to tell the truth, find things out and not let disabled people's oppression go uncontested.

The truth is that these are responsibilities that should have been taken up much more determinedly by political opposition, academic researchers, research organisations, charitable organisations and the like. Most have failed in that responsibility. Instead people like Mo Stewart have risen to the occasion and here take on the task. Mo and others like her, despite the difficulties they face in their own life, the ways in which these welfare reform policies directly negatively impact on their lives, have made a commitment to gain skills, ignore difficulties, put personal pains to one side, to tell truths to power – power that has repeatedly made it clear that it doesn't really want to hear. What a wonderful achievement.

For me, the way in which welfare reform policy has been imposed on the ground against disabled people has had most in common with the appalling behaviour of the First World War committees that sought to send badly wounded and mentally damaged recruits back to the front line, and the arbitrariness of the Nazi military systems that did the same in the Second World War. This is shameful. I say this particularly as a result of hearing repeatedly from my partner, a hospice social worker about the appalling treatment meted out to disabled and distressed service users under this system, people who have either experienced appalling bereavement or themselves have a life limiting condition or illness. It seems there is no such thing to our current political masters as a 'deserving' case. Even the Victorian poor law had that limited understanding. There is also no sign that such thinking is under review. If anything the Conservative government elected in 2015 seems determined to extend the harshness of its welfare policies in relation to disabled and other people in need.

For some conventional analysts and commentators, this book's journey through the horrors and cruelty of welfare reform policy may not be as they expect; it may not read sufficiently modulated, restrained, qualified and 'academicised'. But the point is, it at last offers us the detailed, informed picture that policymakers have always needed, that disabled people have had a right to, but which the powers that be have made minimal effort to develop. Their aim seems more often to have been to deny or hide the truth, rather than seek it out. Mo has sought out and told these truths.

Here we see the realities behind the populist rhetoric of 'welfare reform' exposed; the hidden, often dubious relationships between policymakers and international corporations; the questionable independence of supposedly neutral 'experts' and most of all the scale and severity of the suffering of innumerable disabled people, in some cases resulting in their deaths.

This research and the book that builds on it, highlight yet again the important role that disabled people can play in their own liberation and in reshaping political and public understanding. However, this is also a book that is important to *all* of us, both disabled and non-disabled. This is explicit in its sub-title: 'the planned demolition of the UK welfare state'. The welfare state since its creation has always been something that benefitted the many rather than the few. Its opponents have always sought to enlist the support of the many to undermine it against their own interests. We have seen this campaign developed to its greatest extent in 'welfare reform' policy, where it is presented as the creator of dependency and dependence, rather than of the founding glories of much valued services like the National Health Service.

This book offers a warning for the future as well as from the past. Producing it has been an epic journey for Mo. We owe her an enormous debt of thanks for making it available to us. Within its pages we will find much to help us combat the policies and practices which it brings into the light and subjects to enquiry. What an achievement. Thank you Mo.

CHAPTER 1: INTRODUCTION

In the long run, the sharpest weapon of all is a kind and gentle spirit.
Anne Frank
1929 ~ 1945

This book is the conclusion to what has been a very long voyage of research discovery, conducted voluntarily over the past six years. The content has been described by academics and others as both '*harrowing*' and '*disturbing*' and it identifies the '*atrocities*' of the British government, as yet unknown by and unreported to the British people.

This research has exposed the adoption of American style social security policies by successive United Kingdom (UK) governments, en route to the demolition of the UK welfare state, as all planned a long time ago by a previous Conservative government. The research has also confirmed the influence of a discredited American healthcare insurance giant with the assessment model used to re-assess claimants of Incapacity Benefit (IB), as they are migrated to the new income replacement benefit known as the Employment and Support Allowance (ESA), for welfare benefit claimants who are too ill or disabled to access paid employment.

As the principle researcher, extracts from published research by MS are quoted throughout. The text is not limited by the usual restraints of academic writing that requires the use of diplomatic language, regardless of the identified atrocities exposed by detailed research, and it benefits from the inclusion of illustrations created by the highly talented Dave Lupton, of *Crippen* Cartoons, which can say a thousand words in one detailed picture that adds colour, humour and gravitas to the text. Dave is a wheelchair user and a strong supporter of disabled people.

Cash Not Care: the planned demolition of the UK welfare state

This voyage of research discovery began in September 2009, during almost two distressing years for this disabled female veteran when in a battle with authorities who resisted increasing my War Pension, and challenged my integrity, by presuming that I had lied to access an increase in monthly income. Six years later, evidence from the research has been used in welfare reform debates in the House of Lords and the House of Commons since 2011, the United Nations (UN) have access to the published reports and the UN are now investigating the UK Government for possible breaches of the Human Rights of disabled people.

It has been suggested that perhaps past research by Mo Stewart (MS), available via the Internet, may have encouraged the American corporate UK government insurance '*advisers*' to remove their Income Protection Insurance policies from the open market in 2012, due to the '*relentless negative publicity*' that was possibly assisted by the research, which has attracted global academic interest via ResearchGate as well as being widely promoted online by service users.

The principle research reports of MS, produced from 2010 – 2015, are freely available online and links are listed at the start of the text, together with links to related and significant information from various sources listed in the *Appendices*. Amongst other things, the book content includes extracts from academic research from a variety of UK universities, to identify why the previous help and support offered to chronically sick and disabled people was withdrawn without mercy by the Cameron government(s), whose endless accusations against IB and ESA claimants are demonstrated to be totally without foundation.

During this lengthy voyage of research discovery it has been my great pleasure to have the opportunity to have contact with many significant people, who willingly offered help and support for my efforts. People who have supported the research are listed in the acknowledgements but, more than anyone else, this research was conducted on behalf of those who don't have a voice and who have suffered the most due to a UK government whose cruelty knows no limits. The support of my efforts by other chronically sick and disabled people is valued more than they know and, with the evidence from this research, they may now possibly better understand how a UK government can use neoliberal politics and austerity as an excuse to demolish the welfare state. The research has also confirmed that the identified human suffering following the imposed welfare reforms and austerity measures is due to political ideology not financial necessity.

Over time the research reports improved, became more professional and have attracted approval and endorsements from many people including academics, with some professors referring their students to the published reports and PhD students inviting permission from MS to quote from the research evidence. The book is written for ease of access by people who wish to comprehend why chronically sick and disabled people, who are totally dependent upon welfare benefit for their survival, now live in fear of the UK government and some of the evidence will be considered by many to be disturbing.

The book content may be of interest to students of disability studies, social policy, social sciences and legal studies of Human Rights, both undergraduate and graduate, to journalists and political commentators who want the facts not the fiction offered by politicians, to members of the public who have an interest in social justice and to the chronically sick and disabled population and their carers who have been vilified by successive UK governments.

Reading Access

This book is written so that each chapter can stand alone depending on the reader's interest and preference or the chapters can be read sequentially as each one builds on the content of the previous chapter. I must **advise caution** as the detailed evidence in the text may be considered harrowing by many readers unfamiliar with the implications of government policy decisions, and I should also stress that I am a medically retired healthcare professional and not a professional researcher. Therefore, the text does contain opinions based on the last six years of independent research, which is atypical of professional academic research.

The book exposes the tyranny now adopted by the Department for Work and Pensions, whose Ministers thrive on their perceived authority and who chose to totally disregard all evidence demonstrating that vast numbers of people are suffering and dying in the UK, due to the American influenced welfare '*reform*' policies, which really means welfare destruction.

Chapter breakdown

In **Chapter 2**, the Research Summary confirms the unprecedented political attack against claimants of the Employment and Support Allowance (ESA) that was guaranteed to be reported by the national press to influence the electorate, as all planned long ago to reduce the public support for the welfare state as the UK is covertly moved towards private healthcare funding. Based on what this author has identified as *'Thatcher's Legacy'*, successive British governments have adopted American social security policies, and welcomed the influence of a notorious American healthcare insurance giant with British welfare reforms, as the chapter demonstrates the lengths gone to by the Coalition government to knowingly mislead the British people regarding the welfare budget and the people in need of it. **Chapter 3** identifies the consequences when millionaires are in a position of political power, the expansion of the assessment of 2.5 million Incapacity Benefit claimants being migrated to the ESA when using a totally bogus assessment model, designed to resist benefit funding, with the confirmation that the austerity measures imposed by the Coalition government were identified by academics as '*a political choice, not a financial necessity.*' **Chapter 4** identifies that the political ideology used to favour the rich and terrorise the poor is working well, the Labour Party is still damaged by the '*Blair legacy*' and are a totally ineffective opposition to the point of colluding with the Conservatives to pass the most damaging piece of welfare legislation in the history of this country, and the Liberal Democrats lost all credibility and betrayed their ideology in exchange for a seat at the top table of the Coalition government. **Chapter 5** highlights the dangerous 2001 Malingering and Illness Deception conference that guaranteed, to the everlasting shame of the (New) Labour Party, that in future years countless numbers of the most vulnerable of all would suffer and die because the government adopted the unproven hypothesis of the then DWP Chief Medical Officer, influenced by corporate America, who suggested that vast numbers of people claiming Incapacity Benefit were '*malingering*'. The presumption that most long-term sickness benefit claimants are really just idle, living off the State with a '*money for nothing*' mind-set was generated at the 2001 conference and the Cameron government(s) have disregarded all evidence that confirms that this unsupported hypothesis is incorrect, and was strongly influenced by the American corporate insurance giant who were official government '*advisers*' at the time. **Chapters 6 and 7** offer more detailed and often disturbing evidence as '*Thatcher's Legacy*' becomes a reality for ESA claimants in Britain; with disability hate crimes at an all-time high, aided and abetted by the national press who feed the British people with government propaganda that is subsequently demonstrated to be untrue after the damage has been done. **Chapter 7** also identifies that almost 100,000 chronically ill and/or disabled people have died following the totally bogus Work Capability Assessment, imposed by the welfare reforms and used to access the ESA. **Chapter 8** highlights the research of my original Webmaster, exposing the corruption that was always going to happen as soon as the British government invited corporate America to influence future '*welfare claims management*', with a selection of extracts from important academic research papers from UK universities compiled in **Chapter 9** and this researcher's final thoughts that draws the research to a conclusion in **Chapter 10**.

The *Appendices* include extracts and links to relevant articles by independent journalists John Pring of Disability News Service in *Appendix 2* and Mike Sivier of Vox Political in *Appendix* 3, with extracts from relevant articles by *Private Eye* magazine in *Appendix* 4. The *Appendices* also include a link to the detailed commentary by Bernadette Meaden of Ekklesia in *Appendix* 5, as well as a list of reported deaths, gleaned from the national press and collated by Samuel Miller in Canada, as chronically sick and disabled people were often left with no money due to sanctions, and some would actually starve to death in C21st UK. Links to this information, and other significant further reading, are listed in *Appendix* 6.

This is an evidence based research text and all references are listed at the end of each chapter and, collectively, at the end of the book to allow for ease of reading. I confirm that this research is totally independent, self-funded and the content of it is all my own work.

Mo Stewart
March 2016

CHAPTER 2: RESEARCH SUMMARY

Never underestimate the power of persistence…
Nelson Mandela
1918 ~ 2013

This independent, self-funded research by Mo Stewart (MS) has been conducted during a time when there has been an unprecedented hostile political attack against chronically sick and disabled people, who are financially dependent upon long-term sickness benefit; with the United Kingdom (UK) government using the 2008 global banking crisis as justification for savage welfare reforms that were identified, over 30 years ago, in a plan to eventually demolish the UK welfare state.

Whilst the ongoing welfare reforms touch on many areas of welfare funding and social policy, this research was primarily concerned with the introduction of an identified totally bogus functional assessment model to assess claimants of long-term sickness benefit, the adoption of American social security policies with aspects of the UK welfare reforms and the authority afforded to a handful of inappropriate people. The name of the long-term income replacement benefit used as the long-term sickness benefit changed over time and, as will be demonstrated in the following chapters, the UK government continues to disregard the inevitable death and despair created by the welfare reforms en route to the total demolition of the UK welfare state.

Following previous Conservative government guidelines, the reform of the long-term sickness benefit was introduced in 2008 by the New Labour government, as then led by Gordon Brown, and was significantly accelerated by the Conservative / Liberal Democrat Coalition government following election in 2010. Contrary to the positive comments by Tory devotees, the welfare reforms are identified by this researcher as *'Thatcher's Legacy'* as, according to the National Archives, the future demolition of the welfare state was actively considered by the Thatcher government in 1982; and Margaret Thatcher's famous total disregard for society, claiming *'there is no such thing as society'* [N1] has been emphasised since David Cameron became Prime Minister in 2010. (*Margaret Thatcher was the first elected 'neoliberal' politician, which places *'the market'* at the centre of all economic and social life.)

NOTES

N1: Epitaph for the eighties? *"there is no such thing as society"*

This famous quote was taken from an interview with Prime Minister Margaret Thatcher in the Women's Own Magazine on October 31 1987, reprinted in the Sunday Times and redistributed via the Internet by award winning journalist Brian Deer.

The long-ago planned demolition of the UK welfare state started in earnest in 2010 and is relentless. It has gathered momentum over the past five years, with the Prime Minister and Ministers from the Department for Work and Pensions (DWP) using psychology and the politics of fear to influence the British public regarding their responsibility when claiming unemployment benefit or long-term sickness benefit; which must be justified by the claimants and not expected, whilst misleading the general public with the help of sensational press headlines. The adoption of perjorative language by politicians was reproduced in the national press, with an identified decrease in public sympathy for chronically sick and disabled people who are totally dependent upon welfare benefits for their survival.

As will be demonstrated, the adoption of American style social security policies by the UK government meant that the sick and the poor were suddenly personally responsible for their poverty; which was deemed to be a *'lifestyle choice',* and a punitive stance was adopted towards welfare benefit claimants with often fatal consequences. Elected in May 2010, DWP Ministers in the Coalition government made no distinction between the State financial support for the unemployed and financial support for the long-term sick and disabled benefit claimants who are unable to work due to health restrictions. Sick and disabled people *'languishing for years'* on sickness benefit have been held responsible for the escalating welfare budget that has grown significantly over the past two decades, whilst politicians knowingly disregarded reality. With medical improvements people are now living much longer, even with poor health, which would inevitably dramatically increase the costs of the welfare budget, including the State retirement pension for an ageing population with many people surviving for 25 years or longer post retirement age.

By failing to advise the British people in any detail of the growing demands on the public purse of the increasing elderly population, successive British governments have deceived the public. Clearly, UK governments were alerted to the growing demand given that future welfare reforms, leading to the erosion of the hallowed welfare state, were identified by the Thatcher government over thirty years ago. Meanwhile, regardless of human consequences, a drastic reduction of the long-term sickness benefit costs was deemed necessary to reduce the welfare budget and, by far, the easiest way to begin to do this was to publicly and enthusiastically condemn the recipients of long-term sickness benefit to eventually reduce public sympathy.

The British public have been wilfully deceived since the 2010 election of a Coalition government, with the Secretary of State for Work and Pensions, Iain Duncan Smith, and DWP

Ministers constantly vilifying those deemed to be '*inactive*' due to a '*money-for nothing*' mindset when claiming long-term sickness benefit. Under the protection of the privileges of the House of Commons the Prime Minister, the Chancellor and the Secretary of State for Work

---

Box 2:1 *The truth about spending on disability benefits...*

When the ongoing process of cutting and restricting access to disability benefits began, we were told it was necessary because spending on them was out of control. A new report from the Institute for Fiscal Studies (IFS) shows that, in fact, the exact opposite was the case.

The report says that spending on disability benefits last year was 0.8 per cent of national income, and says, "this is half the level of disability benefit spending when it was at its peak in 1995–96."

So the peak for spending on disability benefits occurred under the Conservative government of John Major. The narrative that the Labour government allowed such spending to get out of control is false – as a percentage of our national income it actually fell during those years.

The report makes another point which disproves the rhetoric about large numbers of scroungers and malingerers who could work, but prefer to claim disability benefits. Whilst the overall number of individuals receiving disability benefits has fallen only slightly since the mid-1990s, "this is in the presence of underlying demographic change that would have tended to push up the numbers receiving considerably – both overall population growth and the baby boomer generation reaching older working ages. The proportion of older men receiving disability benefits has actually fallen sharply since the mid-1990s… Disability benefit receipt among men increases much less steeply with age than it used to."

Of course if we look at spending purely in cash terms, it has risen – but in cash terms, spending on everything has risen. The important figure is what we spend as a share of our national wealth, and that figure has halved.

Disabled people, and families with a disabled member, are more likely to be living in poverty than the rest of the population. As a country we are being less generous, less supportive to them than we were. If politicians wish to defend that as a policy position, they should do so. But they cannot and should not defend cuts to disability benefits by pretending that spending on them is excessive or out of control.

The report, 'The changing characteristics of UK disability benefit recipients' can be seen here http://www.ifs.org.uk/publications/7756

The truth about spending on disability benefits – it's halved [3]

Bernadette Meaden

Ekklesia
27th May 2015
Courtesy of Ekklesia

---

and Pensions have all misrepresented information and statistics[3] to justify often extreme claims, as the tabloid press willingly supported this disturbing political attack against those least able to defend themselves. DWP tyranny soon became the norm as the real '*Thatcher Legacy*' was unleashed onto an unsuspecting public by her devoted disciple David Cameron.

By 2010 this voyage of research discovery had exposed the fact that the Work Capability Assessment (WCA), as used by the DWP to reassess all claimants of long-term sickness benefit, is a replica of the '*disability denial practices*' of an American healthcare insurance giant, which was a consultant to the UK government from 1992 and an official adviser on '*welfare claims management*' to successive UK Governments from 1994.

Following the introduction of the WCA, alarm bells rang out when this researcher learned that for something that claimed to be a '*functional assessment*', the claimant's medical history would be totally disregarded by the DWP. Many assumed that a '*functional assessment*' was an occupational health assessment but, in reality, it is the invention of the healthcare insurance industry when using a '*non-medical*' assessment model to avoid considering diagnosis, prognosis or the medical history of claimants. As will be identified in later chapters, the credit for the creation of '*Disability Assessment Medicine*'[4] in the UK is claimed by a former DWP Chief Medical Officer, who was in post when corporate America was invited to influence the welfare of sick and disabled UK citizens. He left the DWP in April 2005 to be funded by the same American corporate insurance giant at a research centre at Cardiff University.

Given the variety and severity of many debilitating long-term and often permanent illnesses, disregarding diagnosis and prognosis was deemed by this former healthcare professional to be dangerous and irresponsible. Totally disregarding medical history is very high risk with tragic consequences both inevitable and predictable, but the government were being advised by the same former DWP Chief Medical Officer (CMO) as an '*expert*', who introduced the concept of '*malingering*' as a justification for the growing numbers of claimants of long-term sickness benefit. In order to reduce welfare costs successive UK Governments were happy to accept the '*expert*' advice from the former DWP CMO, Professor Sir Mansel Aylward, that failed to offer any detailed credible evidence to support the remarkable theory of the claimed mass epidemic of psychosomatic illnesses… throughout the world!

Historically, chronically sick and disabled service-users did not have a voice of any significance. Their personal experiences of identified oppression or abuse would be dismissed as being '*anecdotal*', as demonstrated so well in Peter Beresford's compelling book: *It's Our*

Lives.[5] In the early years, the often disturbing research evidence was not only dismissed but my own Conservative Member of Parliament refused to accept it or to visit a lone, disabled woman in her home. Now peers and politicians use evidence from the research of MS during welfare reform debates in Parliament and high calibre academics endorse it.

The power of the Internet has permitted supporters to publish the research evidence; from the Centre for Welfare Reform, Ekklesia and the Centre for Disability Studies at Leeds University to grassroots Disabled People's Organisations.(DPO) One of the the most significant, the Black Triangle Campaign, were the first DPO to publish online the evidence from the research to allow access by their supporters, campaigners and other Internet users. Most recently, a research report from January 2015 has attracted a large amount of attention since being published via ResearchGate, which permits access by a global academic audience. As of June 2016 various research reports by MS have been viewed or downloaded via ResearchGate 1100 times, and downloaded in a variety of countries, as the social injustice of the UK welfare reforms, planned to guarantee future corporate financial gain, was exposed.

It's now 2016. We live in a different world and the 'experts' can't disregard or silence the voices of sick and disabled people any longer. With the help of social media, which permits sick and disabled people and their carers to communicate with each other around the country, significant grassroots DPOs have been formed and they now have a voice so strong that they are mentioned during debate in the House of Commons and are publicly acknowledged by professionals, academics, peers and politicians. Their voices will not be silenced again.

REFERENCES

**All references accessed 31st July 2015

3. MEADEN B: 27th May 2015: *The truth about spending on disability benefits – its halved*: http://www.ekklesia.co.uk/node/21740
4. AYLWARD M: 2003: *Malingering and Illness Deception* p290
   Conference papers: ISBN: 0 19 851554 52003:
   http://www.meactionuk.org.uk/Malingering_and_Illness_Deception.pdf
5. BERESFORD P: 2003: *It's Our Lives – A short theory of knowledge, distance and experience* ISBN No 0-9517554-2-0

CHAPTER 3: CASH NOT CARE
~ the creation of DWP tyranny

The only thing necessary for the triumph of evil is for good men to do nothing.
Edmund Burke
1729 ~ 1797

The unprecedented and relentless political attack against the poorest people in society began in earnest in the United Kingdom (UK) following the 2010 general election. With no overall political majority a Coalition government was formed between the Conservative Party and the Liberal Democrat Party and David Cameron, as leader of the Conservative Party, was appointed as the UK Prime Minister in May 2010, with Iain Duncan Smith appointed as the Secretary of State for Work and Pensions.

Regardless of subsequent government rhetoric or banner headlines in the tabloid press, the future demolition of the welfare state was identified long ago as an initiative of the 1982 Thatcher government[6,7] that was to be covertly pursued by all future UK governments **without the mandate of the British people.** As the new Prime Minister, David Cameron furthered the 1982 '*Thatcher Legacy*' by using the 2008 global financial crisis as plausible justification to eventually terrify 2.5 million chronically sick and disabled people, who were all dependent upon long-term sickness benefit for their financial and physical survival.

In October 2008 the UK faced a claimed '*catastrophic*' fiscal deficit, in part caused by the need to fund an additional £37 billion to rescue the banks due to the global financial crisis.[8] This event significantly increased the growing UK fiscal deficit and attention was drawn to the need to urgently reduce government costs. One mechanism used to reduce the deficit was a structural reform of the welfare state, and the welfare budget was placed under close scrutiny. The new 2010 Coalition government enthusiastically accelerated the reform of the welfare budget.

In the recent past chronically sick and disabled people in the UK, who were medically unfit for paid employment for a prolonged period, were supported by the income replacement benefit known as Incapacity Benefit.(IB) Used as the long-term sickness benefit, IB was administered by the Department for Work and Pensions (DWP), with the nation's General Practitioners (GP) responsible for the medical certificate required to recommend the benefit via the Personal Capability Assessment (PCA), as conducted by Atos Healthcare on behalf of the DWP. The family doctor was deemed to understand their patients' health needs, to be able to decide which patients were medically unfit to work and, until October 2008, they were the obvious choice to provide access to essential public funds via their recommendations for IB.

Box 3:1 *Margaret Thatcher's role in plan to dismantle welfare state revealed*

The proposals considered by her cabinet included compulsory charges for schooling and a massive scaling back of other public services. "This would of course mean the end of the National Health Service," declared a confidential cabinet memorandum
by the Central Policy Review Staff (CPRS) in September 1982, released by the National Archives on Friday under the 30 year rule.

The leaked version proposed introducing education vouchers, ending the state funding of higher education, freezing welfare benefits and an insurance-based health service. Nigel Lawson, thenthe energy secretary, said the report by the official thinktank on long-term public spending options caused "..the nearest thing to a cabinet riot in the history of the Thatcher administration."…

But the 1982 cabinet papers show the politically explosive paper was discussed at a special halfday extended cabinet discussion on the 9th September that year. They show that Thatcher and Howe had been encouraging the CPRS thinktank to come up with long-term radical options since February that year and that Howe continued to defend them even after the cabinet "riot" described by Lawson.

As part of that revolt a watered-down version of the CPRS paper was leaked to the press, provoking Labour accusations that Thatcher had a secret agenda to dismantle the post-war welfare state – a charge that continues to echo down the years.

Margaret Thatcher's role in plan to dismantle welfare state revealed.[6]
Alan Travis
Home Affairs Editor – The Guardian

28th December 2012

Courtesy of Guardian News and Media Ltd

Two weeks after the £37 billion banking bail-out in October 2008, IB was replaced by the Employment and Support Allowance (ESA) for all new claimants, with a view to the retrenchment of welfare benefits. Initially, the new scheme was piloted and trialled with new ESA claimants. In theory, this would permit any problems to be identified and rectified before rolling out the new ESA claims process to reassess all IB claimants. Access to the ESA was to be assessed and restricted using a new assessment model with stricter criteria and, over time, all 2.5 million IB claimants[9] would be reassessed using the new Work Capability Assessment.

The 2008 New Labour government introduced the Work Capability Assessment (WCA) to reduce the numbers of new out of work long-term sickness benefit claimants able to access the ESA, and it was an escalation of the corrosive American designed disability assessment model being adopted in the UK. Following the 2010 General Election the ESA was rolled out nationwide far too fast to start to reassess all existing IB claimants. Identified problems with the WCA had not been resolved, a reduction in the welfare budget was the only priority, regardless of human consequences and, eventually, 2.5 million IB claimants would learn to live in fear of the new Coalition government.

Due to the influence of a report by the former City banker David Freud[10], when adviser to the New Labour government in 2007, the WCA was to be out-sourced to a private contractor and the DWP appointed the holding company Atos Origin IT Services Ltd[11], commonly known as Atos Healthcare, to conduct the WCA on its behalf. Atos had been working for the DWP by providing the PCA, so they weren't new providers but were awarded a lucrative new contract. Like Thatcher, Freud is a great fan of the private sector. In his 2007 '*independent*' report Freud referenced research that was co-written by Gordon Waddell, based at the Centre for Psychosocial and Disability Research (the Centre) at Cardiff University. Co-authored by Kim Burton, Waddell's 2006 research report, *Is work good for your health and well-being?*[12] was commissioned by the DWP when the Centre was still sponsored by UnumProvident$_{TM}$ Insurance; official '*advisers*' to the UK government since 1994 and **identified by the American Association of Justice in 2008 as the second worst insurance company in America.**[13]

Research from the Centre invariably concludes whatever the DWP deems necessary, as demonstrated in the very influential DWP commissioned monograph from the same source, namely *The Scientific and Conceptual Basis of Incapacity Benefits,*[14] published in 2005. Authored by Gordon Waddell and Mansel Aylward, the monograph gave authenticity to the introduction of the medical tyranny of chronically sick and disabled people when using an unaccountable imported '*non-medical*' biopsychosocial (BPS) assessment model later identified as the WCA.[15] The ESA was not only introduced to limit claimant numbers, and to remove as many claimants as possible from the income replacement long-term sickness benefit. It was also used to exaggerate DWP claims of Incapacity Benefit fraud, which was listed by the DWP in 2012 as being only 0.3%[16] of the entire welfare budget and the ESA was especially used to manipulate the British public to reduce the national psychological reassurance as historically provided by the welfare state.

To access the ESA, claimants were required to make themselves available for a WCA, as exclusively conducted by Atos Healthcare (AH) '*disability analysts*' at the often inaccessible assessment centres across the UK. As a '*functional assessment*' to determine the '*functioning ability*' of the claimant, the diagnosis and prognosis was not considered by AH staff who did not have access to a claimant's medical history.[17]

The detailed patient knowledge and previous authority of GPs was marginalised by the DWP, whose totally unqualified Jobcentre Plus (JCP) Decision Makers are basic-grade administrators

---

Box 3:2 *Atos Healthcare or Disability Denial Factories?*

This dangerous DWP Contract offers the medical opinion of the AH Disability Analyst as a priority, which the Decision Makers accept verbatim, so all additional specialist medical opinion of Consultants, offered by the patient/claimant, is totally overlooked. Six weeks training as a Disability Analyst does not an expert make - contrary to claims by Atos Healthcare management. By definition, a Consultant is an expert in his field of medicine and it is dangerous nonsense to accept a junior doctor's limited clinical experience over the opinion of a clinical expert. The excuse used is that the Disability Analyst is "trained in disability" and is not making a diagnosis. Consequently, desperately ill people are now being declared fit for work because they are physically capable of collecting a pen from the floor! Patients, welfare advisors and MPs all presume that specialist medical opinion by a Consultant will be accepted because they are unfamiliar with the details of the Contract. The previous DWP Select Committee have commented about this in their last report, which has also been totally ignored by the DWP, together with ignoring all evidence offered in successive annual reports by the President of the Appeal Tribunals, HH Judge Robert Martin.

Medically unqualified Decision Makers, who are administrators with basic skills, now decide the fate of all applicants depending on the conclusions of either a seriously flawed computer tick test and/or Disability Analysts who all have limited clinical experience. Hence AH can claim that they are not responsible for the awarding of government care benefits. Their evaluation system causes a crisis for the many victims of this systematic government medical tyranny, and AH escapes all responsibility whilst Ministers confidently offer unstinting support. It's no wonder that AH is so confident, with an income of £100 million per year from the DWP. The level of unnecessary distress caused to the victims of this tyranny cannot be quantified but is significant and, clinically, totally unjustified and unacceptable.

Atos Healthcare or Disability Denial Factories? [17]
Mo Stewart

June 2010

http://www.whywaitforever.com/dwpatosveteranssummary.html

---

with no medical knowledge or comprehension. Rather than collating and considering all the medical evidence provided by the claimant applying for the ESA that includes Consultant opinion, as was officially required by the DWP, the Decision Makers simply acted as decision-stampers to '*rubber stamp*' the findings from the basic WCA, as identified by Professor Harrington in 2010[18] (p10) in the first of five annual reviews of the WCA.

The total failure of the JCP Decision Makers to comprehend their responsibilities, and to collate all the provided medical evidence, guaranteed that many genuine long-term sick and chronically disabled ESA claimants would be refused the financial support they needed to survive. Human suffering, death and despair were inevitable following the many incorrect decisions by totally unqualified staff, who lacked the confidence and the required knowledge to make decisions based on all the medical evidence. As demonstrated in the first Harrington review in November 2010, with reference to the AH result of the WCA, the Decision Makers confirmed that they '*... don't know enough about it to overrule what they're saying.*'[18] (p 50)

As a researcher, I benefitted from brief personal contact with Professor Harrington in 2010 as he conducted the first annual review of the WCA. I was able to speak with him and we exchanged a number of letters. Harrington dismissed my reservations claiming that the DWP couldn't employ medical administrators, which would be cost-prohibitive. I insisted that no unqualified administrator without a basic comprehension of diagnosis, and all the implications of it, could begin to comprehend the medical evidence that would be provided by the claimants.

It seems I was correct. The JCP Decision Makers admitted that they disregarded all the medical evidence provided by the claimants and confirmed any result of the fatally flawed WCA, as Harrington recommended that the WCA should be improved prior to being rolled out nationwide.[18] As will be demonstrated, there have been many thousands of deaths of ESA claimants. There is growing evidence that many were unnecessary and identified as being linked to the fact that the DWP will not employ qualified staff to make decisions regarding the results of a '*functional assessment*' that, by design, was guaranteed to fail chronically sick people and, inevitably, to link to the death of many genuine claimants, yet to be quantified. Given the public reaction to the last DWP published mortality totals of ESA claimants following a Freedom of Information request[19], the updated and more recent death totals of the victims of this dangerous government '*functional assessment*' system have not been published by the DWP.[N2]

NOTES

N2: Updated mortality totals were finally published by the DWP in August 2015:

DWP: August 2015: *Mortality Statistics: Employment and Support Allowance, Incapacity Benefit or Severe Disablement Allowance* - updated death totals p5

Box 3:3 An independent review of the Work Capability Assessment, year 1

The review has found that many Decision Makers lack the confidence to make a decision that deviates from the Atos advice. In part this appears an issue of training and investment in the Decision Maker role, but it also reflects the lack of time Decision Makers are allowed to devote to particular cases. Several people the review spoke to referred to Decision Makers as "decision-stampers", merely ticking through the advice from Atos.

"The impression drawn from the cases coming before the Tribunal is that decision-makers are not discharging that responsibility in an independently minded manner, carefully weighing up all the evidence, resolving conflicts of fact and opinion, considering the applicable law and reaching a reasoned conclusion. They are simply rubber-stamping the HCP's report."
President, First-tier Tribunal p49

"The design of the WCA is such that Decision Makers are given discretion to place a claimant in either group where there is evidence that they have Limited Capability for Work. However, whether due to a lack of training, a lack of confidence or a lack of authority, they invariably refuse to utilise their discretion, even where there is overwhelming medical evidence from specialist consultants showing the Atos report to be clearly wrong in the circumstances. Instead, in most cases they simply prefer the Atos report without adequate reasons for doing so."
Disability Solutions p49

It is clear that a culture has developed amongst Decision Makers that sees the advice from Atos as forming the decision, and that they are there simply to ratify that decision. This is evident in language officials use about decisions; many talk about 'overruling' the Atos advice rather than making an evidence-based decision, while others reference the difficulty in going against the recommendation of an Atos HCP.
"It's difficult. I mean, they're a doctor. They've assessed the person, I don't know enough about it to overrule what they're saying."
Jobcentre Plus Decision Maker p50

A number of submissions to the review have recommended that greater weighting be given to the medical evidence provided by the claimant. A number of different advantages to using this evidence have been given, including the longer timescales over which this evidence has been obtained, the in-depth knowledge of the effects of the claimant's health condition that their HCP can bring and the ability to assess better particular health conditions, especially those which have fluctuating effects and where the claimant doesn't have insight into the effects of their health conditions.
Centre for Mental Health, Mind, Rethink and the
Royal College of Psychiatrists p50

An Independent Review of the Work Capability Assessment, year 1[18]
Professor Malcolm Harrington

November 2010
The Stationary Office

In the first eleven months of 2011 a total of 10,600 IB/ESA claimants died, with 2,200 people who died before the assessment was completed and 1,300 people who died following the WCA assessment when possibly placed into the wrong group.[19] The underqualified Decision Makers had placed those claimants into the Work Related Activity Group in order to prepare for a return to employment; regardless of diagnosis or prognosis that the DWP fail to consider and the unqualified JCP Decision Makers fail to comprehend.

Of the 10,600 recorded IB/ESA claimant deaths between January to November 2011,[19] the greater majority of 7,100 deaths were of those in the Support Group. Given that the deceased were provided with ESA benefit support due to acknowledged very serious health conditions, these numbers of deaths are not necessarily cause for concern as the deceased were gravely ill and could die naturally due to their serious and failing health. What they had to endure in order to be placed into the Support Group following a WCA remains unknown and may well have accelerated the death of many.

However, the 1,300 claimants who died having been assessed by the WCA and told to prepare for a return to work are surely cause for concern, as are the 2,200 people who died before their ESA claim process had been completed. The added unnecessary stress and anxiety created by the ESA application process may well have contributed to many untimely deaths, but this is speculation and can't be quantified.

There is an identified problem in that the evidence from the DWP mortality figures of 2011 has been misinterpreted, claiming that the recorded deaths were within six weeks of a WCA assessment when, in fact, the reported death totals were recorded within six weeks of the death being reported to the DWP.[19] This misinterpretation of the mortality figures, as reported across social media, may have been the excuse needed by the DWP to resist publishing any updated mortality totals, despite repeated requests and challenges to Ministers and to the Prime Minister in the House of Commons.

WCA Outcome at most recent assessment	Number of claimants leaving ESA with a recorded date of death
Assessment not complete	2,200
Work Related Activity Group	1,300
Support Group	7,100
Total	**10,600**

Table 3:1 Source: DWP report: Incapacity Benefits: Deaths of recipients 2011 p6 [19]

The DWP fails to routinely collate the numbers of deaths of chronically sick and disabled people removed from long-term sickness benefit, when found *'fit for work'* following the ESA assessment process and using the fatally flawed WCA. Perhaps it's time they did, and someone in authority should perhaps question why they don't? How many more people have died due to this dangerous American imported assessment model and when will the DWP publish the updated mortality totals…?? [N2]

Illustration 3:1 Fish In A Barrel ~ Reproduced with kind permission of the artist

In 2010 the cash limits and total welfare budget costs quickly became the only priorities of the new Conservative led Coalition neoliberal government, ably supported by the Liberal Democrats, who rapidly disregarded their party manifesto in exchange for a seat at the top table of government.

Care, concern, dignity, empathy, humanity, common decency and compassion were very quickly demonstrated to be expensive luxuries that could not be justified during the Coalition government's rapidly introduced *'austerity measures'* and DWP tyranny, together with

---

NOTES

N2: Updated mortality totals were finally published by the DWP in August 2015:

DWP: August 2015: *Mortality Statistics: Employment and Support Allowance, Incapacity Benefit or Severe Disablement Allowance* - updated death totals p5

punitive sanctions, guaranteed that the poorest in society would live in fear of the Coalition government.

Following David Cameron's election as Prime Minister in 2010, and over a very short space of time, suddenly we arrived at the '*deserving*' and the '*undeserving*' poor in the UK, to be chosen by the Tory elite, who clearly have no personal experience of poverty but who knowingly make extreme and discredited claims, when using the protection of the '*parliamentary privileges*' in the House of Commons, regarding the numbers of benefit cheats who it seems enjoy a life of idleness with a '*money for nothing*' mindset.

The 2010 Coalition government had a Cabinet of politicians, who were £millionaires or richer, deciding the fate of the poorest people in the UK whilst demonstrating their utter contempt for them. All they identified was the costs to the welfare budget whilst disregarding the need, as the Secretary of State for Work and Pensions, Iain Duncan Smith, excelled at vilifying chronically sick and disabled people by suggesting that many were '*malingering*'. Indeed, Iain Duncan Smith was rarely able to disguise his obvious contempt when referring to claimants of long-term sickness benefit or the long-term unemployed, as he failed to make a distinction between the two groups.

By 2011 the Coalition government deemed that the results of the WCA were not as desired and so changed the WCA descriptors to make it even more difficult to access the ESA benefit. Members of the Disability Benefits Consortium - that comprises over 60 different charities - exposed the claims the government used to justify the WCA changes to be totally false.[20]

In the run up to the 2015 general election the Deputy Prime Minister and then Leader of the Liberal Democrat Party, Nick Clegg MP, insisted that the Liberal Democrats, when sharing the responsibilities of the Coalition government, had '*restrained*' the Conservatives and they had retained the '*centre ground.*' Could Nick Clegg really be totally unaware of the thousands who have died[21,22] and whose deaths were possibly accelerated due to the unprecedented savage '*welfare reforms*' that he willingly supported? Was the Deputy Prime Minister so out of touch with reality that he failed to comprehend that if someone's entire income is arbitrarily stopped, by the over zealous use of sanctions by the DWP, then there is a very real possibility that people will actually starve, sometimes to death, in C21st UK? [23]

Box 3:4 ESA changes to the Work Capability Assessment descriptors

The review which gave rise to the proposals for change to the WCA was carried out based on very limited evidence of how the assessment was working in practice. The DWP has failed to consult widely on the proposals, despite the enormous impact that these could have on disabled people, and they have been subjected to a far lower level of external consultation and scrutiny than both the Harrington review and SSAC's review. The DWP roundly rejected the recommendations of SSAC, which showed a very clear lack of support for the regulations, despite SSAC's recommendations being based on a much wider consultation (with over 160 responses to their call for evidence).

In addition, although the DWP state repeatedly in their response to the SSAC* report that 'A number of external stakeholders including specialist disability groups were closely involved in the department-led review', it is well documented that the disability groups involved (many of whom are members of the DBC**) unanimously rejected the Government's proposals, and highlighted that they did not feel that their input had been adequately considered.

ESA ~ changes to the Work Capability Assessment descriptors [20]
ME Association: Disability Benefits Consortium

January 2011

*SSAC – Social Security Advisory Committee
**DBC – Disability Benefits Consortium

The Coalition government front bench excelled at misdirecting both the House of Commons and the British public. Aided and abetted by the tabloid press, the Cabinet members claimed that a drastic reduction of the welfare budget was essential to *'balance the books.'* They also insisted that the large welfare budget must not only be tackled but, judging by the results of the *'welfare reforms'* when using *'austerity measures',* the welfare budget was to be reduced regardless of the very predictable and often fatal human consequences.[23]

The long ago identified future demolition of the welfare state began in earnest in 2010, masquerading as *'welfare reforms'* [24], as the UK was moved ever closer to the American system, with the poor and the sick being held accountable by government for their circumstances. The blame game also began as, at every possible opportunity, Coalition Ministers reminded the Labour opposition that the 2008 banking crisis[25] happened when there was a Labour government in the UK. What was not mentioned was that the global financial crisis had been encouraged by extremes of speculation by the City of London, which had been made possible due to deregulations set in place years before by the Thatcher government.[26]

Evidence for this reality is not only demonstrated in academic research[26] but also in various academic presentations, as real experts expose the fact that the vilification of welfare claimants, and the expressed urgent need to reduce welfare spending using '*austerity measures*' because the country could not afford the costs, was a total misdirection by the Coalition government. **It was the imposition of Conservative ideology, not fiscal necessity.**

Box 3:5 *The impact of Thatcherism on health and well-being in Britain*

The new economy that emerged in the 1980s was of a seriously unbalanced kind. Manufacturing and extraction industries, public utilities, and collective housing provision were displaced by finance and banking industries, privatized utilities, and rampant property speculation. The "big bang" of 1986 saw the deregulation of the City of London and, with that, the unleashing of hitherto unimaginable forms of financial speculation. The ostensible "giving power back to the people" through privatization in fact led to the radical de-democratization of the power industry—now largely externally owned—and other utilities. And the ambition to create "a nation of homeowners" produced a mushrooming of homelessness due to a chronic shortage of affordable social housing—creating the preconditions for the more recent emergence of a new breed of "buy-to-let" landlords charging "market rents." It also underpinned a new culture of speculation and chronic indebtedness—on which a new breed of amoral "entrepreneurs" in banking and finance would be able to prey. All of this generated—and was designed to generate sharply increased inequalities of income and wealth across Britain and a dramatic increase in poverty. It also put in place most of the prerequisites for the great banking and finance crisis of 2008.

In this way, Thatcher's governments wilfully engineered an economic catastrophe across large parts of Britain and sowed the seeds, later nurtured by Blair's New Labour governments, of a subsequent collapse—which ironically has provided the highly spurious legitimation for a new generation of "uber-Thatcherites" in the current Conservative-Liberal Democrat coalition government to go where Thatcher herself had hesitated to tread—a complete dismantling of the welfare state, including privatization of the NHS in England.

The Impact Of Thatcherism On Health And Well-Being In Britain [26]
Alex Scott-Samuel, Clare Bambra, Chik Collins, David J Hunter
Gerry McCartney and Kat Smith

International Journal of Health Services,
Volume 44, Number 1, Pages 53-71
2014

In his August 2014 presentation: *Austerity, A Failed Experiment on the People*, Professor Martin McKee clearly demonstrated the reality of austerity when compared with government rhetoric. The Professor exposed the fact that the austerity measures imposed on the British people was an experiment that was conducted '..***without any ethical approval..***' [27] The financial crisis of 2008 actually started on Wall Street, in America, in 2006. The then Labour government began the reforms of the welfare state in 2008, claiming that welfare costs were excessive, whilst disregarding the impact of the deregulation of the City. The Professor especially noted the poor judgement of the present Conservative Chancellor, George Osborne, who had promoted the Irish model of investments that was to eventually totally collapse.[27]

Available via *You Tube*, Professor McKee's fascinating explanation of the stock market collapse is explained much better than I ever could, and it is a worthy investment of 44 minutes of anyone's time as, when presenting at a commemorative conference in New Zealand in August 2014[27], he exposes the '*complete bluff* ' regarding the cause of the banking crisis and the fact that welfare dependent claimants are vilified for what was '*..other people's greed.*' Martin McKee explains that the real reason for the financial collapse was that '*.. some very rich and very greedy stupid people were playing with things that they didn't understand..*' and his presentation is very, very entertaining as well as very informative.[27] An academic paper on the same subject, and co-authored by David Stuckler, was published in the Clinical Medicine Journal in 2012. [27b]

The financial crash used to justify the punitive welfare reforms now endured by those least able to protest was inevitable and had actually been predicted because the '*..markets were out of control.*' Indeed, according to Professor McKee, '*... much of what was happening in the financial markets was because we put some very rich and very greedy and very stupid people in charge of it all.*' The conclusion of his presentation is that the argument used for the enforced austerity measures and, subsequently, for all the suffering in the UK '*..just don't stack up..*' and '*... **austerity is a political choice, not a financial necessity.**'* [27] In fact, the UK economy had actually been recovering under Labour, but it all went badly wrong with the 2010 Coalition government and George Osborne's first budget.

Professor McKee's final comments in his presentation to a group of health professionals in Auckland, New Zealand, was that: '*..austerity is not good for the economy, is not good for health, is not good for political stability and it's just not a good idea.*' [27, 27b]

Indeed, the longer this research was conducted, the more deeply disturbing evidence was discovered, confirming that *'Thatcher's Legacy'* was becoming a reality for the British people, as successive UK governments transformed the welfare state into something resembling another American state; regardless of the numbers who suffered and died in the process.[28,28b]

> **Box 3:6** *"Margaret Thatcher left a dark legacy that has still not disappeared."*
>
> The first is what changed in the temper of Britain and the British.
> What happened at the hands of this woman's indifference to sentiment and good sense in the early 1980s brought unnecessary calamity to the lives of several million people who lost their jobs. It led to riots that nobody needed. More insidiously, it fathered a mood of tolerated harshness. Materialistic individualism was blessed as a virtue, the driver of national success. Everything was justified as long as it made money – and this, too, is still with us.
>
> Thatcherism failed to destroy the welfare state. The lady was too shrewd to try that, and barely succeeded in reducing the share of the national income taken by the public sector. But the sense of community evaporated. There turned out to be no such thing as society, at least in the sense we used to understand it. Whether pushing each other off the road, barging past social rivals, beating up rival soccer fans, or idolising wealth as the only measure of virtue, Brits became more unpleasant to be with. This regrettable transformation was blessed by a leader who probably did not know it was happening because she didn't care if it happened or not. But it did, and the consequences seem impossible to reverse.
>
> Margaret Thatcher's legacy [28]
> Hugo Young, 2003
>
> **Hugo Young was a political columnist for the Guardian from 1984 until 2003 and biographer of Margaret Thatcher.*
> *He wrote this piece in 2003, two weeks before he died.*
>
> The Guardian, 11th April 2013
>
> *Courtesy of Guardian News and Media Ltd*

Now that a majority Conservative government has been elected in the UK following the May 2015 general election, David Cameron remains as the UK Prime Minister. As the Conservatives have a predicted £12billion further welfare cuts planned, the future for the long-term chronically sick and disabled people in the UK, who are totally dependent upon long-term welfare funding for their financial and physical survival, does appear to be very bleak. Cameron will continue to try and fail to emulate Thatcher as he gradually moves the UK to the American system of limited, begrudged social security for the few.[29]

The creation of DWP tyranny against those least able to protest has been readily confirmed.

Welcome to Little America…

Box 3:7 *Thatcher's reckless acolytes don't know when to stop*

All can agree that Margaret Thatcher changed the heart of British politics more than any politician since Clement Attlee. She all but erased his political legacy to stamp her own image on the nation, so Britain before and after Thatcher were two different countries. Where once we had stood within a recognisable postwar social democratic European tradition, after Thatcher the country had rowed half way across the Atlantic, psychologically inbued with US neoliberal individualism. Too timid, too in thrall, the 13-year Labour government rarely dared challenge the attitudes she planted in the nation's psyche…

That's history, but what matters to us is her legacy now that her heirs and imitators rule in her wake. The Cameron and Osborne circle are crude copies carried away with the dangerous idea that conviction is all it takes to run a country. Seizing her chariot's reigns to drive it on recklessly, they lack her brains, experience and political skill. Above all, they lack her competence at running the machinery of government…. But on their catastrophic economic policy, it's full-speed ahead into the concrete wall…

The romantic image of the lady in the tank spurs them on. Where she privatised state-owned industries, they go much further, seeking to dismantle the state itself. She usually knew the limits to public tolerance, gauging how much of the spirit of the '45 abided, so even if it was between gritted teeth, she forced herself to say, "The NHS is safe in our hands": she reorganised but did not privatise it. No such alarms ring in Cameron's ears…

Instead, her Big Bang blew the roof off City profits and property booms filled the gap where productive industry should have sprouted. Her heirs have not learned that lesson, with no sign of the promised "rebalancing". No sign they learned from her that markets don't move in to fill the gaps when the state is rolled back – not then, not now…

The endemic worklessness of her era was never repaired – now her successors blame the vicitms. Cameron's crew crudely imagine she intended it. That gives them the nerve to set about cutting benefits and the public realm with a glee they don't bother to hide. They are acolytes of a raw Thatcher cult that they have rough-hewn and exaggerated in their own image.

Thatcher's reckless acolytes don't know when to stop [28b]
Polly Toynbee

The Guardian, 9th April 2013

Courtesy of Guardian News and Media Ltd

NOTES

N2: Updated mortality totals were published by the DWP in August 2015:

DWP: August 2015: *Mortality Statistics: Employment and Support Allowance, Incapacity Benefit or Severe Disablement Allowance* - updated death totals p5
https://www.gov.uk/government/uploads/system/uploads/attachment_data/file/456359/mortality-statistics-esa-ib-sda.pdf

REFERENCES:

** **All references confirmed and accessed 15th May 2015**

Illustration 3:1   *Fish In A Barrel* courtesy of Dave Lupton of Crippen Cartoons:
http://www.crippencartoons.co.uk/

Table 3:1: Incapacity Benefits: deaths of recipients 2011
https://www.gov.uk/government/uploads/system/uploads/attachment_data/file/223050/incap_decd_recips_0712.pdf

6. TRAVIS ALAN: 2012: *Margaret Thatcher's role in plan to dismantle welfare state revealed.*
The Guardian: 28th December 2012 : courtesy of Guardian News & Media Ltd
http://www.theguardian.com/politics/2012/dec/28/margaret-thatcher-role-plan-to-dismantle-welfare-state-revealed

7. SCOTT-SAMUEL et al: 2014: *The impact of Thatcherism on health and well-being in Britain* : Alex Scott-Samuel, Clare Bambra, Chik Collins, David J Hunter, Gerry McCartney, Kat Smith. International Journal of Health Services, Volume 44, Number 1, Pages 53-71, 2014   http://pcwww.liv.ac.uk/~alexss/thatcherism.pdf

8. BBC NEWS 2008: 13th October: *UK banks receive £37bn bail-out*
http://news.bbc.co.uk/1/hi/business/7666570.stm

9. PAC 2010: Support to IB claimants through Pathways to Work Public Accounts Committee: 13th Sept 2010
http://www.publications.parliament.uk/pa/cm201011/cmselect/cmpubacc/404/40405.htm

10. FREUD DAVID: 2007 March: The Freud Report: *Reducing dependancy, increasing opportunity:options for the future of welfare to work.* An independent report by David Freud. Commissioned and published by the DWP. ISBN: 978 1 84712 193 6
http://base-uk.org/sites/base-uk.org/files/%5Buser-raw%5D/11-07/welfarereview.pdf

11. WHO IS ATOS? https://www.whatdotheyknow.com/request/who_is_atos

12. WADDELL & BURTON: 2006: DWP: *Is work good for your health and well-being?* ISBN 0 11 703694 3: 13 digit ISBN 978 0 11 703694 9
https://www.gov.uk/government/uploads/system/uploads/attachment_data/file/214326/hwwb-is-work-good-for-you.pdf

13. AMERICAN ASSOCIATION OF JUSTICE: 2008: *The Ten Worst Insurance Companies in America*
http://www.bulmanlaw.com/wp-content/uploads/2013/03/TenWorstInsuranceCompanies.pdf

14. WADDELL G and AYLWARD M: 2005: DWP: *The Scientific and Conceptual Basis of Incapacity Benefits*: ISBN: 9780117035843

15. STEWART M: 2015: *The influence of the private insurance industry on the UK welfare reforms* http://disability-studies.leeds.ac.uk/library/author/stewart.mo

16. EXELL R: February 2012: *New figures show low level of benefit freud.*
http://liberalconspiracy.org/2012/02/26/new-figures-show-low-level-of-benefit-fraud/

17. STEWART M: June 2010: *Atos Healthcare or Disability Denial Factories?*

http://www.whywaitforever.com/dwpatosveteranssummary.html

18. HARRINGTON M: November 2010: *An independent review of the work capability assessment*, year 1. ISBN: 9780108509476

   https://www.gov.uk/government/uploads/system/uploads/attachment_data/file/70071/wca-review-2010.pdf :

19. DWP: 9th July 2012: Incapacity Benefits: Deaths of recipients
   https://www.gov.uk/government/uploads/system/uploads/attachment_data/file/223050/incap_decd_recips_0712.pdf

20. ME ASSOCIATION: 2011: item 2: *ESA – changes to the Working Capability Assessment descriptors*
   http://www.meassociation.org.uk/2011/02/esa-%E2%80%93-changes-to-the-working-capability-assessment-descriptors/

21. MILLER S: 2014: *Recent recorded deaths related to UK welfare reforms*
   http://blacktrianglecampaign.org/2014/10/21/uk-welfare-reform-deaths-updated-list-october-21st-2014/

22. SOMMERLAD NICK: 2012: *32 die a week after failing test for new incapacity benefit.* The Mirror: 4th April 2012
   http://blogs.mirror.co.uk/investigations/2012/04/32-die-a-week-after-failing-in.html

23. GENTLEMAN AMELIA: 2014: *Vulnerable man starved to death after benefits were cut.* The Guardian: 28th February 2014 http://www.theguardian.com/society/2014/feb/28/man-starved-to-death-after-benefits- cut

24. TRAVIS ALAN: 2012: *Margaret Thatcher's role in plan to dismantle welfare state revealed.* The Guardian: 28th December 2012
   http://www.theguardian.com/politics/2012/dec/28/margaret-thatcher-role-plan-to-dismantle-welfare- state- revealed

25. BBC NEWS 2008: 13th October: *UK banks receive £37bn bail-out*
   http://news.bbc.co.uk/1/hi/business/7666570.stm

26. SCOTT-SAMUEL A et al: 2014: *The Impact of Thatcherism On Health And Well-being In Britain*: International Journal of Health Services, Volume 44, Number 1, Pages 53-71 Alex Scott-Samuel, Clare Bambra, Chik Collins, David J Hunter, Gerry McCartney and Kat Smith http://pcwww.liv.ac.uk/~alexss/thatcherism.pdf (Free access)

27. McKEE M: 29th August 2014: *Austerity, A Failed Experiment on the People* – a presentation to health professionals at Ko Awatea, Auckland, New Zealand:
   https://www.youtube.com/watch?v=G7Fd-uBRPqY
   27b. McKEE M, KARANIKOLOS M, BELCHER P, STUCKLER D: 2012: *Austerity: a failedexperiement on the people of Europe*: Clinical Medicine 2012, Vol 12, No4: 346-50
   https://www.rcplondon.ac.uk/sites/default/files/documents/clinmed-124-p346-350-mckee.pdf

28. YOUNG H: 2003: *Margaret Thatcher's Legacy.* The Guardian: 11th April 2013 Courtesy of Guardian News & Media Ltd
   http://www.theguardian.com/politics/interactive/2013/apr/11/margaret-thatcher-legacy-best-writing

28b. TOYNBEE P: *Thatcher's reckless acolytes don't know when to stop.* The Guardian 9th April 2003 Courtesy of Guardian News & Media Ltd.
   http://www.theguardian.com/politics/interactive/2013/apr/11/margaret-thatcher-legacy-best-writing

29. DAGURRE A & ETHERINGTON D: 30th June 2014
   Welfare reform in the UK under the Conservative-led Coalition government: ruptures and continuities
   http://workfare.org.uk/images/uploads/docs/Welfare_Reform_in_the_UK_PubReady.pdf

CHAPTER 4: CORPORATE INFLUENCE
~ Power, Cash and Corruption

Injustice anywhere is a threat to justice everywhere...
Dr Martin Luther King, Jr
1929 ~ 1968

As the United Kingdom (UK) approached the 2015 general election on May 7th, politicians were all campaigning on subjects they presumed to be of significance to large numbers of the general public, in the distinct hope that more members of the public would be persuaded to use their vote on polling day to secure a majority government and not another coalition government.

Who really could be trusted with the nation's finances as the leaders of the two largest political parties both claimed they had the solution? However, David Cameron had the mighty Tory press behind him, and seemingly unlimited financial resources, so the election result was not really in any doubt as it seems that the Conservative Party attempted to buy democracy in the marginal constituencies[30], despite the suggestion of the pre-election polls that the election result was too close to call.

The extension of the '*Right To Buy*' for housing association tenants to purchase their homes, with generous government financial support, was offered by the Conservative Party manifesto.[31] Of course, David Cameron was continuing one of Thatcher's policies as it was a previous Conservative government that permitted residents of council houses to buy their homes for this '*property-owning democracy*' that was one of Thatcher's rallying calls for the 1980 Housing Act.[32] Her disciple was simply continuing in her footsteps, hoping the British people would fall for the rhetoric; whilst overlooking the fact that there is a catastrophic shortage of affordable social housing in the UK, which has caused problems for a generation with '*buy-to-let*' landlords charging '*market rents*'. Cameron also overlooked the fact that he claims that the UK cannot justify the welfare budget funded by the Department for Work and Pensions (DWP) yet, when he needs to influence voters in the run up to a General Election, the Prime Minister can find unlimited amounts of '*tax payers' money*' for the latest scheme to bribe the gullible electorate, by offering to help tenants with the costs of a deposit to purchase their social housing properties.

Surely, if this nation cannot afford to care for genuine chronically sick and profoundly disabled people then no government should have the ability to give away tax payers' cash to help people living in social housing to buy property? This is yet more government policy introduced following ideology and totally unrelated to the needs of a nation. If social housing tenants can afford a mortgage then they should find another property and free the social housing to make it available for those who are in desperate need of it. Is that not common sense or perhaps, as Brian May would say, '*Common Decency*' [33], as morality and ethics seemed to escape David Cameron and his Cabinet.

Meanwhile, during the 2015 general election campaign, Ed Miliband MP was attempting to be all things to all men. He was attempting to demonstrate that only the next Labour government could really secure the National Health Service (NHS), whilst claiming that an appointment with a General Practitioner (GP) would be available within 48 hours if Labour were elected to government [34], without any detail of how that could possibly be achieved. Miliband was trying very hard to distance himself from the last New Labour government and the accusation that under their leadership the UK's deficit grew significantly, supposedly leaving '*no cash*' for the incoming Coalition government in 2010.

In the last five years this claim was constantly thrown at the Labour front bench by Ministers of the Coalition government, whilst being very careful to overlook the fact that the banking collapse in 2008, which had required an additional injection of £37billion from the New Labour government, was created thanks to previous policies of the Thatcher era that had foolishly deregulated the City of London. [35]

As the leader of the Liberal Democrats in the 2010 Coalition government Nick Clegg MP, having tasted power, didn't want to let it go in 2015. Instead of campaigning for the Liberal Democrats, Clegg was busy reminding voters of the choices for the next predicted UK coalition government. [36] Following the polls, Clegg predicted the election choice was between the Liberal Democrats once again sharing power or the Scottish National Party in a possible coalition with the Labour Party and the UK Independence Party (UKIP) no doubt in a coalition with any other party who would accept them. Clegg proclaimed that, as the Deputy Prime Minister of the UK over the last five years, he had governed with '*compassion and a sense of fairness*.' [36] So that's another political leader in the UK who failed to acknowledge the many thousands of chronically sick and disabled people who have died[37,38] due in no small part to welfare reform policies he willingly supported when in government. It appears that the needs of the long-term chronically sick are invisible to all political leaders. It's as if they don't exist except, of course, as a financial burden to the '*hard-working tax-payer.*'

The May 2015 general election produced a small Conservative majority, with Prime Minister David Cameron now free to continue to cause more destruction to the lives of the poorest, with very little objection from within his own party. Nick Clegg and Ed Miliband resigned as leaders of the Liberal Democrat and Labour parties, and Nigel Farage initially stepped down as leader of the UKIP party whilst the country recovered from the shock of a Conservative majority government once again leading the UK following a low turnout at the polls.

Regardless of the general election, the fact remains that the Employment and Support Allowance (ESA) is still the long-term sickness benefit, badly administered by the DWP, for all those without independent means who are not well enough or physically capable of considering paid employment. Maximus Health and Human Resources Ltd replaced Atos Healthcare, contracted to the DWP as the Work Capability Assessment (WCA) provider[39], with effect from March 2015. This is another highly discredited[40] foreign corporate giant, totally unaccountable to the General Medical Council, awarded a £multi-million DWP contract to assess this nation's most vulnerable citizens for access to long-term sickness benefit. As previously reported, the WCA assessment has already been linked to thousands of 2011 deaths[41] and, since 2012, the DWP have refused to publish the official updated mortality totals of ESA claimants[N2], following a WCA when conducted by Atos Healthcare, despite public demand and Freedom of Information requests. This begs the question as to what are they hiding?

Over the past five years of the Coalition government a lot has been written about the WCA, and the many victims of it. The Secretary of State for Work and Pensions, Iain Duncan Smith, together with all DWP Ministers, totally disregarded all evidence against the fatally flawed assessment model, dismissed all evidence of the increasing numbers who have died as an indirect result of the ESA assessment process and rejected all suggestions that the WCA should be '*scrapped*', regardless of which medical representative body was providing the evidence.[42]

I would venture so far as to suggest that the WCA is here to stay as this DWP nightmare was a done deal with UnumProvident_TM Insurance back in 1994.[43] The research demonstrated long ago that the WCA was completely bogus and a replica of the '*disability denial practices*' of the American corporate healthcare insurance giant UnumProvident_TM Insurance.[44] Now known as Unum Insurance, the company have had significant influence with the long-term

NOTES

N2: Updated mortality totals were finally published by the DWP in August 2015: DWP: August 2015: *Mortality Statistics: Employment and Support Allowance, Incapacity Benefit or Severe Disablement Allowance* - updated death totals p5

sickness benefit reforms of successive British governments thanks to the authority of just one man, Professor Sir Mansel Aylward. He was the government principle medical officer when the company became official government '*advisers*' in 1994 and his influential '*academic research*,' since leaving the DWP in 2005, was sponsored by Unum (Provident) Insurance via Cardiff University and was used to justify the introduction of the totally discredited WCA.[44]

Illustration 4:1 Hit Men ~ reproduced with kind permission of the artist

Yet, what is often unreported is the fact that, in 2007 in America, Professor John Langbein of the Yale School of Law produced a paper identified as '*The Unum Provident Scandal*'[45] that exposed Unum's policy of disability denial that continues to be referenced to this day and, in November 2007, BBC News reported that the British government were being advised by an American insurance company with a reputation for '*racketeering*'.[46]

The American corporate healthcare insurance giant certainly presumed that they would gain from the ongoing demolition of the British welfare state, as large uptake of private healthcare insurance was anticipated when the company began their mass TV advertising for their income protection insurance (IPI) in 2011.[47] The TV marketing was soon stopped, presumably by the Office of Fair Trading (OFT), who were alerted by disability activists who exposed Unum (Provident) Insurance as benefitting from '*insider knowledge*' having been government advisers on '*welfare claims management*' since 1994. The adverts stopped shortly after the OFT had been so informed.

In the ongoing attempt to transform the United Kingdom (UK) into Little America, their ambition to swamp the UK market with their IPI policies failed. Unum Insurance subsequently removed their IPI policies from the open market in 2012[48] and concentrated on selling their '*back-up plan*' to industry, to be funded by workers via wages.[49] The long ago planned mass sales of IPI policies by Unum (Provident) Insurance had failed thanks to the efforts of the disability lobby in the UK. The company and the DWP had both underestimated the significance of the Disabled Peoples' Organisations (DPO) and their supporters, who share the research evidence of MS online, or link to it, and they are all very well informed regarding the influence of the American company with the UK government's '*welfare reforms.*'[50]

Regardless of government protests and mutterings, reports or debates, the fact is that the Work Capability Assessment (WCA) is an identified and confirmed totally bogus assessment model, causing '*preventable harm*' to many, and discredited by both the British Medical Association[51] in 2012 and the Royal College of Nurses in 2013[52]; who both demanded that the WCA should be '*scrapped.*' The DWP disregarded their protests.

The DWP disregards all protests against the WCA. Indeed, the Coalition government clearly demonstrated that using the excessive authority provided by '*financial privilege*'[53] - an ancient authority of the House of Commons used to totally disregard all suggested amendments to the Welfare Reform Bill as hard won in the House of Lords in 2011[54] - the government has carte blanche to wreak havoc to millions of lives in the UK. They can and do disregard all evidence against the WCA, regardless of the growing numbers of identified associated deaths, as demonstrated in the very disturbing and detailed evidence in 'Calum's List'[55] and others.

Given the fact that the design of this '***non-medical***' WCA assessment model was influenced by Unum (Provident) Insurance, a foreign healthcare insurance giant with an ulterior motive, and **identified in 2008 by the American Association of Justice as the second worst insurance company in America**[56], this evidence alone should be enough to have the WCA stopped and the ESA reconsidered.

The claims management of Unum (Provident) Insurance was identified as being '*illegal*' by the American Association of Justice[56], so someone needs to ask why the DWP use the identical claims management process, by using the modified and bogus biopsychosocial (BPS) model of assessment in the UK, better known as the WCA, together with totally unqualified Job Centre Plus (JCP) Decision Makers to resist funding benefit? If the principle reason for the *'welfare reforms'* is to reduce the DWP welfare budget, regardless of human consequences, there can be no surprise that the DWP is totally resistant to all legitimate evidence against the WCA.

Box 4:1 *The influence of the private insurance industry on the UK welfare reforms*

The influence of Unum Provident Insurance is demonstrated in the memorandums provided for past WPSC* reports that clearly list the transformation of Incapacity Benefit to ESA. The requirement to 'resist diagnosis', 'revise the 'sick note', 'encourage the Government to focus on ability and not disability', 'change the name of Incapacity Benefit' and 'benefits not to be given on the basis of a certain disability or illness but on capacity assessments' have all come to pass as Unum Provident Insurance have influenced UK Government welfare policy since 1994.

'At UnumProvident we have a non-medical, enabling model
of rehabilitation and we are working with our partners at the
UnumProvident Centre for Psychosocial and Disability
Research at Cardiff University to better understand what places
people at risk of long-term or chronic illness. Further
information about this model can be made available
to the committee'

Supplementary memorandum submitted by UnumProvident(TM)
2006

The SCBIB** was, essentially, the blue print for the future introduction of the WCA, using a discredited biopsychosocial (BPS) model of assessment as planned following the New Labour conference in November 2001: Malingering and Illness Deception, with Aylward as a contributor and "malingering" very firmly planted as being the motivation for claimants of disability benefits. Guilty until proven innocent was the mind-set that continues to this day. "And the methodology used by Waddell and Aylward is the same one that informs the work of UnumProvident."

The influence of the private insurance industry on the UK welfare reforms [50]
Mo Stewart
January 2015

ResearchGate

*WPSC – the Work and Pensions Select Committee
**SCBIB – the Scientific and Conceptual Basis of Incapacity Benefits

---

The moderated BPS assessment model, known as the WCA, was designed to remove as many as possible from access to ESA on route to the demolition of the welfare state, to be eventually replaced by private healthcare insurance.[57] The assessment model and the welfare reforms were planned for one reason and one reason only which was financial gain, with medical 'experts' employed by corporate giants heading both the Faculty of Occupational Medicine and the Society of Occupational Medicine, as Aylward and colleagues from the then UnumProvident™ Insurance introduced '*rehabilitation*' to politicians in 1992 as a panacea to reduce costs.

This convinced the John Major Conservative government that General Practitioners (GP) know nothing about their patients' health in relation to work, and so all clinical opinion could be marginalised in favour of using '*Disability Analysts*' from the private sector. Breath-taking though it now seems, this misdirection and medical fiction actually worked, and over three million people are now being potentially harmed by a '*rehabilitation*' model, masquerading as a '*functional assessment*', which was expected to guarantee to save the government £millions in welfare benefits and to persuade middle England to invest in private healthcare insurance.

Chaired by the indomitable and disabled Dame Anne Begg MP, the tri-party Work and Pensions Select Committee (the Committee) published a damning report[58,59] in July 2014, providing detailed evidence of the needless suffering caused by the WCA, and the Committee recommended that the ESA should be completely redesigned. Replacing one corporate giant with another to conduct the WCA was not good enough. However, the omnipotent Minister for Disabled People, Mark Harper, totally dismissed the select committee's report seemingly without a second thought.[60]

Illustration 4:2 Spin ~ reproduced by kind permission of the artist

With *Cash Not Care* being demonstrated as the only government priority when using the enforced government '*austerity measures*' and '*financial privilege*', the DWP presumed an authority to totally disregard all evidence of wrong doing. The growing numbers of fatalities and victims linked to the dangerous ESA assessment system that uses unqualified JCP Decision Makers to decide benefit entitlement, are demonstrated to be nothing more than disposable lives and acceptable collateral damage.[61] It seems that this is the price being paid for the completion of '*Thatcher's Legacy*' to ensure that the former security of the welfare state will be totally demolished, and few will regard it as the safety net it was designed to be.

When researching the background to the WCA and the ESA it was the activities of Atos Healthcare that was originally investigated. Over time, the discovered evidence took this researcher on a voyage of research discovery to uncover the sinister influence of an American corporate healthcare insurance giant within the DWP, and the influence the company have had with consecutive UK governments. The entire national press, collectively, refused to expose to the British people the confirmed involvement of Unum (Provident) Insurance with the UK welfare reforms claims management since 1994 so all information was, of necessity, shared via the Internet. Is this the power of an American corporate giant or the influence of the UK government to control and to silence the national press….??

If not for the courage of journalist John Pring, the Editor of the UK's only Disability News Service, the link between the DWP and Unum Insurance would not have been exposed in the public domain[62] other than via the online disability support groups. Despite John's best efforts, he writes for a limited market and the vast majority of the able bodied British people, indoctrinated by the verbal abuses of the Coalition DWP Ministers against the long-term sick, as reported in banner headlines in the tabloid press, remained in total ignorance of the long – ago planned demolition of the British welfare state.[63]

Someone should surely ask why the national press refused to expose this American corporate giant's influence with government welfare policies as the UK moves, with each passing year, ever closer to resembling another American state.[63] In reality, the majority of the national press reproduced government rhetoric and, most of them, terrorised chronically sick and disabled people with the endless Tory accusations against them, as increases in disability hate crimes climbed. We are meant to have a free press in the UK. What we have in reality is a national press that conducts Tory party propaganda.[64,65]

When attempting to alert people to this American corporate influence with the UK welfare reforms, disabled IT Consultant and my original Webmaster '*Mike Bach*', was already exposing the influence of Unum Provident[TM] Insurance on his website at *Why Wait Forever*[66], whilst academic Jonathan Rutherford had been trying to expose the influence of Unum, and the failure of the Labour Party to resist the influence, since 2007.[67,68]

Box 4:2 *Unum bragged about 'driving government thinking' on incapacity benefit reform*

Unum even launched a major media campaign in 2011 just as the coalition began a three-year programme to reassess about 1.5 million existing IB claimants through the new, stricter test, the work capability assessment (WCA). Now DNS has secured a copy of a Unum document on the assessment of "incapacity", which was published in 2005.

The document was written by Michael O'Donnell, then the company's chief medical officer and now in the same role at Atos Healthcare, which carries out WCAs on behalf of the government. O'Donnell says in the document that Unum has "always been at the leading edge of disability assessment and management". He adds: "We know that our views and understanding are not yet in the mainstream of doctors' thinking, but Government Policy is moving in the same direction, to a large extent being driven by our thinking and that of our close associates, both in the UK and overseas."

Unum bragged about 'driving government thinking' on incapacity benefit reform.[62]
John Pring

Disability News Service
15th February 2013

Over the last six years, the research evidence exposed the true realities behind the welfare reforms that were totally unrelated to the 2008 banking crisis.[69] The future demolition of the welfare state was identified by Thatcher in 1982[70], then supported by all subsequent British governments. Regardless of evidence, protests or death totals, all British governments since 1982 have committed to the future demolition of the welfare state, in keeping with the 2007 *Freud Report*[71], by former banker David Freud, when adviser to the last (New) Labour government. The influential report was written prior to Freud joining the Conservative Party, his elevation to the House of Lords and his appointment as the unelected Parliamentary Under Secretary of State, better known as the Minister for Welfare Reform, in the 2010 Coalition government.

Despite being unelected, Freud was rewarded with unlimited authority. As Minister for Welfare Reform, any suggestion he made to reduce the DWP budget was welcomed by the Coalition government, such as the under-occupancy penalty[72], commonly known as the *'bedroom tax '* that again jeopardised the welfare of only the poorest people in the land, regardless of predictable human consequences. With cash reduction as the only priority, since being appointed as a DWP Minister Freud's suggestions of how to reduce the DWP budget have been adopted by government. They have created relentless harm to chronically ill and profoundly disabled people, as he designed endless ways to force them back into abject poverty and isolation.

Box 4:3 *E pluribus Unum*

In 1994, the Tory government hired John LoCascio, second vice-president of giant US disability insurance company, Unum, to advise on reducing the numbers successfully claiming IB. He joined the "medical evaluation group". Another key figure in the group was Mansel Aylward. They devised a stringent "all work test". Approved doctors were trained in Unum's approach to claims management. The rise in IB claimants came to a halt. However, it did not reduce the rising numbers of claimants with mental health problems. The gateway to benefit needed tightening up even more.

E pluribus Unum[67]
Jonathan Rutherford

The Guardian ~ Comment is Free
17th March 2008

Courtesy of Guardian News & Media Ltd

In the 2007 *Freud Report* [73] the former banker referenced the 2006 research as co-authored by Gordon Waddell[74] based at the Centre for Psychosocial and Disability Research (the Centre), at Cardiff University, as sponsored until 2009 by the American healthcare insurance giant Unum (Provident) Insurance. Freud used the research evidence as justification for his conclusions, whilst overlooking the easily demonstrated coincidence that any claimed *'independent'* research commissioned by the DWP, as conducted at the Centre and sponsored by Unum (Provident) Insurance, routinely demonstrated whatever conclusion was deemed necessary by the DWP. That conclusion was that regardless of diagnosis or prognosis, one million sick and disabled people needed to find a job. *Cash Not Care* began in earnest due to the influence of Freud's report, who had freely admitted that he knew nothing about welfare…

This travesty was very well documented by Professor Alison Ravetz in her detailed critique of the New Labour government's 2006 Green Paper on Incapacity Benefit Reform: *A New Deal for welfare: empowering people to work.*[75] The Professor exposed the fact that the Green Paper used commissioned DWP research from the Centre as the main reference in the Green Paper.[76]

Box 4:4 *The 'Freud Report'*

To achieve its 80% aspiration, the Government will need to target its welfare strategy at tackling all of the inactive groups. It will require about one fifth of the "economically inactive" population to move into work. This would include 300,000 lone parents (relative to a current population of 780,000 claiming Income Support); one million more older people in work (relative to 20 million people aged over 50 in total) and reducing the numbers claiming incapacity benefits by 1 million (relative to 2.68 million.) (p 5)

DWP: Reducing dependency, increasing
opportunity: options for the future of welfare to work
[71]

David Freud

The Scientific and Conceptual Basis of Incapacity Benefit [77] (SCBIB) was authored by Gordon Waddell and Mansel Aylward, when commissioned by the DWP and sponsored at the Centre by Unum (Provident) Insurance, and was identified by Professor Ravetz as being politically motivated. In other words, the monograph used to justify the future devastation of millions of lives was written to support the '*Thatcher Legacy*' and to justify the planned future demolition of the welfare state.

The SCBIB was used in the 2006 Green Paper to justify the reform of Incapacity Benefit. Academics do not accept research evidence provided by the Centre as being truly independent, as used by the DWP to justify any major changes to funding of long term sickness and disability benefits required by the DWP. Whilst official DWP reports offer '*academic research*' from the Centre to justify political decisions, regularly quoted research demonstrates the DWP as having an ulterior motive. The SCBIB research evidence '*…is not research undertaken in the spirit of open enquiry. It is commissioned research and, as such, pre-disposed towards ideologically determined outcomes*' [78] and is, therefore, lacking credibility.

Yet, the welfare of over three million chronically sick and disabled people, dependent upon long-term sickness benefit, was threatened due to this one report that the government accepted as justification to terrorise all those who, according to the 2010 Coalition Government, had a presumed '*money-for-nothing*' mentality and a lack of work ethic. Thanks to the SCBIB, suddenly every sick and disabled claimant of IB or ESA benefits was presumed guilty unless proven innocent, when using Unum as official '*government advisers*' for welfare claims management; despite the company being identified in 2005 as **'*an outlaw company*'** by the California Department of Insurance Commissioner, John Garamendi.[79]

In 2005 in America, there were so many serious complaints against Unum (Provident) Insurance that there was a multi-state settlement of 48 American states that exposed the company as knowingly conducting '*bad faith*' claims practices, and Unum were ordered to reverse 42% of previously denied disability claims, at an estimated cost of $676 million.[80] By October 2008, Unum Insurance were identified by a Boston federal jury as having '*committed fraud*' by requiring claimants to apply for Social Security benefits when the company '*knew they were not eligible.*' [81] **The obvious question remains as to why this American corporate insurance giant were ever permitted to become official UK '*government advisers.*' ??**

In the UK, by using the WCA '*non-medical*' assessment model, as introduced to resist funding long-term sickness benefit, detailed medical opinion was marginalised and claimants had to prove their illness and lack of ability to go to work, all because Waddell and Aylward proclaimed that '*illness is a belief*' and that claimants could '*think themselves well*'; and '*motivational tools*' [82] (p166) were recommended as '*incentives*', [82] which would be translated by the DWP into savage sanctions. What remains incredible is that, regardless of the inevitable death and destruction it would cause, this medical fiction as copied from corporate America was welcomed by British governments whose only concern was *Cash Not Care*.

The planned abolition of the security of the welfare state was easier to enforce so long as all authentic medical opinion by General Practitioners (GP) and Consultants was totally disregarded by unqualified JCP Decision Makers, as demonstrated by Professor Harrington in the first review of the WCA.[83] (p 50) Sick and disabled people were despondent but there is always strength in numbers…

By 2012 the Disabled Peoples' Organisations (DPO) were more co-ordinated and their voices were being heard by a larger audience. They had many highly competent supporters who were more than capable of exposing the realities of the bogus WCA assessments, and the manipulation of the British public by the government in this ongoing social engineering, to persuade the British people that it was their responsibility to work and to challenge anyone who didn't regardless of diagnosis, prognosis or fatal consequences.

Box 4:5 *An independent assessment of the arguments for proposed Incapacity Benefit reform*

He is now head of the Centre whose remit 'to develop special lines of research into the psychosocial factors related to disability, vocational rehabilitation, and the ill-health behaviours which impact on work and employment. (p 6) Unum Provident, an American company, is the largest disability insurance company in the world and is involved in a number of lawsuits for 'bad faith' in refusing to honour disability insurance claims. This reinforces the caution against taking this apparently impressive body of work at face value. It is not research undertaken in the spirit of open enquiry. It is commissioned research and, as such, pre-disposed towards ideologically determined outcomes. (p 7) ......

GPs, who first certify claimants, do not 'understand the importance of work for health' or 'consider carefully whether sick certification is really necessary and in the patients' best long-term interests.' (S/C Basis* p 106) This reviews different ways of bypassing them... 'For common health problems and future capacity for work, the doctors' opinion... is unfounded, of limited value and can be counter-productive'... (S/C Basis p145-146) (p 10) ......

(1)...We are expected to be impressed by the unacceptable and spiralling numbers of claimants and to agree with bland generalisations about their conditions, but we are not presented (as would be the case in genuinely objective research) with the data from which to evaluate the conclusions drawn.

(2) Those on benefits are depicted as victims of the benefits system, so by implication passive, idle and helpless. This suggests that holding the 'status' of sickness on benefits is a doddle – 'something for nothing' according to the Secretary of State when contrasting his offer of 'something for something.' The actual experience of those with serious and long-term illness/disability could not be more different. (p 13) With pain, weakness, exhaustion and (often) sleeplessness, not to mention self-reproach and huge anxiety and despair about the future, serious illness/disability calls for self-management of a high order... (3)

(4)... By implying that they are parasites, it excludes them more insidiously from the body politic than the system it seeks to replace. The people in question, like the 19th-century poor, are not asked to speak for themselves about their health conditions and resulting problems and needs. For example, the study of the early Pathways clients in *DWP Research Report 259* was only interested in their reactions to the service provided, so useful information that could have been extracted from even this tiny sample was missed. In countless DWP-commissioned studies, the voices of sufferers are only heard through, and interpreted by, researchers and officials. (p 15) ... the DWP is turning the clock back, to a time before National Insurance when the cost of sickness was born by the individual and the family. (p 25)

Green Paper: A New Deal for Welfare: empowering people to work. 2006
An independent assessment of the arguments for proposed incapacity benefit reform.[78]

Alison Ravetz MA, PhD
March 2006

Centre for Disability Studies, Leeds University

*S/C Basis – The Scientific and Conceptual Basis of Incapacity Benefits

After delivering a keynote speech at another gathering of like-minded individuals, Aylward was *'ambushed'* by members of the Black Triangle Campaign and Disabled People Against Cuts and defensively claimed to know nothing about the WCA and the harm it was causing. Witnessed and reported by John Pring from Disability News Service,[84] it seems that this former DWP Chief Medical Officer, who is the leading UK *'expert'* in the [manipulated] BPS model

---

Box 4:6 *Insurer Unum Group Reverses 42% of Previously Denied Claims*

According to a press release from Tennessee Department of Commerce and Insurance, the Unum Group and 48 states, plus the District of Columbia, have reached an agreement that will reverse 42% of previously denied or terminated disability claims from 1997 to 2004.

In addition to the reversals, which are estimated to total $676 million, the agreement will also require Unum to make "significant changes to corporate governance such as adding three new directors subject to approval of state insurance regulators to its Board of Directors, implementing new claims procedures and standards for claims processing, enhancing and implementing new internal quality controls and requiring hands-on involvement of its Board of Directors in ensuring successful implementation of the new processes. The original agreement also included strong oversight, such as quarterly evaluations and monitoring the company by Tennessee's insurance regulators as well as other lead states."

Insurance Bad Faith [80]
Attorney Pages
2005

---

of disability assessment, as used for the WCA, suddenly claimed that he had always insisted that the *'social model'* must be a consideration of the assessment used by government. Aylward also claimed that he had just advised the audience at the Unum sponsored September 2012 International Forum on Disability Management that the BPS model of assessment was *'unsatisfactory'*, and that he now believed it *'no longer addresses the real needs of disabled people and the exclusion of disabled people from society.'* Aylward further claimed that *'I think I am a man of integrity. If I think the WCA is not proper I will speak against it.'* [84] Access to the published papers from that 2012 International Forum is unobtainable.[85]

This was big news... The lead 'expert' whose research was responsible for the introduction of the fatally flawed WCA was now admitting that the [manipulated] BPS model of assessment, as used by both Unum Insurance and the DWP to deny insurance claims and welfare benefit, had suddenly changed his mind; regardless of the numbers of papers, articles and books he has written and the speeches he has given to confer on him the title of BPS *'expert'* ... Needless to say, the press release by MS that announced this change of mind by the leading expert in his

---

Box 4:7 *A Tale of Two Models*

When the links between the profiteers in the misery of disabled people and the ideologies of denial are exposed what are we left with? First, this is not about getting people into work, whatever the Tories and previous governments claim they don't care if you work or not. Media rhetoric[27] on scroungers, workshy and other protestations of undeserving poor were part of the strategy to change public opinion helped along by misleading DWP press releases. This is about denying benefits, denying illness and denying incapacity. It is not even about 'thinking yourself well' or other tortured nonsensical models shored up by dubious academics: It's about something Unum have a successful history of: it's about denying pay outs and capitalising on fear and risk. (Page 12)

The denial of pay outs may be through Unum's insurance policies or it may be through denying pay outs after an individual has paid a life-time of national insurance contributions to the state – but is put on time limited Employment and Support Allowance – the outcome will be the same. Who better to work with ex-banker Freud and MPs in denying people their rightful entitlements than a company which has been publically named as : "an outlaw company – it is a company that for years has operated in an illegal fashion[28]" by California Insurance Commissioner John Garamendi in 2005, where Unum were charged with more than 25 violations of state law and fined $8 million. Among the charges were: ... 'that the company knowingly applied the wrong legal definition of disability in denying claims or ruling claimants were able to go back to work, targeted high-cost claims for denials to save firm money, misused claimants' medical records and even the opinions of in-house medical personnel to deny benefits and wrongly sought to file cases under a federal benefits law that severely limits claimants' ability to successfully sue their insurers.' (Page 13) ....

Rutherford argues: in the 1980s Unum, and insurance companies Provident and Paul Revere were in trouble in the US. They had increased profits by sharing similar policies on disability and sickness insurance and selling to professionals. A combination of falling interest rates and the growth of diagnosed illnesses which were not subject to the insurance sector's tests appeared to be increasing, affecting the professionals who had taken out policies with the companies, and in turn affecting company profits. These illnesses included: Myalgic Encephalomyelitis (ME) or Chronic Fatigue Syndrome (CFS), Fibromyalgia, Chronic Pain, Multiple Sclerosis, Lyme disease. (Page 13) ....

It meant that specific illnesses were targeted in order to discredit the legitimacy of claims. This 'strategy' was to prove useful in dealing with the UK's welfare reform and in overriding the basis of medical opinion on a whole set of conditions. As the state joined in the denial with its set of private companies and supporting academics Unum achieved more market returns while disabled people began to see their own support rapidly diminishing. ....

It amounts to the biggest government benefit fraud in social welfare and human rights in contemporary history. (Page 15)

A Tale of Two Models: Disabled People vs Unum, Atos, Government and Disability Charities [86]

Debbie Jolly
March 2012

Centre for Disability Studies, Leeds University

field was totally disregarded by the national press. Informed academics reacted to Aylward's comments. Debbie Jolly had already demonstrated the aftermath of '...*the links between the profiteers in the misery of disabled people and the ideologies of denial.*' [86]

Social Sciences lecturer, researcher and author Angela Kennedy was '*somewhat surprised*' to learn of Aylward's sudden change of academic opinion, as published by the Black Triangle Campaign website.[87]

Box 4:8 *Angela Kennedy responds to Professor Sir Mansel Aylward*

I was somewhat surprised to see Mansel Aylward's changing view on the 'biopsychosocial' model, claimed by him as he was confronted by those representing disabled people vicitimised by this model for many years. But I am not confident Aylward has actually understood what the problems of this model are...

It is often claimed that the 'biopsychosocial' approaches are merely 'holistic' approaches to people's health, a much-needed move away from the medical-model for which Aylward claims so much distaste. And, in this extent, objections from patients might seem rather odd. Why on earth would patients seek to move away from being seen as 'whole persons', in all their social and psychological complexity, from being cared for 'holistically'? ...

Patients facing a 'biopsychosocial approach' therefore find themselves facing an over-emphasis on the 'psycho' (and only then with regard to alleged causation rather than impact of their illness), leading to psychogenic dismissal of their illness and malign constructions of their characters (hypochondriacs, malingerers, wimps etc). Whatever the ostensible 'patient as a whole person' philosophy claimed by the proponent of 'biopsychosocial' approaches, it is used most often to assume a physical illness is caused by psychopathology and deviance, and to advocate treatment management approaches based on this belief.

Aylward's distaste for the 'medical model' bears commenting upon as well. Many patients have come to actively seek to reduce medical inquiry for their physical bodies. This is most likely to be a rational attempt to prevent iatrogenic risks to their physical, psychological and social health caused by an approach that is not holistic at all; but in real-life practice, an irrational pyschogenic dismissal by doctors of physical illness is the last thing patients need.

Angela Kennedy responds to Professor Sir Mansel Aylward's Statements to Black Triangle and DPAC [87]

Angela Kennedy
September 2012

Meanwhile....

.... academic Gill Thorburn was a little more forthright in her reaction to Aylward's claims, and gave a very detailed explanation as to why the Professor's claims of innocence just '*don't stack up*'... [88]

Box 4:9 *A response to Professor Aylward's statement*

Few people have been involved in as many return to work or rehabilitation initiatives as Professor Mansel Aylward.

In my article on the subject (2) I believe I argue convincingly quite the opposite to Professor Aylward's current assertions, providing examples that indicate how this has been achieved. It is an ideas trail that leads directly back to the esteemed Professor and his (and his various colleagues) efforts (in concert with the insurance firm, *Unum*), to revolutionise the way in which our health related benefits are administered – with its overwhelming emphasis on 'proving', in the words of Chris Grayling, almost everyone capable of 'some work'. What the WCA most certainly is *not*, contrary to claims otherwise, is a fair, impartial and objective method of assessing someone's capacity for work…

Ruthless promotion of the BPS model

Examining Professor Aylward's recent defence of his position on BPS, and the links that have been made between his work and the rearrangement of our welfare system, it would seem that he is now claiming to have had no influence upon the changes which have been wrought. That is an astonishing claim in light of the manner in which he and others of his cohort have ruthlessly promoted and applied some very specific ideas about illness. These academics, including Professor Aylward, within what I have previously termed the *'BPS lobby',* have consistently and persistently pushed their 'new' notions about illness and disability until they, first successfully penetrated, and then became the sole authoritative discourse within official literature in this area. They were able to do so through drawing on their privileged positions as leaders of medical and scientific authoritative discourse and doctrine. We should remind ourselves too that welfare policy is to all intents and purposes a form of law, which in the case of welfare benefits is very strenuously applied. Results of failure to comply are severe, and punished mercilessly by the modern system. Those stigmatised as 'scroungers' or 'malingerers' are afforded zero tolerance and enthusiastically chased to ground and pilloried in our contemporary society. All the more reason, then, for the ideas which have fed into those administrative instruments by which people's health is assessed to be above criticism, and fair and just, avoiding adding to any stigmatisation of illness and disability.

On 11th September Professor Aylward claimed to 'sympathise' with the 'grievances' raised by the disabled community. He hints that the address he had just given about the BPS model contained criticism of its current application with respect to disabled people; that he now finds it *'unsatisfactory'*, because it *'no longer addresses the exclusion of disabled people from society.'* When did it ever, professor? It is not the BPS model itself that people are outraged by, sir, but the uses to which it has been put. And that has been to *further* 'exclude' sick and disabled people from society by *further disabling* them through adding demonization to their stigmatisation, and financial penury to their already disadvantaged economic situation. And all this has been accomplished via the Atos administered WCA, built as it was on ideas about 'illness' culled from *your* literature, and that of the insurance firm Unum, whose processes have been aptly described as *'disability denial factories.'*

A response to Professor Aylward's statement to Black Triangle and DPAC [88]
Gill Thorburn
18th September 2012

Professor Aylward did not speak out regarding any investigation into the WCA, as mentioned during his discussion when challenged outside the 2012 International Forum on Disability Management.[89] Indeed, since that meeting, the Professor has been lecturing around the world to help to introduce the same welfare reforms to New Zealand and to other nations when using the [manipulated] BPS model of assessment.[90,91,92]

Box 4:10 *Work tests concern disability organisations*

Disability services group CSS says it has "grave concerns" about plans to introduce work capability assessments, influenced by controvertial tests conducted in Britain.

From July, the invalid's benefit, paid to about 85,000 New Zealanders, will be replaced by the supported living payment, as part of wide-ranging welfare changes.

Social Development Minister Paula Bennett has said this would mean little change, although in a speech to health professionals late last year she signalled a new assessment regime which "echoes" the British process.

......

CSS Disability Action chief executive David Matthews cited research showing the British Government had spent £42.2million (NZ$80.5m) on appeals against these tests, about 40 per cent of which overturned Atos' findings.

The tests were developed partially on the work of disability expert Professor Sir Mansel Aylward, who has visited New Zealand to advise on health reform, meeting Mrs Bennett. (My emphasis. MS)

Mr Matthews said most government policy focused on how society builds barriers for the disabled, whereas a key part of Professor Aylward's work focused on the extent to which a disabled person could overcome barriers.

"The whole philosophy and approach to disability in New Zealand is based on the social model… which looks at barriers to employing people, rather than what's wrong with the individual," he said. "We have grave concerns about basing welfare changes in New Zealand on such a flawed approach."

A work ability test would be an extra requirement for the disabled.

Mrs Bennett's spokeswoman said details of the assessments were being considered by a select committee and had not been finalised.

Work tests concern disability organisations [90]
Hamish Rutherford

Business Day, New Zealand
11th January 2013

Courtesy of stuff.co.nz/FairfaxNZ

NOTES

N2: The new and updated DWP mortality figures were released in August 2015 as this manuscript neared completion. The reference to the figures are identified as notes.
https://www.gov.uk/government/uploads/system/uploads/attachment_data/file/456359/mortality-statistics-esa-ib-sda.pdf

REFERENCES

** **All websites accessed 18th July 2015**

Illustration 4:1:
Hit Men courtesy of Dave Lupton of *Crippen* Cartoons: http://www.crippencartoons.co.uk/

Illustration 4:2
Spin courtesy of Dave Lupton of *Crippen* Cartoons: http://www.crippencartoons.co.uk/

30. BBC NEWS: 10th April 2015: *Liberal Democrats cry foul in election race*
    http://www.bbc.co.uk/news/uk-england-32248326
31. Conservative manifesto: 14th April 2015:
    http://www.bbc.co.uk/news/election-2015-32295970
32. THE DAY: 15th April 2015: *Cameron revives 'home-owning democracy' dream*
    http://theday.co.uk/politics/cameron-revives-home-owning-democracy-dream
33. MAY B: Common Decency, colour blind politics: www.commondecency.org.uk
34. BBC NEWS: Labour manifesto: 14th April 2015:
    http://www.bbc.co.uk/news/election-2015-32284159
35. SCOTT-SAMUEL A et al: 2014: *The Impact of Thatcherism On Health And Well-being In Britain* : International Journal of Health Services, Volume 44, Number 1, Pages 53-71 Alex Scott-Samuel, Clare Bambra, Chik Collins, David J Hunter, Gerry McCartney and Kat Smith http://pcwww.liv.ac.uk/~alexss/thatcherism.pdf
36. BBC NEWS: 15th April 2015: Nick Clegg: The choice is me, Salmond or Farage
    http://www.bbc.co.uk/news/election-2015-32311736
37. MILLER S: October 2014: UK Welfare Refom Deaths – updated list
    http://blacktrianglecampaign.org/2014/10/21/uk-welfare-reform-deaths-updated-list-october-21st-2014/
38. DWP: 9th July 2012: Incapacity Benefits: Deaths of Recipients
    https://www.gov.uk/government/uploads/system/uploads/attachment_data/file/223050/incap_decd_recips_0712.pdf
39. GOV.UK: 30th October 2014: Maximus appointed to carry out health assessments for the DWP
    https://www.gov.uk/government/news/maximus-appointed-to-carry-out-health-assessments-for-the-department-for-work-and-pensions
40. PRIDE T: September 2014: *Meet MAXIMUS (the new ATOS) and its list of scandals in the US*
    https://tompride.wordpress.com/2014/09/13/meet-maximus-the-new-atos-but-even-worse/
41. BLACK TRIANGLE CAMPAIGN: 4th October 2012: *10,600 sick and disabled people died last year…*
    http://blacktrianglecampaign.org/2012/10/04/10600-sick-disabled-people-died-last-year-within-six-weeks-of-their-claim-ending/

42. BMA: June 2012: *Scrap work capability assessment, doctors demand*
http://bma.org.uk/news-views-analysis/news/2012/june/scrap-work-capability-assessment-doctors-demand

43. STEWART M: June 2010: *Atos Healthcare or Disability Denial Factories*
http://www.whywaitforever.com/dwpatosveteranssummary.html

44. STEWART M: January 2015: *The influence of the private insurance industry on the UK welfare reforms.*
http://disability-studies.leeds.ac.uk/files/library/The%20influence%20of%20the%20private%20insurance%20industry%20%20-%20FINAL%20-%20Jan%202015.pdf

45. LANGBEIN J: Yale School of Law: The Unum Provident Scandal & Judicial Review of benefit denials under ERISA: 2007
http://papers.ssrn.com/sol3/papers.cfm?abstract_id=917610 – abstract
– full paper may be downloaded as a PDF.

46. BBC 10PM NEWS: 6th November 2007: VIDEO: Mark Daly.
http://www.meactionuk.org.uk/UNUM_on_BBC_News_061107.wmv

47. ADVISER – CORPORATE: September 2011: *Income protection ads in Downtown Abbey as Unum launches £15m TV campaign*
http://www.corporate-adviser.com/home/income-protection-ads-in-downton-abbey-as-unum-launches-15m-tv- campaign/1038714.article

48. BENEFITS AND WORK: 15th March 2012: *Unum withdraws from individual income protection*
http://www.benefitsandwork.co.uk/news/1805-unum-withdraws-from-individual-income-protection166

49. UNUM Back-Up plan: 29th September 2011: You Tube
https://www.youtube.com/watch?v=v8zPl6rHRJw

50. STEWART M: January 2015: *The influence of the private insurance industry on the UK welfare reforms*
http://www.researchgate.net/publication/271199429_The_influence_of_the_private_insurance_industry_on_the_UK_welfare_reforms

51. BMA: June 2012: *Scrap work capability assessment, doctors demand*
http://bma.org.uk/news-views-analysis/news/2012/june/scrap-work-capability-assessment-doctors-demand

52. RCN: April 2013: *Congress resolved that the disability assessments in the UK were unfit for purpose.*
http://www.rcn.org.uk/newsevents/congress/2013/agenda/1-disability-assessments

53. PARLIAMENT UK: APPENDIX 2: FINANCIAL PRIVILEDGE:
http://www.publications.parliament.uk/pa/ld201011/ldselect/ldconst/97/9705.htm

54. GREY-Thompson T: HOL: Welfare Reform Bill Second Reading: 13th September 2011: column 701
http://www.publications.parliament.uk/pa/ld201011/ldhansrd/text/110913-0002.htm

55. CALUM'S LIST: http://calumslist.org/

56. AAJ: 2008: *The Ten Worst Insurance Companies in America* The American Association of Justice http://www.bulmanlaw.com/wp-content/uploads/2013/03/TenWorstInsuranceCompanies.pdf

57. STEWART M: 10th June 2013: *From the British Welfare State to Another American State*
http://blacktrianglecampaign.org/2013/06/10/final-report-from-the-british-welfare-state-to-another-american-state-by-mo-stewart/

58. W&P 2014: July: *ESA needs fundamental redesign, says MPs:* Work & Pensions Select Committee: 23rd July 2014: News Release
http://www.parliament.uk/business/committees/committeesaz/

59. W&P 2014: July: Report: *Employment and Support Allowance and Work Capability Assessments*
http://www.publications.parliament.uk/pa/cm201415/cmselect/cmworpen/302/302.pdf

60. DNS: John Pring: 28th November 2014: *Concern over government's 'dreadful' response to MPs' fitness for work report.*
http://www.disabilitynewsservice.com/concern-governments-dreadful-response-mps-fitness-work-report/

61. MILLER S: October 2014: UK Welfare Refom Deaths – updated list
http://blacktrianglecampaign.org/2014/10/21/uk-welfare-reform-deaths-updated-list-october-21st-2014/

62. DNS: John Pring: 15th February 2013: *Unum bragged about 'driving government thinking' on incapacity benefit reform'*
http://disabilitynewsservice.com/2013/02/unum-bragged-about-driving-government-thinking-on-incapacity-benefit-reform/

63. STEWART M: 10th June 2013: *From the British Welfare State to Another American State*
http://blacktrianglecampaign.org/2013/06/10/final-report-from-the-british-welfare-state- to-another-american-state- by-mo-stewart/

64. CHORLEY M: Mail on Line: 23rd October 2012: *More than half of people who have been claiming incapacity benefit are 'fit for work.'*
http://www.dailymail.co.uk/news/article-2221954/More-half-people-claiming-incapacity-benefit-fit-work.html

65. PEEV G: 26th January 2011: Daily Mail: *400,000 'were trying it on' to get sickness benefits: 94% of incapacity claimants CAN work.*
http://www.dailymail.co.uk/news/article-1350359/400-000-sickness-benefits-cheats-94-incapacity-claimants-CAN-work.html

66. BACH M: 2012: *Why does the Government allow such a company to operate in the UK?* http://www.whywaitforever.com/dwpatosbusinessunum.html#performance

67. RUTHERFORD J: 17th March 2008: *E pluribus Unum*
http://www.theguardian.com/commentisfree/2008/mar/17/epluribusunum

68. RUTHERFORD J: Summer 2007: *New Labour, the market state and the end of welfare*
http://blacktrianglecampaign.org/2011/09/07/new-labour-the-market-state-and-the-end- of-welfare/

69. BBC NEWS: 13th October 2008: *Banking crisis*
http://news.bbc.co.uk/1/hi/business/7666570.stm

70. TRAVIS ALAN: 2012: *Margaret Thatcher's role in plan to dismantle welfare state revealed.* The Guardian: 28th December 2012 Courtesy of Guardian News & Media Ltd http://www.theguardian.com/politics/2012/dec/28/margaret-thatcher-role-plan-to-dismantle-welfare- state-revealed

71. FREUD D: 2007 March: The Freud Report: *Reducing dependancy, increasing opportunity:options for the future of welfare to work.* An independent report by David Freud
http://webarchive.nationalarchives.gov.uk/20130128102031/http://dwp.gov.uk/docs/welfarer eview.pdf

72. BROWN C: 2014 January: *Freud: Bedroom tax loophole 'to be closed in March.'*
http://www.insidehousing.co.uk/freud-bedroom-tax-loophole-to-be-closed-in-march/7001634.article

73. FREUD D: 2007 March: The Freud Report: *Reducing dependancy, increasing opportunity:options for the future of welfare to work.* An independent report by David Freud.
http://5.79.19.119/sites/default/files/policy_downloads/freud_review.pdf

74. WADDELL G & BURTON K: 2006: *Is work good for your health and well-being?* https://www.gov.uk/government/uploads/system/uploads/attachment_data/file/214326/hwwb- is-work-good-for-you.pdf

75. DWP: GREEN PAPER: Jan 2006: *A new deal for welfare: Empowering people to work* https://www.gov.uk/government/uploads/system/uploads/attachment_data/file/272235/6730.p df

76. RAVETZ A: 2006: *An independent assessment of the argument for proposed Incapacity Benefit reform* Re: Green Paper: A New Deal for Welfare: Empowering People to Work http://disability-studies.leeds.ac.uk/library/author/ravetz.alison

77. WADDELL G and AYLWARD M: 11th October 2005: *The Scientific and Conceptual Basis of Incapacity Benefits* ISBN: 9780117035843

78. RAVETZ A: 2006: *An independent assessment of the argument Incapacity Benefit reform for proposed* Re: Green Paper: A New Deal for Welfare: Empowering People to Work http://disability-studies.leeds.ac.uk/library/author/ravetz.alison

79. ONLINE LAWYER SOURCE: Unum Complaints: http://www.onlinelawyersource.com/unum/complaints/

80. ATTORNEY PAGES: *Insurance Group Reverses 42% Of Previously Denied Disability Claims*: http://attorneypages.com/hot/unum-group-reverses-denied-disability-claim.htm

81. WILLIAMS WALSH M: 23rd October 2008: New York Times: *Disability Insurer Found Guilty of Social Security Freud*: http://www.onlinelawyersource.com/unum/complaints/

82. WADDELL G and AYLWARD M: 11th October 2005: *The Scientific and Conceptual Basis of Incapacity Benefits* ISBN: 9780117035843

83. HARRINGTON M: November 2010: *An independent review of the work capability assessment*, year 1. ISBN: 9780108509476 http://www.nationalarchives.gov.uk/doc/open-government-licence/version/3/

84. PRING J: DNS: 14th September 2012: *Former DWP medical boss Sir Mansel Aylward makes WCA pledge to protesters.* http://blacktrianglecampaign.org/2012/09/14/former-dwp-medical-boss-sir-mansel- aylward-makes-wca-pledge-to-protesters-disability-news-service/

85. INTERNATIONAL JOURNAL OF DISABILITY MANAGEMENT 2012: *Abstracts for the International Forum on Disability Management (IFDM), London, England, Sept 10 – 12, 2012* http://connection.ebscohost.com/c/abstracts/98801873/abstracts-international-forum- disability-management-ifdm-london-england-september-10-12-2012

86. JOLLY D: March 2012: *A Tale of Two Models: Disabled People vs Unum, Atos, Government and disability charities.*: http://disability-studies.leeds.ac.uk/files/library/A-Tale-of-two-Models-Leeds1.pdf

87. KENNEDY A: 19th September 2012: *Academic responds to Professor Sir Mansel Aylward's statements to Black Triangle and DPAC* http://blacktrianglecampaign.org/2012/09/19/academic-angela-kennedy-responds-to-professor-sir-manselaylwards-statement-to-black-triangle-and-dpac

88. THORBURN G: 18th September 2012: *Academic response to Aylward's claims* https://dl.dropboxusercontent.com/u/32109159/Aylward/ResponseToAylward.pdf

89. PRING J: DNS: 14th September 2012: *Former DWP medical boss Sir Mansel Aylward makes WCA pledge to protesters.* http://blacktrianglecampaign.org/2012/09/14/former-dwp-medical-boss-sir-mansel- aylward-makes-wca-pledge-to- protesters-disability-news-service/

90. RUTHERFORD H: 11th January 2013: Business Day New Zealand: *Work tests concern disability organisation* http://www.stuff.co.nz/business/industries/8165236/Work-tests-concern-disability- organisation

91. NZ SOCIAL JUSTICE BLOG 2013: Medical and Work Capability Assessments – based on the controvertial bio-psychosocial model.
https://nzsocialjusticeblog2013.wordpress.com/2013/09/02/medical-and-work-capability-assessments-based-on-the-controversial-bio-psycho-social-model/

92. ACC FORUM: NEW ZEALAND:
http://accforum.org/forums/index.php?/topic/15188-medical-and-work-capability-assessments-based-on-the-bps-model-aimed-at-disentiteling-affected-from-welfare-benefits-and-acc-compo/page__st__20

CHAPTER 5:
MALINGERING AND ILLNESS DECEPTION
~ New Labour's Dangerous Legacy

Oh what a tangled web we weave, when first we practise to deceive
Sir Walter Scott
1771 ~ 1832

The moral compass of the United Kingdom (UK) government totally disappeared during the last Parliament, with the Coalition government being very successful at misleading the British public, and the House of Commons, regarding the welfare budget and those who are in need of financial support due to health and disability restrictions.

The Coalition government's reported vilification of the long-term sick and disabled population demonstrated the dangers of the Tory dominated national press[93], where the majority of the British public seem to obtain their news and, apparently, actually believe what they read. Of equal concern perhaps is what the national press will not publish; such as the influence of a notorious American healthcare insurance giant with British welfare reforms since 1992.[94] Nothing else could explain the Conservative victory at the recent general election, when so many people in the UK have suffered, and so many have died; with many deaths linked to the '*welfare reforms*' imposed by the Coalition government.[95,96]

The UK is not now too far away from the adoption of the American style healthcare insurance system, to be funded by private healthcare insurance with many companies that will not, if at all possible, pay out when a claim is made.[97] The British people will continue to be manipulated via the press and, since May 2015, by the new majority Conservative government; which is likely to be even more callous than the previous Coalition government regarding the welfare and the financial security of this nation's chronically sick and disabled people.

Iain Duncan Smith was re-appointed as the Secretary of State for Work and Pensions in the new Conservative government. Therefore, the long-term sick and disabled claimants of the Employment and Support Allowance (ESA) can anticipate another five years of hostile speeches, filled with pejorative language, as the Prime Minister, the Chancellor and Iain Duncan Smith continue their mission to '*help*' as many '*inactive*' people as possible to find work, by intimidating and terrifying them with their hostile rhetoric that appears to have encouraged a dramatic increase in disability hate crimes.[98]

75% on sick are skiving, 26/1/11
Workshy to lose benefits, 18/2/11
Blitz on Britain's benefits madness, 21/4/11
Blitz on benefits: 887,000 fiddlers exposed, 28/4/11

Illustration 5:1 Banner headlines ~ courtesy of Express Newspapers/N&S syndication

Using the imposed '*austerity measures*' as justification for all decisions that were guaranteed to harm the poorest people in the country, the Coalition government routinely disregarded all reports by the Work and Pensions Select Committee that highlighted many problems, including the influence of the national press and the pejorative language used by the press when reporting government welfare reforms.[99] It seems likely that the reason for the ongoing hostile government rhetoric could be to successfully reduce public sympathy, to justify the long- ago planned demolition of the welfare state that remains largely unknown by the majority of the British people.[100]

BOX 5:1 *The role of incapacity benefit reassessment in helping claimants into employment*

40. Sections of the media routinely use pejorative language, such as "work-shy" or "scrounger", when referring to incapacity benefit claimants. We strongly deprecate this and believe that it is irresponsible and inaccurate. The duty on the state to provide adequate support through the benefits system for people who are unable to work because of a serious health condition or illness is a fundamental principle of British society. Portraying the reassessment of incapacity benefit claimants as some sort of scheme to "weed out benefit cheats" shows a fundamental misunderstanding of the Government's objectives.

41. Whilst fully accepting that the Government, and this Committee, have no role in determining the nature and content of media coverage, we believe that more care is needed in the way the Government engages with the media and in particular the way in which it releases and provides its commentary on official statistics on the IB reassessment. In the end, the media will choose its own angle, but the Government should take great care with the language it itself uses and take all possible steps to ensure that context is provided when information about IB claimants found fit for work is released, so that unhelpful and inaccurate stories can be shown to have no basis.

[Emphasis as published in text of report. MS]

The role of incapacity benefit reassessment
in helping claimants into employment. [99]
Sixth Report of Session 2010-2012
Volume 1

House of Commons
Work and Pensions Committee
13th July 2011

At the same time as the Work and Pensions Select Committee were expressing concerns about the hostile press coverage, a major study was being conducted by Glasgow University, sponsored by Inclusion London, and the report: *Bad News for Disabled People: How newspapers are reporting disability* [101] was deposited in November 2011. The results of the long-awaited research paper were much worse than was first feared, and demonstrated the significant transformation of press coverage of sick and disabled people and of sickness and disability benefit claimants. Detailed analysis of painstaking research exposed the significant amount of tabloid press focus on the *'deserving'* and the *'non-deserving'* disabled community, together with the disturbing negative impact such reporting appeared to be having on the readership. [101]

BOX 5:2 *Bad News for Disabled People:*
how the newspapers are reporting disability

In the light of our findings in relation to the changes in the way disability is being presented and reported in the media, we were interested in trying to find out if or how this change had impacted on and effected people's views of disability and benefits. This topic was a major element of the focus groups and one of the questions we asked the groups to consider was what they thought the percentage of people who were fraudulently claiming benefits was. The responses varied from 'about 10%' right up to 70%. (p61)

This was a view shared, not surprisingly, by all the disabled participants and they talked about how difficult it is to get benefits. One of the participants described the benefits system as, 'going through a minefield, to get a pittance that sustains you just above the poverty line.' (p62)

Disabled people also expressed significant anger at some of the press reporting and at the accusations linking disabled people with benefits, scrounging and fraudulent claims. A number of disabled people suggested that there was a major issue of disabled people not receiving what they do need. Not only, they argued, was there 'huge unmet need', a great deal of people who were entitled to benefits were not receiving the level of support they required and this was a bigger scandal than fraud… Disabled people also emphasised that fluctuating conditions can make the process of applying for benefits significantly more difficult, and accusations of fraudulence more likely. It is not uncommon for example for people to be able to walk one day and the next be unable to leave the house. (p63)

** The vitriolic approach adopted by articles in some papers today, and the way they have reported disability and disabled people in the period following the Comprehensive Spending Review adds further weight to these claims. Much of the coverage in the tabloid press is at best questionable and some of it is deeply offensive. The increased focus on benefit fraud with outlandish claims of 70% of people on disability benefits are frauds is an example of this type of reporting. (p68)

** There is a danger that much of the reporting that we have discussed in this report could lay the groundwork for the removal of some of the support structures and processes that are currently in place. This fear was expressed openly in one of the focus groups of disabled people and is one the press should take seriously. By simply replicating the government's position on disability and disability benefit, without checking either their statistics or the basis on which the claim is made, the partisan approach they adopt has the danger of further adding to oppression disabled people are experiencing. (p70)

Bad News for Disabled People:[101]
how the newspapers are reporting disability

Emma Briant, Nick Watson, Greg Philo
University of Glasgow
November 2011

Research sponsored by Inclusion London

As the Secretary of State for Social Security in the John Major Conservative administration, it was Peter Lilley who hired John LoCascio of UnumProvident[TM] Insurance (Unum) in 1992 to advise the UK government on welfare claims management, to reduce the identified rising numbers of claimants of long-term sickness benefit.

Box 5:3 *Problems in the assessment of psychosomatic conditions in social security benefits and related commercial schemes*

The medical community must recognize that support of claims for Incapacity Benefit and related commercial schemes places the patient in a small and special sub-population of clinical practice which may require specialist investigation, treatment, and documentation. Determination of functional capacity and of disability requires knowledge either not available or unfamiliar to most physicians with caring and therapeutic roles, especially of legal or contractual provisions and occupational data. However, it is not necessary for them to determine disability and they should not be asked to do so. The new, medical assessment procedures for Incapacity Benefit in the UK do not require this, and the largest provider of related commercial schemes (Long Term Disability; Permanent Health Insurance) has already eliminated this requirement from its application process.

When such application is anticipated or requested, the medical record should be prepared and appropriate consultation obtained. Subjective issues should be identified and addressed. Comprehensive psychiatric evaluation, especially in subjective impairment, is critical in chronic incapacity. The estimation of functional capacities in the absence of objective data is particularly troublesome, but, clinicians can provide the Disability Medical Analyst with appropriate medical documentation.

Problems in the assessment of psychosomatic conditions in social security benefits and related commercial schemes [102]

Mansel Aylward and John LoCascio
Journal of Psychosomatic Research

Volume 39, Issue 6, Pages 755-765
August 1995

By 1994, Unum were official '*government advisers*' on future welfare claims management. Mansel Aylward was the then Principal Medical Officer for the Department for Social Security (DSS) (1991-1995)[X], later to become the Chief Medical Officer for the Department for Work and Pensions (DWP)(1995-2005)[X]. By 1995, Aylward and LoCascio were co-authoring academic papers to suggest that General Practitioners (GP) should not be expected to determine patients' levels of disability or incapacity to work.[102] This one paper effectively justified the future removal of the authority of GP opinion to permit claimants access to the long-term DWP sickness benefit. The 1995 academic paper by Aylward and LoCascio[102] opened the door to the future marginalisation of the clinical opinion of GPs and for the government to, eventually, offer a lucrative contract to the unaccountable foreign corporate IT giant, commonly known as Atos Healthcare, to conduct the Work Capability Assessment. (WCA)

The WCA was designed to resist funding the Employment and Support Allowance (ESA)[103] and it has been working well, as the demolition of the welfare state moves ever closer year by year as predicted by Professors Martin McKee and David Stuckler in December 2011.[104]

BOX 5:4 *The assault on universalism: how to destroy the welfare state*

"Martin McKee and David Stuckler watch aghast as American examples are followed to destroy the European model of the welfare state"

The direction of travel should now be clear. More and more, the middle classes will ask why they are paying into a system that gives them little back. The idea that the state is an insurance system, from which they can benefit if they are in need, is steadily eroded. Even the word "insurance" will be taken out in Chancellor George Osborne's plans to merge national insurance with taxation. There will be ever greater reductions in the funding, and inevitably the quality, of those remaining services used by the middle classes, such as primary and secondary education and healthcare, persuading them that they would be better off seeking private options. Public services will become like public hospitals in the United States, a service for the poor. As Richard Titmuss famously said, a "service for the poor" inevitably becomes "a poor service," as the vocal and the politically active middle class abandon the system. The ground rules are already being laid in healthcare, as the health secretary has sought to weaken his responsibility for a comprehensive health system. At some stage in the future all vestigial safeguards could disappear and commissioning consortiums, by then funded by personalised budgets, would become, in effect, insurance companies, with all sorts of ways to limit whom they enrol and what they cover.

The assault on universalism: how to destroy the welfare state [104]
Martin McKee and David Stuckler

BMJ Christmas 2011

Courtesy of the BMJ

Fifteen years ago UnumProvident$_{TM}$ Insurance (Unum) was exposed in Parliament in the 1999 Permanent Health Insurance debate, where Members of Parliament (MP) identified the suffering of constituents as Unum refused to pay out on income protection insurance policies.[105] At the time of the debate, Unum were already *'official government advisers'* for *'welfare claims management'*, yet no-one it seems made the connection… Why not??

Six years later, concerns were expressed in a 2005 government inquiry regarding Aylward's long association with Unum (Provident) Insurance, including links with the American corporate insurance giant when Principle Medical Officer/Chief Medical Officer at the DSS/DWP from 1991 – 2005. To date there has been no formal investigation following the evidence by Professor Malcolm Hooper to the Gibson Parliamentary Inquiry, despite the exposure of a *'clear financial conflict of interest and possible breach of Civil Service protocol'* by Aylward.[106]

BOX 5:5 *Concerns about a commercial conflict of interest underlying the DWP handbook entry on ME and CFS*

There would also appear to have been a clear financial conflict of interest and possible breach of Civil Service protocol, in that a senior Civil Servant such as Aylward could not have been unaware while he was in post at the DWP that Unum Provident was already financing his next employment, which would allow him to indulge in his existing conviction that syndromes such as ME/CFS are affected by 'cultural' factors and are 'behavioural' in nature. It is also a matter of concern that a senior Civil Servant accepted sponsorship from a company with Unum's track record.

Concerns about a commercial conflict of interest
underlying the DWP handbook entry on ME and CFS [106]

Evidence by Professor Malcom Hooper
The Gibson Parliamentary Inquiry

December 2005

Since the escalation of the *'welfare reforms'* by the Coalition government, which should really read as 'welfare destruction', many have wondered what happened to common decency, care, compassion and basic humanity as the list is growing of those who have suffered preventable harm due to the WCA or the fear of it, which is linked to many new reported deaths[107] that the DWP still resist publishing.[N2]

As previously mentioned, in 2012 the DWP did publish the mortality figures of the claimants who had died in 11 months in 2011, whilst claiming ESA, with 10,600 people dying in total

---

NOTES

N2: Updated mortality totals were finally published by the DWP in August 2015: DWP: August 2015: *Mortality Statistics: Employment and Support Allowance, Incapacity Benefit or Severe Disablement Allowance* - updated death totals p5

and 1300 people dying after being removed from the guaranteed monthly benefit, placed into the Work Related Activity Group regardless of diagnosis, forced to prepare for work and then died trying.[108]

A large part of this ongoing preventable harm may be due to the fact that government departments, for reasons best known to themselves, don't appear to communicate with each other. As demonstrated so well in the 2010 paper by Steve Griffiths, *Dark Times For Those Who Cannot Work*[109], if the DWP communicated with the Department of Health (DoH) then many serious problems could have been averted. Griffiths exposed the fact that the New Labour claim that there were over one million people receiving Incapacity Benefit (IB) who should not be '...*was based from the beginning on selective use of evidence.*'[109]

Illustration 5:2 DWP death totals ~ reproduced with kind permission of the artist

Griffiths continues by asking the same question asked ever since the New Labour government introduced the ESA in 2008, which was always a disaster waiting to happen, and the death totals started climbing... '*How many successful appeals against disallowance does it take to suggest a wider problem?*' He also noted that '...*hundreds of thousands of people who are unfit for work appear to have been disallowed benefits wrongly.*'[109] Now five years old, this is a very significant paper, with a collection of relevant references that led Griffiths to conclude that: '*This paper catalogues a failure of compassion, unacknowledged incompetence and injustice on a massive scale: a social policy tragedy.*'[109]

BOX 5:6 *Dark times for those who cannot work*

No competence, no compassion in Incapacity Benefit reform

The existence of 2 million people unfit for work, many of them suffering from the very conditions so central to the Department of Health agenda, should be seen in this context. But the connection seems never to have been made between two major Government work streams serving the same people. People on Incapacity Benefit die early, that is acknowledged by Government. But it is as if in benefit terms, they were just expected to drop off their perches rather than suffer chronic illnesses and be the beneficiaries of a progressively vanishing 'security for those who cannot work'.[17] ...

One small piece of research did look at the demands on the NHS and receipt of incapacity benefit... Seven out of nine indicators showed a strong and significant correlation with emergency hospital admissions (all causes, age under 65). But the distribution of incapacity benefit claimants showed the strongest association of all seven with the emergency admissions indicator...

There was a disassociation between the connections being made across the academic world and the reach of much health policy development on the one hand, and the 'Reducing Dependency' agenda of New Labour. Where did that disconnect come from? One explanation for the immense stress and error imposed by the introduction of ESA is that there has been a major policy misdiagnosis based on selective attention to evidence.

Dark Times For Those Who Cannot Work [109]
Incapacity Benefit Reforms

Compass Think Pieces No 67

Steve Griffiths
October 2010

Whilst the concentration of concern is now with the ESA, the WCA needed in order to access the benefit and the growing catalogue of deaths and despair that is a result of the unwelcome influence of the private healthcare insurance industry with the UK Government; nevertheless, before the ESA there were other policies used to attempt to limit claimant numbers.

More and more private contractors were introduced to conduct welfare policy and, without exception, they have all been an unmitigated failure. How many more £millions of *'tax-payers' cash'* will successive UK governments waste before they realise that, regardless of the opinion of Lord Freud, private contractors have demonstrated that they are not the best use of DWP funding; be it for the assessment of the chronically sick and the long-term disabled people or the IB claimants forced to improve skills via the Pathways to Work initiative, using private contractors, for the non-existent millions of new jobs that remain unavailable?[110] According to a 2010 report by the National Audit Office: '*More recent evaluation results from later phases of Pathways roll out have been far less positive and have shown that once accepted for incapacity benefits, new claimants are just as likely to move into employment without Pathways support as they are with it.*' The same report identified that: '*Contractors have underperformed against targets and have achieved a greater proportion of jobs from voluntary rather than 'mandatory' participants compared with Jobcentre Plus areas.*'[110]

This unmitigated social policy disaster must have started somewhere and, it appears, it all began at a conference, near Oxford. Justification for the future demolition of the welfare state was created in November 2001 at the 'Malingering and Illness Deception' conference, held at Woodstock, near Oxford, with the conference attended by like-minded individuals including Aylward and LoCascio, from UnumProvident[TM] Insurance, who both made a contribution.[111]

Published by Oxford University Press, the conference papers were subsequently collated in 2003,[111] with the overwhelming commentary that '*malingering*' was a lifestyle choice for many claimants of long-term sickness benefit, due to the more generous benefits that had become widely available over the previous 30 years. It seems unlikely that any of the conference speakers had actually attempted to live on these identified '*generous*' benefits, as commentary overlooked the rise in the cost of living which justified the increases in benefit. As a consequence of the 2001 conference, it is no accident that since 2008 all future claimants of the ESA are presumed to be bogus until proven otherwise by the DWP. The theory of claimants being guilty until proven innocent, regardless of diagnosis or prognosis, was actually created at the 2001 Woodstock *Malingering and Illness Deception* conference.[111]

There were lots of '*experts*' at the Woodstock conference who were offering opinions that would, eventually, adversely impact on the welfare of over two and a half million claimants of IB in the UK. At least one expert compared chronically sick and disabled people to APES [111] (p 54) and, of course, there were a number of '*experts*' in Psychology waxing lyrically about the causes of psychosomatic illnesses and illness deception. (p 156, 243, 267) [111] The influence of the conference wasn't difficult to sell to future UK governments. All these '*experts*' were authorities in their relevant academic fields and all had strong opinions about '*malingering*' and so, gradually, the planned future demolition of the welfare state would be brought into being as there was no representative at the conference to challenge this collected opinion. Throughout his presentation at the Woodstock conference, Aylward's principle references were to his own research, together with references to the paper he co-authored in 1995 with LoCascio from UnumProvident$_{TM}$ Insurance and to papers from his future colleague at the

---

BOX 5:7 *Wilful deception as illness behaviour*

The fact that health and non-health related deception is commonly practiced within society and that public attitudes towards fraud and deception are largely equivocal, suggests that it is reasonable to view illness behaviours from several conceptually non-medical perspectives. This is clinically and theoretically important, since disagreements both within and outside the medical community about the fundamental nature of illness deception are still largely framed in the medical parameters given the absence of credible or acceptable non-medical accounts. Discussion of illness deception outside medicine is meaningless without an explicit recognition and acceptance that an individual's choice to feign or exaggerate symptoms is a legitimate explanation for some illness behaviours associated with personal or financial incentives.

Over the past 30 years, more generous benefits have become more widely available. It seems unlikely that medical factors alone can adequately explain the large uptake in work-related incapacity benefits in most countries since the 1970s, despite improvements on most objective measures of health. Significantly, most of the conditions associated with this increase are symptom-based illnesses which ultimately rely on the credibility of the subject's report. The key factor in any discussion of illness deception is the extent to which a person's reported symptoms can be considered a product of free will, 'psychopathology' or psychosocial influences beyond his/her volitional control or perhaps all. Distinguishing illness deception from psychiatric illness on the basis of a subject's assumed motives is not practical or always possible; there are no reliable or valid methods for objectively determining consciously motivated intention. Medical models of illness are rendered more congruent with existing sociologic models of human nature, when they acknowledge and consider the capacity for patients (as human beings) to influence illness behaviour by choice and conscious intent. (p3-4)

Malingering and Illness Deception [111]

Halligan, Bass and Oakley
2003, p3-4

UnumProvident$_{TM}$ Centre for Psychosocial and Disability Research at Cardiff University, namely Gordon Waddell. Funded by the DWP, it appears to have been a conference that demonstrated how to preach to the converted. These 'experts' were all in the same or related fields and it seems likely that they were all very familiar with each other's work. Of course, the vast majority of politicians had no knowledge of the 2001 conference[111], or the implications drawn from it but, in years to come, the systematic political attack against the claimants of long-term sickness and disability benefits would be justified due to the opinions reported at the conference; which was funded by the DWP and enjoyed *'enthusiastic support'* from Aylward.

BOX 5:8 *Origins, practice, and limitations of Disability Assessment Medicine*

The development of this specialty, which recognizes the importance of distinguishing clearly between symptoms and disability in clinical practice and as a basis for sick certification and social security benefits, has been driven by dramatic increases in sickness and incapacity for work associated with musculoskeletal disorders, mental health problems, and 'subjective health complaints' in Britain and other more developed democracies. A biological explanation for these observed increases in chronic disability is hard to adduce, set against a background of improvement in most objective measures of health. How more objective standards are achieved by which disability can be judged and 'malingering' defined, offering security to the vulnerable while protecting public funds on behalf of the taxpayer, poses a significant social policy dilemma in the twenty-first century. Disability Assessment Medicine has offered some tools for a more robust and expert advisory service for decision makers. However, new conceptual frameworks, methodologies, and reasoned professional judgements based upon biopsychosocial models of disability have moved the discipline away from its foundation on the biomedical model to address complex analysis of inappropriate illness behaviours and to seek out reasons for discrepancies between functional capacity and performance... (p287)

It necessarily follows that the disability analyst will also need to be satisfied that the symptoms, functional limitations, and restrictions which a person reports are adequately explained by a medically recognized disease or definitive neurobiological or psychological dysfunction... (p288)

Moreover, both definitions stress that physical impairment may result either from *pathological or anatomical loss* or *abnormality of structure* or *physical loss or limitation of function,* or indeed some combination of both types of physical impairment. This is equally applicable to mental impairment since the medical disease model assumes that this follows from structural and functional changes that originate primarily in the brain... (p289)

As a consequence, disability assessment medicine recognises that reported and observed activity and performance may be due to the interaction of a variety of factors: (a) actual loss of function, (b) restrictions of function, (c) premature termination of activity, (d) sub-optimal performance, (e) environment and (f) motivation and attitude. In many of these pain or fatigue states *per se*, expectations of pain or fatigue and indeed other perceived adverse effects of an activity can act to limit function, resist activity and thus performance... (p289)

Biopsychosocial models provide powerful..frameworks... But their apparent failure to acknowledge that illness behaviours may also be driven by the subject's choice and intent is a formidable barrier... when deception is strongly suspected. (p296)

Malingering and Illness Deception [111]

Mansel Aylward
2003, p287 - 296

The endless comparisons to the activities and reported experiences in America dominated the conference, which included 13 contributors from the United States (US) and Canada, suggesting that evidence from America could be replicated in the UK, so the seeds were sown for the future desecration of the British welfare state. In the UK the DWP now liken themselves to a private insurance contractor and have adopted the American analysis, which doubts all clinical opinion of GPs and the evidence of all claimants. Hence, the bogus WCA was designed to discredit the claimant in a decision used to favour the DWP and to resist funding the ESA benefit. **Illness is never mentioned**, only incapacity or disability. With *Cash Not Care* as the only priority, the welfare of the claimants is of no consequence to the DWP. The only priority is the budget.

This challenge to the integrity of all long-term sickness benefit claimants, and their GPs, was also applied to sick and disabled veterans from the British military forces, to resist increasing War Pensions, as well as to the civilian population. There is a chapter in the published conference papers[111] claiming that American doctors exaggerate their patients' needs to guarantee payment by the healthcare insurers, with the suggestion that British doctors do the same thing to support claimants of long-term sickness benefit.[111] (p197- 205)

Needless to say, John LoCascio – a Unum 'consultant' advising the UK government - also contributed to the conference. LoCascio went to great lengths to demonstrate what a significant contribution the healthcare insurance industry made to society, and identified the duties of the healthcare insurance industry: '*..to pay valid claims promptly and fairly, and to simultaneously avoid the depletion of a necessary resource by identifying claims that are not valid.*'[111] (p 301 – 310)

Whilst it is encouraging to learn that one of the claimed duties of the corporate giant is to '*pay valid claims promptly*', judging by the thousands of inquiries of Linda Nee's consultancy service in the US[112], as a disability insurance consultant, this claim by LoCascio may well be interpreted by the insurance industry as the ability to challenge any claim and to delay claims as long as possible, as exposed by the 2007 BBC News report, when Unum Insurance were identified as '*racketeers.*'[113]

BOX 5:9 *Malingering, insurance medicine and the medicalisation of fraud*

Malingering is a concept that spans law and medicine and has important societal consequences. Disability-related programmes in both the public and private sectors are faced with increasing numbers of disability claims despite improved health care and job design (the disability paradox). As a result, medical providers face questions of malingering and related issues with increasing frequency. However, there is a paucity of data as to the demographics and exact magnitude of the problem. Changes in medical technology, confusion between medical and legal concepts, and unrecognized clinical assumptions make malingering difficult to analyse and document, and may result in risk to unskilled analysts. To be most effective, the analyst must: distinguish malingering from fraud; understand the difference between the clinical and analytical role; know the limits of medical data; and apply functional concepts in a disciplined manner... (p301)

This charge has grown increasingly difficult as law, medicine, and the workplace evolve: as work becomes less physical and more intellectual; as claims for benefit become less 'objective' and more 'subjective'. As a result, insurers are faced with a disability paradox: an increasingly healthy society; safer and less physically demanding workplaces; but more reported disability (Aylward and LoCascio 1995; see also Baron and Poole, Chapter 19). (p302)

This has awakened the modern interest in malingering. Thus, the object of this chapter is to consider some of the ways medicine relates to law and insurance in questions of malingering, and how medical providers can most effectively present this knowledge to insurers and to the greater society... (p302)

When the medical resource becomes a functional analyst, it is necessary to recall that the cases that are referred for disability benefit are not the rule of clinical practice, but the exception. That is to say, they are in the minority of cases that, despite the best efforts of the medical system, fail to improve enough to resume normal life activities, including gainful employment. When such a case also lacks objectification, especially in this day of advanced chemical, imaging, and histological techniques, they are part of an even smaller minority. In other words, they are the clear exceptions to the clinical rule... (p306)

This volume compiles many stimulating perspectives and approaches in a newly invigorated field. Some of us are compelled by the structure of our work to analyse the individual's behaviour, others the behaviour of groups. Perhaps one day a technician will directly address questions of intent through a practical method of 'lie detection' (see Craig and Hill, Chapter 26). (p309)

Malingering and Illness Deception [111]

John LoCascio – Unum Provident Insurance
2003, p300 - 310

NOTES

N2: The new and updated DWP mortality figures were released in August 2015 as this manuscript neared completion. The reference to the figures are identified in the footnotes. https://www.gov.uk/government/uploads/system/uploads/attachment_data/file/456359/mortality-statistics-esa-ib-sda.pdf

REFERENCES

X http://www.debretts.com/people-of-today/profile/20192/Mansel-AYLWARD

** **All websites accessed 5th August 2015**

Illustration 5:1
Banner headlines ~ courtesy of Express Newspapers/N&S syndication

Illustration 5:2
DWP Death totals ~ courtesy of Dave Lupton of Crippen Cartoons:
http://www.crippencartoons.co.uk/

93.   A LATENT EXISTENCE blog: press headlines: 26th July 2011: *Twisting the facts, printing lies. How the DWP and tabloids are wrong about fit for work stats.*
http://www.latentexistence.me.uk/government-launch-new-attacks-even-as-select-committee-condemns-propaganda/
94.   STEWART M: January 2015: *The influence of the private insurance industry on the UK welfare reforms.*
http://www.researchgate.net/publication/271199429_The_influence_of_the_private_insurance_industry_on_the_UK_welfare_reforms
95.   MILLER S: October 2014: UK Welfare Reform Deaths – updated list
http://blacktrianglecampaign.org/2014/10/21/uk-welfare-reform-deaths-updated-list-october-21st-2014/
96.   DWP: 9th July 2012: Incapacity Benefits: Deaths of Recipients
www.gov.uk/government/uploads/system/uploads/attachment_data/file/223050/incap_dec_d_recips_0712.pdf
97.   AAJ: 2008: *The Ten Worst Insurance Companies in America*: The American Association of Justice
http://www.bulmanlaw.com/wp-content/uploads/2013/03/TenWorstInsuranceCompanies.pdf
98.   RILEY-SMITH BEN: 19th June 2012: *Hate crimes against disabled soar to record level:*
The Independent:
http://www.independent.co.uk/news/uk/crime/hate-crimes-against-disabled-people-soar-to-a-record-level-7858841.html
99.   HOC WORK & PENSION COMMITTEE Report: 13th July 2011: *The role of incapacity benefit reassessment in helping claimants into employment.*
http://www.publications.parliament.uk/pa/cm201012/cmselect/cmworpen/1015/1015.pdf
100. STEWART M: November 2011: *The truth behind the welfare reforms*
http://www.whywaitforever.com/dwpatosveteransreport20111120.html
101. BRIANT E, WATSON N: PHILO G: November 2011: *Bad News for Disabled People:How the newspapers are reporting disability.* Glasgow University
http://eprints.gla.ac.uk/57499/1/57499.pdf
102. AYLWARD M DSS & LO CASCIO J Unum Ltd: August 1995

Problems in the assessment of psychosomatic conditions in social security benefits and related commercial schemes. Journal of Psychosomatic Research 1995, Vol 39, No 6, pp755-765
http://www.sciencedirect.com/science/article/pii/002239999500037J

103. STEWART M: August 2010: *Atos Healthcare or Disability Denial Factories* – research summary
http://blacktrianglecampaign.org/2011/08/23/important-read-circulate/

104. MCKEE M and STUCKLER D: December 2011: BMJ: *The assault on universalism: how to destroy the welfare state*: BMJ2011;343:d7973:
http://users.ox.ac.uk/~chri3110/Details/Universalism%20McKee%20Stuckler.pdf

105. HOC 1999: *Permanent Health Insurance debate; Westminster Hall, 21st December 1999.* Unum Provident Insurance exposed during debate.
http://www.publications.parliament.uk/pa/cm199900/cmhansrd/vo991221/halltext/91221h01.htm#91221h01_head0

106. GIBSON PARLIAMENTARY INQUIRY: Dec 2005: Evidence
http://www.meactionuk.org.uk/HOOPER_CONCERNS_ABOUT_A_COMMERCIAL_CONFLICT_OF_INTEREST.htm

107. MILLER S: October 2014: *UK Welfare Reform Deaths* – updated list
http://blacktrianglecampaign.org/2014/10/21/uk-welfare-reform-deaths-updated-list-october- 21st-2014/

108. DWP: 9th July 2012: Incapacity Benefits: Deaths of Recipients
ww.gov.uk/government/uploads/system/uploads/attachment_data/file/223050/incap_decd_recips_0712.pdf

109. GRIFFITHS S: October 2010: *Dark Times for Those Who Cannot Work.*
http://www.compassonline.org.uk/wp-content/uploads/2013/06/Dark-Times- Benefit-Reform-Thinkpiece-67.pdf

110. NAO: DWP May 2010: Support to incapacity benefits claimants through Pathways to Work: page 9
http://www.nao.org.uk/wp-content/uploads/2010/05/101121es.pdf

111. VARIOUS AUTHORS: CONFERENCE PAPERS: Malingering and Illness Deception ISBN: 0 19 851554 52003:
http://www.meactionuk.org.uk/Malingering_and_Illness_Deception.pdf

112. NEE LINDA: Disability Claims Solutions Inc:Licensed Disability Claims Consultant   http://www.disabilityclaimssolutions.com

113. BBC NEWS: UNUM INSURANCE: 7th November 2007 – 6 minutes - VIDEO
http://www.meactionuk.org.uk/UNUM_on_BBC_News_061107.wmv

CHAPTER 6: THE SHAME OF BRITAIN
~ Thatcher's Legacy In The Making

There are none so blind as those who will not see.
John Heywood
1546

By definition, 'welfare' is meant to be concerned with '*the health, happiness, and fortunes of a person or a group.*'[114] However, following five years of the Coalition government, the ongoing '*welfare reforms*' permitted disability discrimination to become a policy of State in the United Kingdom (UK), when following guidance from an American corporate insurance giant for the assessment of claimants of long-term sickness benefit.[115]

Over time, it became very obvious to this researcher (MS) that the enforced welfare reduction in the UK was following some form of template, which had to be found. Whilst certain politicians and 'experts' sympathetic to the Coalition Government claimed that the '*welfare reforms*' were needed due to claimed prolific welfare spending by the last Labour government, and the 2008 banking crash, it had been apparent for quite some time that this was an excuse and not a justification for the adoption of the Welfare Reform Act 2012[116]; that would introduce perceived government funded tyranny into UK welfare policies.

Look no further than America, and Margaret Thatcher's well reported close relationship with the American President Ronald Reagan[117] that would appear to have opened the door for American social security policies to be adopted in the UK in the future as '*Thatcher's Legacy*' still rules supreme in the Conservative Party. '*It's just another way in which Thatcher shaped the Britain we're living in today.*'[118] The close bond between the former political leaders of America and the UK came to the fore following the death of Mrs Thatcher in 2013, when the national press had a field day on both sides of the Atlantic, and David Cameron presumed to spend in excess of £3.6 million of '*tax-payers' cash*' on her funeral.[119]

During her reign, from 1979 to 1990, Thatcher was at times identified as acting as a President rather than a Prime Minister, and her funeral certainly confirmed that the Tories afforded her a unique position in the history of their party, as the poorest people in the UK are forced to live with her legacy every day; that was demonstrated so well in Danny Dorling's 2015 book *Injustice ~ why social inequality still persists*, as explained via the author's website in a detailed introduction to the book.[120] It should be remembered that Thatcher was elected as the UK Prime Minister in 1979 and, according to academic experts, injustice has increased ever since.

BOX 6:1 *An introduction to Injustice ~ why social injustice still persists*

Principally: Injustice can be seen as the result of five social evils, namely the effects of elitism, exclusion, prejudice, greed and despair. Underlying each social evil are views which, when propagated, strengthen the harm done. These are views that most of us hold in small measure, and we often think there is not much harm in them. However, when such views begin to pervade society from top to bottom, the results can be extremely damaging to the fabric of our lives... (p1)

We live in an increasingly hierarchical society. We talk about some people being way above and others way below other people. And yet we are not that different from each other. This sham hierarchy has been created by elitism, exclusion, prejudice, and greed. The end result is increasing amounts of despair, not only among the poor, but also among groups like the children of aspirational parents. If we want a content and happy society, we are currently going in the wrong direction... (p2)

It has been estimated that in the UK, as 2015 draws to a close, almost 7.1 million of the nation's 13 million youngsters will be in homes with incomes judged to be less than the minimum necessary for a decent standard of living. In contrast, relatively few people would describe themselves as poor and needing to take out loans 'just to get by' in countries as diverse as Japan and the Netherlands, whereas in Britain and the US, relative and now absolute rates of poverty have grown greatly in recent decades, simply because inequality has grown... (p3)

Human beings are not mentally immune to the effects of rising elitism, exclusion, prejudice and greed. They react like rats in cages to having their social environments made progressively more unpleasant. Part of the mechanism behind the worldwide rise in diseases of despair – depression and anxiety – is the insecurity caused when particular forms of competition are enhanced... (p5)

Not making children and adults anxious, tearful, fearful and stressed in the first place is the best place to start. By looking at different places and at different countries, and by noting the extraordinarily rapid increase in despair in the UK and the US, it is apparent that the proportion of desperately unhappy people is not currently so very high by some law of nature, but the result of policies and attitudes that can be changed.(p5)

An introduction to Injustice: [120]
why social inequality still persists

Danny Dorling
3rd June 2015

Courtesy of Professor Danny Dorling
Published by Policy Press

As this research progressed it was clear that independent academic research would expose the true realities behind the UK welfare reforms, and that evidence was demonstrated when the significant 2008 paper of Dr Anne Daguerre of Middlesex University was accessed. Her paper *'The Second Phase of US Welfare Reform, 2000-2006: Blaming the poor again?'*[121] demonstrated the savage American social security policies as now replicated in the UK.

BOX 6:2 *The second phase of US Welfare Reform*
~ blaming the poor again?

In 1992, Bill Clinton's promise 'to end welfare as we know it' set the stage for a radical revolution in American social policy... The new Republican administration (G. W. Bush became President in January 2001) wanted to build upon the existing programme, and was also keen to strengthen work requirements. Thus the second phase of welfare reform was about policy consolidation as opposed to radical change. In February 2002, President Bush published the White House reauthorization proposals, entitled *Working Towards Independence*. Between 2002 and 2005, Congress passed eleven short-term extensions of the 1996 law. Welfare reform reauthorization was included as part of the Deficit Reduction Act of 2005   and was signed by the President on 8 February 2006. The new legislation strengthened the Work First Approach which had dominated TANF* in 1996 as well as the family values agenda promoted by Republicans... In the second section, the analysis is devoted to the politics of the second phase of US welfare reform (2001-6). The final legislation strengthens work requirements while putting additional burdens on both states and welfare recipients. States have now lost a great deal of administrative freedom, and are increasingly required to police welfare claimants' behaviour if they want to avoid financial sanctions...

The Human Capital Approach clashed with the punitive Work First Approach endorsed by conservative intellectuals such as Murray (1984) and Mead (1986)... While Murray (1984) suggested that all forms of social assistance should be repealed, Mead was more nuanced and therefore more influential in policy terms... His arguments justified the development of a regime of sanctions and regular work controls. These principles were at the core of the Work First Approach, which was based on the idea that welfare recipients should be pushed into paid employment as quickly as possible regardless of the quality of the job offer. The Work First Approach was part of the 'rhetoric of blaming the poor' which explained poverty in terms of personal inadequacies as opposed to structural social factors such as a lack of suitable, decently paid jobs in the formal labour market.

The Second Phase of US Welfare Reform, 2000-2006:[121]
Blaming the Poor Again?

Anne Daguerre

Social Policy & Administration
Volume 42, Issue 4, p362-378
August 2008

*TANF – Temporary Assistance for Needy Families

The key findings of the Daguerre 2008 paper[121] make for disturbing if expected reading, and confirmed this researcher's experience to date. Quite clearly, the reforms introduced by previous UK administrations, and especially since Cameron became Prime Minister, are a replica of the *'welfare'* reforms as adopted in America and introduced in the UK by misleading the British people. The previous New Labour Prime Ministers Blair and Brown were just as addicted to the American social security policies as Cameron, and they had both continued the *'Thatcher Legacy'* between 1997 - 2010, although with less vitriol than now endured; including the introduction of the Employment and Support Allowance (ESA) in 2008.

There was more to come from Middlesex University. To acknowledge the conclusion of a two-year Economic and Social Research Council (ESRC) research project *'Welfare reform in the US and the UK: an interdiscipliniary analysis'*, Associate Professor Dr Anne Daguerre led a one day conference on 20th March 2015.[122] The preamble to the conference identified the close links between the US and the UK welfare policies:

BOX 6:3 *Assessing 20 years of welfare reform in the US and the UK Conference, London, March 2015*

Almost 20 years have passed since the adoption of the Personal Responsibility Work Opportunity Act in the United States, which made work requirements a condition of receiving cash… American policies inspired British policy makers on both sides of the political spectrum, from the New Deal for Young People (1997) to the Welfare Reform Act 2012 (stringent work requirements and increased use of benefit sanctions). Despite ongoing controversies regarding the negative impact of benefit sanctions on vulnerable claimants, Secretary of State for Work and Pensions Iain Duncan Smith says that the United Kingdom is a model of effective welfare policies. In the run up to the May 2015 general election, it is time to reassess the experience of welfare reform on both sides of the Atlantic, in political, economic, social and legal terms.

This one-day conference concludes a two-year ESRC* research project 'Welfare reform in the US and the UK: an interdisciplinary analysis led by Associate Professor Dr Anne Daguerre.' The research shows that the erosion of social assistance rights has been a central feature of social policy reforms in both countries, a trend that has not been reversed by the presidency of Barack Obama, with the notable exception of health care.

Assessing 20 years of welfare reform in the US and the UK [122]

Conference London
20th March 2015

*ESRC - the Economic & Social Research Council

Just before the conference, in March 2015, Dr Anne Daguerre co-authored a paper with Dr David Etherington: '*Workfare in 21st century Britain – the erosion of rights to social assistance.* '[123] Again funded by the ESRC, the research demonstrated a similar conclusion to the 2008 independent paper by Anne Daguerre.

BOX 6:4 *Workfare in 21st Century Britain*
~ the erosion of rights to social justice

In order to legitimize these cuts, the coalition government has called back the spectre of the 'moral underclass'. Under this vision, poverty and unemployment are being caused by individual failings such as alcohol or drug addiction, chaotic lifestyles, idleness and lack of purpose (dissolution). To address these issues a strong focus is being placed on stable relationships and family life as opposed to 'the poverty plus a pound approach' that characterized the Labour government approach. The Secretary of State for Work and Pensions Iain Duncan Smith has said that 'Marriage should be supported and encouraged'. This agenda resembles American welfare reform in the 1990s, which aimed to end dependence of needy parents on government benefits by promoting job preparation, work and marriage... (p6)

This report is part of an ESRC* funded research which analyses the evolution of welfare reform in the US and the UK. It is argued that workfare policies represent a test case for exploring the redefinition of socio-economic rights in the early 21st century, when rights-based entitlements are being increasingly replaced with conditional rights dependent on the fulfilment of obligations. The research explores the socio-legal constructs that justify this rebalancing of rights and responsibilities in two mature liberal welfare states, the US and the UK. The report summarises the provisional findings regarding welfare to work in the UK, with a particular focus on the decision making processes behind the expansion of workfare schemes endorsed by the coalition government (2010/present). Trickey and Walker (2001) define workfare as 'a programme or scheme that requires people to work in return for social assistance benefits'. Non-compliance with work requirements carries the risk of loss of benefits, a temporary withdrawal of benefits or a reduction in benefits (Trickey and Walker, 2001, p. 203). In practice, most sanctions entail a temporary reduction of benefits (up to three years in the UK since the Welfare Reform Act 2012). The intention is to send a clear message according to which non-compliance will not be tolerated and will have serious negative financial consequences. Workfare policies, with their reliance on compulsion, carry strong authoritarian and disciplinary tendencies. Their explicit aim is to modify individual behaviour through the use of persuasion and coercion. (p7-8)

Workfare in 21st Century Britain [123]
the erosion of rights to social assistance

ESRC

Dr Anne Daguerre & Dr David Etherington
November 2014

*ESRC - the Economic & Social Research Council

Whilst not including the welfare reforms imposed on the claimants of Incapacity Benefit (IB) being migrated to the Employment and Support Allowance (ESA), nevertheless, the Daguerre and Etherington 2014 research paper[123] demonstrated that the erosion of rights to social assistance - benefits - in the UK are a replica of American social security policies.

As identified in the 2014 research paper[123], the recent legal judgement against the government caused problems for the Department for Work and Pensions (DWP) and Daguerre and Etherington's paper concluded that: '*This also explains why the coalition government is looking to ways into which they could replace the Human Rights Act with a UK Bill of Rights, and are on record for criticising interference from the European Court of Justice as well as the European Court of Human Rights.*' [123] (p8)

Clearly, as Prime Minister, John Major continued the '*Thatcher Legacy*' following her departure from office in 1990. It is no coincidence that John Major's then Secretary of State for Work and Pensions, Peter Lilley, invited John LoCascio of UnumProvident™ Insurance to offer guidance on welfare claims management in 1992[124] that coincided with the introduction of Bill Clinton's '*radical revolution in American social policy;*' as identified in Anne Daguerre's 2008 paper '*Blaming the poor again?*'[125]

Illustration 6:1 Cameron's message ~ reproduced by kind permission of the artist

71

Given that almost half of all the long-term sickness benefit claimants have a mental health diagnosis[126], and the Freud Report[127] would cause them to be intimidated by government policies, Danny Dorling had some thoughts about the manipulation of the public regarding the victims of mental health illness, if and when their liberty should be removed, and about the *incorrect figures* [128] as used by Freud in his 2007 Report.

BOX 6:5 *The Real Mental Health Bill*

Incidentally don't be fooled by the figures in the (DWP commissioned) Freud report suggesting spectacular falls in the number of Incapacity Benefit claimants in pathways pilot areas (a 9.5% fall on page 44 of his report). David Freud got his numbers wrong (to verify this simply read the sources he cites – they do not apply to all claimants as he implies, most of whom have been claiming for years, but only to a small minority), but then he is not a social scientist but a banker – so why should counting be his strong point? David's report is titled "independent", but both commissioned and published by the DWP. Independent no longer means independent. The point of independent reports to government and ministers today is that they are not written by people who are independent of government but by folk whose lives and connections are intimately wound up in the machinery of government and elite civil society. For those who enjoy unravelling these connections, and given the journal this is written in, it is relevant to point out that David is the great grandson of Sigmund, and Sigmund was briefly associated with the Institute for the Scientific Study and Treatment of Delinquency (CCJS, 2007). Delinquency was thought then and still by many now to be a mental illness, possibly inherited. Although such thinking is now discredited the use of some of Sigmund's thinking to sell ideas to the public is continuous and underpins a huge consultancy industry: public relations (PR).

The Real Mental Health Bill [128]

Danny Dorling
Guest Editorial
Journal of Public Mental Health
6(3), 6-13 May 2007

As with all significant academic essays and research, Danny Dorling's paper is published in an academic journal that few outside the academic world will ever access, unless and until the detailed information is rescued from obscurity and reproduced in the public domain. Danny Dorling's identified flaws in Freud's report, and that identified incompetence of Freud, is now available in the public domain for all to note.[128]

In keeping with most DWP funded reports by '*independent*' experts, they wax lyrically but are often sparce with reality. The 2007 Freud Report was no different. He gleefully acknowledged that he '*didn't know anything about welfare*' [129] before he wrote the 2007 report at the behest of the New Labour Party and now, eight years later, he frequently demonstrates that he has gained power but no knowledge since being awarded a Ministerial post by Cameron. Certainly, if nothing else, the ongoing *'welfare reforms'* in the UK have demonstrated that with Freud's help, when Cameron walked into No 10 for the first time in 2010 humanity left via the back door, as demonstrated so well in Mary O'Hara's critically acclaimed new book, 'Austerity Bites.' [130]

BOX 6:6 *Austerity Bites*

The book demonstrates how, despite government claims that drastic cuts to public spending and sweeping reform of the welfare state were necessary and 'fair', this was, in fact, a fallacy. What was implemented was a regime that disproportionately affected the most vulnerable people in society while leaving the well-off unscathed.[2] By examining the lived experience and 'real-time' reactions of those most affected by a whole raft of bruising austerity measures – the poorest and those most reliant on public services – the rest of the book lays bare the extraordinary damage inflicted during what has become known as 'the age of austerity'. And it looks too at one of the most important factors explaining how austerity was so forcefully applied: the fact that policies were deftly propped up by shrewd political narrative which both painted cuts as inevitable and depicted people who were living in poverty, out of work or who were victims of austerity as 'scroungers', to blame for their own predicament.[3](p1)…

Paraded in the language of 'fairness', step by step the government undermined six decades of core social security protections such as Child Benefit and support for people with disabilities. The previous Labour administration had got away with a profligate public spending, the Coalition cried (to barely a whimper from a timorous Labour Party which feared – correctly – that public opinion blamed them for the deficit.) The global economic crisis and banking catastrophe of 2008 was unprecedented and therefore warranted an exceptional response, the austerians declared. Austerity was right, necessary, unavoidable and (most memorably false) the population were 'all in this together'. However… rampant public spending was not the primary culprit of the UK's difficulties… Rather, it was the billions of taxpayers' cash pumped into bailing out a failed global banking system. (p5)

AUSTERITY BITES [130]
Mary O'Hara
2015

Courtesy of Policy Press

Mary travelled the length and breadth of the UK to interview the many whose lives have been adversely impacted by the government's identified austerity measures and *'welfare reforms'*, as copied from America, and demonstrating the human consequences of the imposed fear and suffering in disturbing detail. Supporting the evidence exposed in Mary O'Hara's book,[130] others have been attempting to draw attention to their fate via publications such as the New Statesman, as demonstrated so well by 25 year old Rosie Fletcher in her very strong essay: *Memo to David Cameron: I have all the incentives I need to stop being ill. It's called 'being ill.'* [131]

BOX 6:7 *Memo to David Cameron:*

Another day, another rummage down the back of the benefits sofa to find a spare £12bn. This week: changing Employment Support Allowance to incentivise ill people to get back to work.

One problem: I already have the best incentive to stop being ill and get back to work. It's called "being ill"…

Disease isn't like a gas meter. It has no notion of economics. It doesn't switch off because you've stopped putting money in. This isn't some kind of elaborate con I've been running, shutting myself away from the world to trick you out of the princely sum of £48 a week. Cutting my benefits won't get me back into work. It will make my life smaller, more stressful. It will make me sicker.

Please do not be taken in by the weaselly misuse of the word incentive. Incentives are nice things, rewards, like cream cakes or that video of Michael Gove falling over. Cutting the money that sick and disabled people receive isn't an incentive to work, it's a disincentive and a punishment for being ill. You can paint it orange and call it a carrot as much as you like, but if you're beating people into the ground with it, it's still a stick.

This isn't just a question of economics, of ideological war on the welfare state. This is the insidious, callous notion that sick and disabled people are ultimately not trying hard enough. This says what people with chronic illnesses and disabilities hear all too much from their friends, from their families, from even their doctors: we do not believe that you are ill.

If you think that eventually you can make people so sad and stressed and poor that they will "get over" being ill, that you can starve them out and they'll end their little displays of sickness, then you are very much mistaken. We have all the incentives we need to get back to work; cutting ESA will only make it harder to do so.

Memo to David Cameron: I have all the incentives I need to stop being ill. It's called "being ill". [131]

The Staggers – The New Statesman's rolling politics blog

Rosie Fletcher
3rd July 2015

Courtesy of New Statesman

In the MS 2014 research report: '*UK Government refuses to accept responsibility for identified crimes against humanity*' [132] the evidence of the ongoing human suffering, death and despair in the UK linked to the 'welfare reforms' was identified. The 2014 report confirmed the fact that the often critical annual reports by the President of Appeal Tribunals were cancelled by a UK government intent on removing all legitimate protest against what was identified as government funded tyranny against those least able to protest.[132]

BOX 6:8 *UK government refuses to accept responsibility…*

The new report by The Mental Health Welfare Commission for Scotland, regarding a woman's suicide after being '*stripped of disability benefits*', was reported by John Pring at the Disability News Service (DNS) and by many others.(g) The Coalition government knew this carnage would happen. Three years ago a list of distinguished academics, together with politicians and disability support groups, identified the future in a letter as published in The Guardian newspaper: *'Welfare reform bill will punish disabled people and the poor.'*(h) Now, 3 years after this letter was published, questions are being asked as to why the appointed and totally unsuitable Lord Freud, in his capacity as the Minister for Welfare Reform - who was <u>unelected</u> by anyone in the usual democratic way - deemed it necessary for the DWP to stop collating the numbers of deaths recorded of claimants found fit to work and removed from the long-term sickness and disability benefit, now known as the Employment and Support Allowance (ESA), regardless of confirmed catastrophic and permanent diagnosis…

Identified claimant suffering includes dramatic increases in the onset of mental health problems (r). The General Practice (GP) service is close to collapse due to overwhelming numbers of patients needing support with DWP paperwork that limits GP time spent with other patients who are ill, and the BMA(p) and the RCN(q) have both exposed the WCA as causing 'preventable harm' in breach of the Hippocratic Oath. Yet this dangerous UK government, with a Cabinet full of £millionaires who fail to comprehend need, dismiss all other evidence regardless of source. They disregard the obvious fact that the 'reforms' are falling disproportionately onto chronically disabled people, and those who are very ill and in need of guaranteed long-term welfare benefits, as the government sell the UK and transform a once great nation
into UK plc...

UK government refuses to accept responsibility for
identified crimes against humanity [132]
Mo Stewart
May 2014

ResearchGate

Whilst there are those who have an extreme reaction to the use of the words '*crimes against humanity*', with claims against their use resorting back to the atrocities of the Second World War, nevertheless, by definition of the International Criminal Court,[133] which include '*intentionally causing great suffering or serious bodily or mental injury*', crimes against humanity have been identified in the ongoing *'welfare reforms'* by the UK government as led by David Cameron. There has been plenty of published academic research that has identified the failures of the Coalition government's social policies, and the enforced suffering of the chronically sick and disabled people of the UK due to the *'welfare reforms'*. In the April

---

BOX 6:9 *Shifting the Goalposts*

Quantitative longitudinal studies investigating the health and wellbeing of long-term IB* and ESA** recipients are largely absent from the current social policy literature and so there has been no empirical basis upon which the claims made by politicians and the media or public perceptions of the relationship between benefit receipt and ill health can be tested. Previous UK studies of IB receipt have largely focused on evaluating the effects of welfare-to-work interventions amongst this group and have tended to employ experimental or evaluation methodologies with employment (rather than health) as the main study outcome… (p3)

The introduction of ESA and ongoing welfare reform means that there is a risk of IB recipients' administrative health status changing overnight, despite no actual change in their health state. For example, following a WCA, someone can be found 'fit for work' even though their health status has not altered, thus creating further obstacles for IB recipients to face, with all of the implications of a 'deserving' and 'undeserving' rhetoric that accompanies such a change… The results of the study presented in this paper show that the IB recipients have multiple health conditions, that their levels of ill health are stable over time, and that their health status is well below the general population level… (p19)

Taken together, the two data sources show that those in long-term receipt of IB experience significant – and constant – ill health and other barriers to labour market participation, and that their lives are difficult and limited by both illness and the stigmatisation of benefit receipt. This is coupled with shifting interpretations of 'work readiness' that are being attached to benefits recipients; what constitutes ill health for benefit recipients – or at least ill health of a sufficient level to receive state support – is a constantly changing and politically determined state, which may bear no relation to the real health or lived experiences of recipients. Adopting a 'health-first', together with a 'life-first', approach could allow for a consideration of the intricacies of the experiences of sick and disabled benefits recipients. (p20)

Shifting the Goalposts:[134]
A longitudinal mixed-methods study of the health of
long-term Incapacity Benefit recipients during a period of
substantial change to the UK Social Security System

The Journal of Social Policy
Kayleigh Garthwaite, Clare Bambra, Jonathan Warren,
Adetayo Kasim, Graeme Greig

Volume 43, Issue 02, April 2014

*IB – Incapacity Benefit   **ESA – Employment and Support Allowance

---

2014 paper '*Shifting the Goalposts: A longitudinal mixed-methods study of the health of long-term incapacity benefit recipients during a period of substantial change to the UK Social Security System*',[134] the acclaimed team in the Department of Geography at Durham University identified the often catastrophic implications of the impact of the enforced ongoing '*welfare reforms*', and the **stigma and shame** now experienced by those who are too ill to work but who are constantly under suspicion by the UK government.

The 2014 paper [134] is of significance as it exposed the fact that the often scathing attacks on the long-term chronically sick and disabled community, by politicians and by the media, were not based on any quantitative longitudinal studies of those in receipt of IB, which was not a '*lifestyle choice*' as so often suggested by DWP Ministers to manipulate the general public.

This reality was also well demonstrated by Bernadette Meaden, via the Ekklesia blog, in her essay: *New report ~ The Psychological Impact of Austerity* [135] as she highlighted the report by Psychologists Against Austerity.[136]

BOX 6:10 *The Psychological Impact of Austerity*

Humiliation has also been highlighted as a central experience for those affected by the changes to disability benefits. (17) Both shame and humiliation are social emotions. Humiliation arises when people are made to feel that they are lesser in status or worth, while shame occurs when people are made to feel that they have violated a social or moral standard[18]. These feelings have been compounded by the punitive benefits rhetoric used to drive through austerity policies, which has promoted the idea that those who use welfare benefits are worth less ('shirkers') than those who work ('strivers'[19])...

Fear and distrust are central to many mental health problems. Life events which are rated as dangerous are known to cause experiences of serious anxiety[34]. Societies that are less trusting also tend to be less equal, and have higher levels of mental health diagnoses[35]. High levels of distrust are associated with an 80% increase in overall reported poor health[36]. Low levels of trust also increase the chance of being diagnosed with depression by nearly 50 per cent[37]. People who live in neighbourhoods that have high levels of distrust also have increased levels of all mental health problems, particularly psychosis[38]. Loss of trust in the world and others is also known to be a precursor to suicide[39]. Policies that increase distrust within and between communities are therefore poisonous to both community cohesion and individual mental health.

The Psychological Impact of Austerity ~ a briefing paper [136]
Psychologists Against Austerity

L McGrath, V Griffin, E Mundy

March 2015

It's thanks to the vast and growing online participation by people like Bernadette, demonstrating the ongoing impact of austerity and the brutal welfare reforms that permit readers to gradually become much better informed. Academic research is being reported more and more and readers, often desperate for information, have learned that academic papers are not exclusive to academic study.[136]

As demonstrated in the 2015 paper by Psychologists Against Austerity,[136] the austerity policies being pursued by the government are toxic and '..*poisonous to both community cohesion and individual health'*.[136] There are a multitude of studies, academic papers, conference contributions and other data that demonstrate the dramatic increases in suicides,[137] the disturbing dramatic rise in disability hate crimes[138] and the catastrophic loss of confidence by the very people who have a need for the security of the welfare state in order to survive.

BOX 6:11 *British people are committing suicide to escape poverty…*

The Mullins had physical and mental disabilities to contend with and had spent months fighting the notoriously complex disability process at the Department for Work and Pensions. Starved, literally, of sufficient financial assistance, the couple's weekly food intake was bolstered by the vegetables they received from a soup kitchen in Coventry, a 12-mile round trip that they made weekly on foot.

The Mullins couldn't afford a fridge and so kept food in the garden shed. Eventually they could no longer stretch their non-existent budget to heating their home and they spent their remaining months living in one room. Captured on camera by a roving reporter shortly before their death, Mr Mullins, criticised the system: "They have no problems suspending benefits," he said, "They just put a tick in a box and they alter your life." So it was that the Mullins' life was altered irreparably and, dreading another cold and hungry winter, they were found side by side, in an apparent suicide pact in November 2011… What is the difference between people dying from starvation and people killing themselves before they have to face that certain misery?..

Some have been pushed to the brink by the Coalition's continued use of the much criticised ATOS system, designed to tell how 'fit for work' someone is… The current 'new thing' for our disabled and sick to endure is the anxious wait for 'the brown envelope' from the DWP. So far a thousand or so disabled people have received instructions about getting back to work even though some have been given fewer than six months to live…

British people are committing suicide to escape poverty.[137]
Is this what the State wants?

Sonia Poulton
Mail Online
20th March 2012

Courtesy of Solo Syndication

The sinister manipulation of the poorest people in society did not end with the introduction of the Welfare Reform Act 2012.[139] On the contrary, the more evidence that demonstrated that the policy was failing, such as the increasing numbers of successes at Appeal Tribunals, meant that the government would introduce measures to prevent access to appeals.[140]

BOX 6:12 *People stripped of benefits could be charged for challenging decision*

Critics said the proposal, contained in an internal Department for Work and Pensions document leaked to the Guardian, would hit some of the poorest people in Britain, who have been left with little or no income. In the document about the department's internal finances, officials say the "introduction of a charge for people making appeals against [DWP] decisions to social security tribunals" would raise money...

Earlier this week figures showed that in the past year nearly 900,000 people have had their benefits stopped, the highest figure for any 12-month period since jobseeker's allowance was introduced in 1996. In recent months, however, 58% of those who wanted to overturn DWP sanction decisions in independent tribunals have been successful. Before 2010, the success rate of appeals was 20% or less."...

The policy proposal leak comes as the prime minister and senior religious leaders clash over the benefits system. In a letter to the Daily Mirror, 27 Anglican bishops blamed David Cameron for creating a "national crisis" in which hundreds of thousands of people have been forced to survive on the charity of food banks because of "punitive sanctions" and other DWP failures. It followed similar criticisms from Vincent Nichols, the highest ranking Catholic in England and Wales, that the government was stripping away the welfare safety net – a charge dismissed as "an exaggeration" by Nick Clegg, the deputy prime minister...

Neil Bateman, a long-serving welfare rights lawyer, also described the policy idea as a disgrace. He said: "Stopping people from challenging bad decisions actually strikes at the heart of our democratic arrangement." He said many of the people he had successfully represented over the years at tribunals would not have got justice if they had been made to pay a fee and that even £5 would be too high a charge for them. Bateman said that from his experience, a very high proportion of appeals were caused by mistakes and poor-quality decision-making by the DWP. He said this had risen in recent years because the department had got rid of experienced DWP decision-makers, social security law had become more complex and attitudes had changed.

People stripped of benefits could be charged
for challenging decision [140]

Shiv Malik and Patrick Butler
The Guardian
20th February 2014

Courtesy of Guardian News & Media Ltd

The combination of austerity plus the welfare reforms is causing death, damage and despair but no acknowledgement from the government. Knowingly using fake figures and manipulating evidence to gain banner headlines in the tabloid press, to mislead the British public, is the act of a bully not a statesman but it's been routine for UK governments in recent years, and it has been working very well as politicians are creating a society where people are, literally, *Getting Away With Murder*.[141]

BOX 6:13   *Getting Away With Murder*

In July 2007 Christine Lakinski, a disabled woman, collapsed in a doorway on her way home. As she lay dying a man threw a bucket of water over her, covered her in shaving foam and urinated on her.
One of his friends filmed the incident on a mobile phone.

In March 2005 Keith Philpott, who had learning difficulties, was falsely accused of being a paedophile, tortured, disembowelled and stabbed to death in his own home.

In May 2006 Raymond Atherton, a 40 year old man with learning difficulties, was severely beaten, had bleach poured over him and was thrown in the River Mersey, where his body was later found by police.
His attackers were people he considered his friends.

Kevin Davies, who had epilepsy, was kidnapped and held captive in a garden shed for four months before he died in September 2006. He was fed scraps, brutally tortured and his money was
stolen. Again, he considered his captors friends.

In April 2007 Colin Greenwood, a blind father with young children, was kicked to death by two teenagers. Before his murder Mr Greenwood had stopped using his white stick in public for fear of being targeted.

Getting Away With Murder [141]
Disabled people's experiences of hate crime in the UK

The UK Disabled Peoples' Council

Katherine Quarmby
August 2008

[**NB:** *The above quotes are taken from a report written in 2008.
As of January 2015, campaigners suggest there has been
a 213% increase in disability hate crimes.* [142, 143] MS]

Courtesy of SCOPE

With campaigners now identifying a 213% increase in disability hate crimes, as '...*fuelled by benefits propaganda*,' it's time these atrocities were stopped.[142, 143]

BOX 6:14 *213% Rise in Disability Hate Crime*
"Fuelled"
by Benefits Propaganda

Last year former director of public prosecutions, Ken
MacDonald, said the police and CPS* were often
overlooking cases of
disability hate crime, despite disabled people being
"abused, injured or murdered."

213% Rise in Disability Hate Crime [142]
"Fuelled" by Benefits Propaganda,
say Campaigners

Welfare Weekly
12th January 2015

*CPS – Crown Prosecution Service

<u>REFERENCES</u>

**All references confirmed and accessed 15th August 2015

<u>Illustration 6:1</u>
Cameron's message ~ courtesy of Dave Lupton of Crippen Cartoons:
www.daveluptoncartoons.co.uk

114. WELFARE definition: http://www.collinsdictionary.com/dictionary/english/welfare 115. STEWART M: 22nd January 2015: *The influence of the private insurance industry on the UK welfare reforms*: Centre for Disability Studies, Leeds University http://disability-studies.leeds.ac.uk/files/library/The%20influence%20of%20the%20private%20insurance%20industry%20%20-%20FINAL%20-%20Jan%202015.pdf

116. WELFARE REFORM ACT 2012:
http://www.legislation.gov.uk/ukpga/2012/5/contents/enacted

117. SCOTT-SAMUEL BAMBRA C, COLLINS C, HUNTER D, McCARTNEY G, SMITH K: 2014: *The impact of Thatcherism on health and well-being in Britain* http://pcwww.liv.ac.uk/~alexss/thatcherism.pdf

118. HUDSON T: 15th April 2013: *Of prime ministers and presidents* http://www.politics.co.uk/comment-analysis/2013/04/15/of-prime-ministers-and-presidents-thatchers-forgotten-legacy

119. STAFF: THE TIMES: 10th August 2013: *Thatcher funeral cost the taxpayer £3.6m* http://www.thetimes.co.uk/tto/news/uk/article3749333.ece

120. DORLING D: 2015: An introduction to *Injustice~why social injustice still persists* http://www.dannydorling.org/books/injustice/injustice-anintroduction.pdf

121.DAGUERRE A: August 2008: *The Second Phase of US Welfare Reform, 2000-2006: Blaming the Poor Again?* http://onlinelibrary.wiley.com/doi/10.1111/j.1467-9515.2008.00609.x/abstract?userIsAuthenticated=false&deniedAccessCustomisedMe ssage=

122. MIDDLESEX UNIVERSITY: one day conference: 20th March 2015: *Assessing 20 years of welfare reform in the US and the UK* http://www.mdx.ac.uk/events/2015/03/assessing-20-years-of-welfare-reform-in-the- us-and-the-uk

123. DAGUERRE A, ETHERINGTON D: November 2014: *Welfare in 21st century Britain – The erosion of rights to social assistance* http://workfare.org.uk/images/uploads/docs/workfarein21stcenturybritain.pdf

124.STEWART M: 22nd January 2015: *The influence of the private insurance industry on the UK welfare reforms*: ResearchGate http://www.researchgate.net/publication/271199429_The_influence_of_the_private_i nsurance_industry_on_the_UK_welfare_reforms

125. DAGUERRE A: August 2008: *The Second Phase of US Welfare Reform, 2000-2006: Blaming the Poor Again?* http://onlinelibrary.wiley.com/doi/10.1111/j.1467-9515.2008.00609.x/abstract?userIsAuthenticated=false&deniedAccessCustomisedMe ssage

126. BRIANT E, WATSON N: PHILO G: November 2011: *Bad News for Disabled People:How the newspapers are reporting disability.* Glasgow University http://eprints.gla.ac.uk/57499/1/57499.pdf

127. FREUD D: 2007: *Reducing dependency, increasing opportunity: options for the future of welfare to work* ISBN: 978 1 84712 193 6

128. DORLING D: May 2007: *The Real Mental Health Bill*
http://www.dannydorling.org/wp-content/files/dannydorling_publication_id0514.pdf

129. SYLVESTER AND THOMSON: 2nd February 2008: *Welfare is a mess, says adviser David Freud.* Daily Telegraph
http://www.telegraph.co.uk/news/politics/1577313/Welfare-is-a-mess-says-adviser- David-Freud.html

130. O'HARA M: 2015: *Austerity Bites:* Policy Press: ISBN 978-1-4473-1570-4 Reproduced courtesy of Policy Press

131. FLETCHER R: 3rd July 2015: *Memo to David Cameron: I have all the incentives I need to stop being ill. It's called "being ill".* Reproduced courtesy of New Statesman.
New Statesman – The Staggers ~ The New Statesman's rolling politics blog
http://www.newstatesman.com/politics/2015/07/memo-david-cameron-i-have-all- incentives-i-need-stop-being-ill-its-called-being-ill

132. STEWART M: May 2014: *UK Government refuses to accept responsibility for identified crimes against humanity*
http://www.researchgate.net/publication/263673446_UK_GOVERNMENT_REFUSE S_TO_ACCEPT_RESPONSIBILITY_FOR_IDENTIFIED_CRIMES_AGAINST_H UMANITY_-a_report

133. INTERNATIONAL CRIMINAL COURT: CRIMES AGAINST HUMANITY:
Definition: http://www.icc-cpi.int/en_menus/icc/about%20the%20court/frequently%20asked%20questions/Pages /12.aspx

134. GARTHWAITE K, BAMBRA C, WARREN J, KASIM A, GREIG G: February 2014: *Shifting the Goalposts: A Longitudinal Mixed-Methods Study of the Health of Long-Term Incapacity Benefit Recipients during a period of Substantial Change to the UK Social Security System*: The Journal of Social Policy, 43, pp 311-330: Abstract
DOI: http://dx.doi.org/10.1017/S0047279413000974
http://journals.cambridge.org/abstract_S0047279413000974

135. MEADEN B: 12th March 2015: *New Report:* http://www.ekklesia.co.uk/node/21505 136. McGRATH L, GRIFFIN V, MUNDY E: March 2015: *The Psychological Impact of Austerity – a briefing paper:* Psychologists Against Cuts
https://psychagainstausterity.files.wordpress.com/2015/03/paa-briefing-paper.pdf

137. POULTON S: 20th March 2012: *British people are committing suicide to escape poverty. Is this what the State wants?* Mail online. Courtesy of Solo Syndication
http://www.dailymail.co.uk/debate/article-2117718/British-people-committing-suicide-escape-poverty-Is-State-wants.html

138. WHEELER C: 11th January 2015: EXCLUSIVE: *Hate crimes on disabled up 213%*
http://www.express.co.uk/news/uk/551327/EXCLUSIVE-Hate-crimes-on-disabled-rise-by-213

139. WELFARE REFORM ACT 2012:
http://www.legislation.gov.uk/ukpga/2012/5/contents/enacted

140. MALIK S and BUTLER P: 20th February 2014: The Guardian: *People stripped of benefits could be charged for challenging decision*
http://www.theguardian.com/politics/2014/feb/20/people-stripped-benefits-charged- decision

141. QUARMBY K: August 2008: *Getting Away With Murder*: ISBN: 0946828989
http://www.scope.org.uk/Scope/media/Images/Publication%20Directory/Getting-away-with-murder.pdf?ext=.pdf

142.   WELFARE WEEKLY: 12th January 2015: *213% Rise in Disability Hate Crimes 'fuelled' by benefits propaganda, say campaigners*
http://www.welfareweekly.com/disability-hate-crime-fuelled-by-propaganda/

143.   WHEELER C: 11th January 2015: EXCLUSIVE: *Hate crimes on disabled up 213%*
http://www.express.co.uk/news/uk/551327/EXCLUSIVE-Hate-crimes-on-disabled- rise-by-213

CHAPTER 7: THE DEMONISATION OF SICK AND DISABLED PEOPLE

Money, money, money, Must be funny,
In the rich man's world.
ABBA*

To recap, the latest income replacement benefit for chronically sick and/or disabled people, namely the Employment and Support Allowance (ESA), was introduced in 2008 by the then New Labour government. Influenced by the research of the former Department for Work and Pensions (DWP) Chief Medical Officer, Professor (Sir) Mansel Aylward, it was claimed at the time that the Work Capability Assessment (WCA) was a *'functional assessment'*, conducted by an unaccountable private contractor (Atos Healthcare) at a huge cost to the public purse to determine genuine claimants of the ESA.[144] In reality, the WCA is a totally bogus assessment model, a replica from corporate America, and introduced to resist funding ESA to as many people as possible by disregarding diagnosis, prognosis and the claimant's medical history.[144] The difficulty for the New Labour government, as led by Gordon Brown from 2007, was that under the previous leadership, Tony Blair had acted as if he was Margaret Thatcher's 'heir'.[145]

BOX 7:1 *Fair Play...*

New Labour was new. What was new was that it was not progressive. Its term of office failed to coincide with social progress but instead were more closely associated with a rapidly dividing society. (p66)

For most of the period 1997-2010 Prime Minister Blair, born in the same year as Margaret Thatcher's twins, behaved as if he was her heir. No single person is that important, neither Margaret nor Tony Blair. But it can help to summarise periods of political history to use the surnames of people as long as we remember we are talking about the actions of a group of people, not one woman or one man. Over the 1997-2010 New Labour period of office, the majority of other rich countries in the world managed to achieve a far better record on inequality, so the problem was not 'globalisation'. In almost all OECD* countries inequalities were lower than in the UK, and in many, when measured by income, wealth, or health, they were found not to be rising. The question we need to ask is not whether New Labour failed but why it failed. (p67)

FAIR PLAY [145]
a Danny Dorling reader on social justice

Danny Dorling
2012

*OECD – The Office for Economic Co-operation and Development

Courtesy of Policy Press

Since May 2010 there has been the constant claim by the government and, especially, by Iain Duncan Smith (IDS) as Secretary of State for Work and Pensions, that there were countless numbers of '*skivers*' milking the sickness benefit system with vast numbers committing benefit fraud when, according to the evidence from the DWP, there have never been vast numbers of people stealing long-term sickness and disability benefits from the State.[146] So why the need to terrorise in excess of two million chronically sick and disabled people, other than to influence the public support for the welfare state to allow it to be, ultimately, demolished?

Illustration 7:1 Skeletons ~ reproduced by kind permission of the artist

For example, evidence published by the DWP for 2011/12 confirmed that for Incapacity Benefit (IB) - the long-term sickness benefit replaced by the ESA - fraud was listed as being only 0.3% of the entire budget.[147] For Disability Living Allowance (DLA), which is not an out of work benefit but is the financial support provided for chronically sick and disabled people, used to contribute to the additional costs of disability, the DWP's own figures demonstrated that DLA fraud was only 0.5%.[147] [DLA recipients are now threatened with the loss of this vital financial support as DLA is being replaced by the Personal Independence Payment (PIP) that of course requires yet another new assessment, by a private contractor, who is totally unaccountable to the General Medical Council when working on behalf of the government. With the removal of DLA, or the failure to be awarded PIP, many disabled people **will lose**

their jobs as, without it, they lose access to personal transport via a Motability car.]

Therefore, the welfare reforms forced on to the long-term chronically sick and disabled people of this nation were built on government propaganda at best, or were they more realistically government lies for ideological purposes...? Is there any difference?? With official DWP errors every year costing more money to the British taxpayer than the very minimal identified fraud and errors by claimants of long-term sickness and/or disability benefits[147], I think not...

Following a WCA by an unaccountable foreign corporate giant, [now Maximus as of March 2015 after Atos Healthcare stepped away from the DWP contract] claimants can be awarded one of three possible decisions by totally unqualified Jobcentre Plus (JCP) Decision Makers:

(1) 'Fit For Work', which means the claimant will be placed on to Jobseeker's Allowance (JSA) for the unemployed and will be expected to search for work, with severe penalties/sanctions if the local JCP staff don't think the claimant is trying hard enough to find paid employment.

(2) A time limited award of contributory ESA and an allocation to the Work Related Activity Group (WRAG), with the expectation by the DWP that ESA claimants will miraculously recover from their diagnosed health problem within 12 months and prepare for a return to work; with sanctions enforced as punishment and benefits removed if claimants fail to actively prepare to return to paid employment. There is no comprehension or consideration of profound illness, fluctuating conditions, diagnosis or prognosis; just a badly administered dangerous system when using a bogus and totally discredited assessment model, imported from the private health insurance industry that places far too many people into the wrong group when using unqualified JCP Decision Makers. [Consequently, the death toll is rising and there is now evidence of seriously ill people actually starving to death in C21st UK to this nation's everlasting shame.]

(3) An award of ESA and an allocation to the Support Group, which means that the claimant will receive the full benefit without the conditionality of being expected to prepare for a return to work in the near future. Entry to the Support Group means the DWP have accepted that the claimant has a profound health problem that is not expected to improve in the short-term, and claimants are not reassessed so often. Administered by Jobcentre Plus (JCP), claimants in the Support Group still live in fear of the DWP and the arrival of the brown envelope to summons them to another WCA assessment.

Estimated DWP overpayments 2011/12	Fraud	Customer Error	DWP Official Error
Incapacity Benefit	0.3% £10m	0.9% £40m	**1.2% £60m**
Disability Living Allowance	0.5% £60m	0.6% £80m	**0.8% £100m**

Table 7:1 Source:DWP Fraud and Error in the Benefit System 2011/12 Estimates p13[147]

As the British government continues to disregard all evidence against the fatally flawed WCA, that causes '*preventable harm*', the despair of its victims mounts. Yet more and more evidence exposed the extent to which the Coalition government would go to further reduce funding for welfare benefits, regardless of human consequences, and the shocking increase of benefit sanctions against the chronically sick and disabled population was revealed but the DWP failed to explain the sanction increases following a 2014 Freedom of Information (FOI) request.[148] The impact of cruel and unnecessary sanctions on genuine chronically sick and disabled benefit claimants was revealed in November 2014 by John Pring of Disability News Service (DNS).[148]

The information confirmed the callous disregard of chronic illness, or the fluctuations of it, as working age claimants awarded ESA, and placed into the WRAG by basic grade administrators at the Jobcentre, were given no leeway for the fact that there would be times when many would be too ill to keep appointments with JCP staff.

No doubt due to DWP propaganda, it seems that the under qualified and very poorly trained JCP Decision Makers fail to comprehend that anyone in the WRAG is actually ill. It should not be necessary for anyone in the WRAG to live under the threat of ESA sanctions. However, JCP Decision Makers hand out sanctions without mercy and, in June 2014, a total of 5,132 sanctions[148] were made against ESA claimants placed into the WRAG, with claimants advising that they had called the Jobcentre, to explain why they could not attend a meeting due to illness, only to discover that they were **disregarded and sanctioned** without any concern for the serious consequences.[149]

It seems unlikely that the British public fully comprehend the meaning of DWP benefit '*sanctions*'.[150] Survival on DWP benefit is difficult at the best of times but a sanction means that the claimant's only source of income is stopped and, in the UK, that only source of income **can be stopped for up to a maximum of three years** for unemployed people on Jobseeker's Allowance (JSA) with an '*open ended sanction*' for ESA claimants.[151]

BOX 7:2   *No explanation from ministers for soaring ESA sanctions*

Ministers have again refused to offer any explanation for the soaring use of sanctions against claimants of out-of-work disability benefits.

Figures published this week by the Department for Work and Pensions (DWP) show that the number of decisions to sanction claimants of employment and support allowance (ESA) reached 5,132 in June 2014.

This compares with 4,770 the previous month, 3,230 in January 2014, 2,698 in December 2013 and 1,091 in December 2012.

This means the use of sanctions – all applied to those in the work-related activity group (WRAG) of ESA – has risen by 370 per cent in just 18 months. About nine in 10 sanctions were for a failure to participate in work-related activity, with the others imposed for a failure to attend a mandatory interview.

Claimants lose at least a week's benefit for missing a single appointment or session of work-related activity.

A DWP spokesman said that sanctions were "nothing to do with saving money and the number of sanctions is entirely dependent on how many people do or do not fulfil all their obligations"... But he has so far failed to explain why the number of ESA sanctions has risen so sharply in the last 18 months...

No explanation from ministers for soaring ESA sanctions [148]
John Pring

Disability News Service
14th November 2014

Whose authority deemed it necessary to arbitrarily stop a claimant's only source of income for up to **three years** for JSA claimants, when many of them are sick and disabled people who are, in reality, too ill to work but who were given an incorrect decision following the totally discredited WCA and haven't had the strength or the resources to challenge that decision?

How, precisely, is anyone meant to survive, including able bodied Jobseekers, if they have no money for food let alone heating, water and power?? Why can underqualified basic grade JCP administrators have authority that means that chronically ill people now **starve to death** in the UK,[152] or they may decide that life just isn't worth the struggle any longer, and **so kill themselves as a way of removing that guaranteed and impending starvation.**[153]

BOX 7:3 *DWP: benefit sanctions – ending the 'something for nothing' culture*

The new JSA sanctions regime, which was introduced from 22 October 2012 has the following sanctions:

- higher level sanctions (for example for leaving a job voluntarily) will lead to claimants losing all of their JSA for a fixed period of 13 weeks for a first failure, 26 weeks for a second failure and 156 weeks for a third and subsequent failure (within a 52 week period of their last failure)
- intermediate level sanctions of 4 weeks for a first failure, rising to 13 weeks for a second or subsequent failures (within a 52 week period of their last failure) may be applied following a period of disallowance for not actively seeking employment or not being available for work
- lower level sanctions (for example for failing to attend an adviser interview) will lead to claimants losing all of their JSA for a fixed period of 4 weeks for the first failure, followed by 13 weeks for subsequent failures (within a 52 week period of their last failure)

The new sanctions regime for people on ESA in the Work Related Activity Group (WRAG) was introduced from 3 December 2012. Under the new rules ESA claimants in the WRAG who fail to comply with the conditions for receiving benefit receive an open ended sanction, followed by a fixed period sanction when they re-comply. The fixed period sanction will be 1 week for a first failure, 2 weeks for a second failure and 4 weeks for a third and subsequent failures in a 52 week period.

DWP: benefit sanctions – ending the [151]
'something for nothing' culture

DWP
6th November 2013

The British people have not given any politician or government department a mandate to starve people to death, or to intimidate the most vulnerable to the point where they can't justify living. [153]

Iain Duncan Smith (IDS) when thriving due to his position, power and authority as the Secretary of State for Work and Pensions, still resisted and at times manufactured evidence claiming, via a TV interview, that he had no knowledge of suicides related to the ESA, only to be challenged as the Green Party demanded a formal apology[154] because IDS had been *'misleading the public'*.[155]

The DWP of course totally disregarded the fact that the benefit sanctions were identified in 2014 by Dr David Webster of Glasgow University as *'a grave attack on the rule of law...'* [156]

BOX 7:4 *British people are committing suicide to escape poverty ...*

The Mullins had physical and mental disabilities to contend with and had spent months fighting the notoriously complex disability process at the Department for Work and Pensions. Starved, literally, of sufficient financial assistance, the couple's weekly food intake was bolstered by the vegetables they received from a soup kitchen in Coventry, a 12-mile round trip that they made weekly on foot.

The Mullins couldn't afford a fridge and so kept food in the garden shed. Eventually, they could no longer stretch their non-existent budget to heating their home and they spent their remaining months living in one room. Captured on camera by a roving reporter shortly before their death, Mr Mullins, criticised the system: "They have no problems suspending benefits," he said, "They just put a tick in a box and they alter your life." So it was that the Mullins' life was altered irreparably and, dreading another cold and hungry winter, they were found side by side, in an apparent suicide pact in November 2011…

What is the difference between people dying from starvation and people killing themselves before they have to face that certain misery?.. Some have been pushed to the brink by the Coalition's continued use of the much criticised ATOS system, designed to tell how 'fit for work' someone is… The current 'new thing' for our disabled and sick to endure is the anxious wait for 'the brown envelope' from the DWP. So far a thousand or so disabled people have received instructions about getting back to work even though some have been given fewer than six months to live…

British people are committing suicide to escape poverty. [153]
Is this what the State wants?

Sonia Poulton
Mail Online
20th March 2012

Courtesy of Solo Syndication

The shameful increase in sanctions/conditionality has helped to ensure that those chronically sick and disabled people, whose health can't ever improve regardless of DWP intimidation, were guaranteed to live in fear of the UK Government, as **the death toll continues to mount** and the DWP tries to hide the evidence for as long as possible.

The latest mortality statistics, finally published in a very defensive report by the DWP on 27th August 2015,[157] have identified **a death total of 81,140** ESA and IB claimants following a WCA, between December 2011 and February 2014, after the DWP resisted publishing the updated death totals for over 2 years until ordered to publish by the '*information watchdog*', the Information Commissioner's Office.[158]

It was thanks to a FOI request in May 2014 by freelance journalist Mike Sivier of *Vox Political* that the figures were invited to be provided by the DWP. We now know that since January 2011, the death totals are collectively close to **100,000 people who have perished** following the '*non-medical*' assessment for access to long-term sickness benefit.[159]

BOX 7:5 *Green Party calls on Duncan Smith to apologise…*

The Green Party has requested that Iain Duncan Smith, Secretary of State for Work and Pensions, issue a formal apology for misleading the public after he denied knowledge of the number of benefit claimant deaths shown to be caused by suicide…

Commenting on the exposure by the DNS, Jonathan Bartley, Green Party Spokesperson for Work and Pensions, said:

"It is utterly shameful for Iain Duncan Smith to have misled the public and the families of those affected by these tragic deaths. It's not enough that his Department appears to have sat on research revealing the immense damage his welfare policies are causing to families up and down the country. To deny all knowledge of the reports is heartless and blinkered - hardly the kind of approach we want the person in charge of national welfare to be taking.

"On behalf of the Green Party I'm requesting that Mr. Smith issue a formal apology for his misleading of the public and that the research discovered by the DNS be made publicly available on the website of the Department for Work and Pensions. Understanding the impact of government policies is essential in helping us improve and inform future government decisions so that we can ensure they are working in the best interests of the public. That is exactly why it needs to be shared publicly and in an open and democratic manner."

Green Party Calls On Duncan Smith To [154]
Apologise For Misleading Public Over
Benefit Claimant Deaths

The Green Party
6th May 2012

Indeed, following the strong public reaction to the previous DWP mortality totals, as published in 2012 that exposed the fact that 10,600 people on ESA had died following a WCA between January to November 2011[160], the DWP developed a resistance to publishing any more mortality statistics; until demand for the information grew to include a petition with in excess of 200,000 signatures demanding the information and, in particular, how many people had died following a WCA that resulted in claimants being found '*fit for work*' regardless of diagnosis or prognosis. [161] That particular information is still unavailable from the DWP as Lord Freud

---

DWP Mortality Statistics: ESA, IB or SDA

The figures in this release are derived from administrative data held by the Department for Work and Pensions (DWP) and the analysis only applies to working age recipients. Some of the figures supplied are derived from unpublished information and have not been quality assured to National Statistics or Official Statistics publication standard. They should therefore be treated with caution. (p2)

Any causal effect between benefits and mortality cannot be assumed from these statistics. (p2)
Additionally, these isolated figures provide limited scope for analysis and nothing can be gained from this publication that would allow the reader to form any judgement as to the effects or impacts of the Work Capability Assessment. However, the combination of an historical time series and comparable rates in the related statistical publication on mortality rates for out-of-work working age benefit claimants allows users to analyse the information more easily and look at the longer term trends. (p2) …

Total number is IB/SDA and ESA off-flows with a date of death at the same time (p5)	**81,140**

of which:

*ESA	(p5)	50,580
*IB/SDA	(p5)	30,560

DWP Mortality Statistics: [157]
[between December 2011 – February 2014]
Employment and Support Allowance,
Incapacity Benefit or
Severe Disablement Allowance

DWP
August 27th 2015

Table 7:2 Source:DWP Mortality Statistics Dec 2011 – Feb 2014 [157] p5

it seems deemed it no longer necessary, so **he stopped the collection of the data. Why does this unelected junior Minister have such authority?**

IDS, together with the unelected Lord Freud, as Minister for Welfare Reform, and successive DWP Ministers for Disabled People - who don't tend to stay in post for too long - all dismissed concerns about the WCA, claiming there was the opportunity to appeal any decision, whilst knowing that the Appeal Tribunals were in meltdown due to the vast numbers of applicants and the limited resources. *'In one six month period alone, 37,100 people had waited up to a year to have their ESA benefit reinstated following appeal, yet no-one is asking what would have happened to these genuinely sick and disabled people if they had not had the strength to pursue their claim to appeal?'* [162]

DWP 'Mortality Statistics' following a WCA	Confirmed death totals
January 2011 to November 2011	10,600 [*]
December 2011 to February 2014	81,140 [**]
Total confirmed deaths January 2011 to February 2014	**91,740**

Table 7:3 Source: Combined DWP mortality totals, created by MS
*DWP: Published July 2012: Incapacity Benefits: Deaths of recipients [160] *p6*
**DWP:Published August 2015:Mortality Statistics: ESA, IB and SDA [157] *p5*

Given the deeply disturbing death totals eventually and reluctantly published by the DWP, it can't be a coincidence that Iain Duncan Smith (IDS) found himself making a high profile speech on work, health and disability[163] just three days before the latest DWP mortality statistics were finally published in August 2015. The Secretary of State continues to be selective with the evidence he uses to justify the fear and despair the DWP welfare reform policies have created, whilst IDS disregards any and all evidence demonstrating that the Tory ideology adopted long ago, aided and abetted by the influence of a former DWP Chief Medical Officer and an American private healthcare corporate insurance giant is, actually, **killing people**.[164]

Of course, as long as all protest is aimed at the DWP and politicians, the main culprit behind the creation of the WCA is spared. As the former DWP Chief Medical Officer, Professor Sir Mansel Aylward advised the government to disregard the opinion of General Practitioners (GP), and to totally disregard diagnosis, prognosis and the past medical history of claimants as he avoided all public accountability when recommending the use of a *'non-medical'* assessment model.[165] (p287-296)

Aylward claims fame for the introduction of *'Disability Assessment Medicine'* into the UK[165] (p287 -296) and, more to the point, he persuaded the UK government that a modified version of the biopsychosocial (BPS) model of disability assessment was necessary to remove large numbers of bogus claimants, for which **there is no evidence** apart from his presumption of an

BOX 7:6 *The Hidden Agenda*

This is how the UK welfare state will be destroyed. There is a BPS 'expert' in place, and an American corporate insurance giant has influenced the UK government to totally disregard human suffering, in favour of a reduced welfare budget, using an identified bogus 'assessment'. Unum Insurance have begun their mass marketing to encourage able bodied members of the British public to invest in their 'Income Protection Insurance' or their 'Back-up Plan' that's only available via the workplace, and these are the healthcare insurance policies that the company has historically tried very hard to resist funding when a claim is made.(20)(21)

Given that the unacceptable practice of Unum (Provident) Insurance was previously exposed by MPs during a House of Commons debate in 1999 (22), the question remains as to why was this highly discredited American corporate insurance giant ever permitted to influence UK welfare reforms and why the national press, en masse, refuse to expose this insurance company's confirmed influence despite it being identified by a BBC News report in 2007? (23) The recent exposure of a 2005 internal Unum report, that actively boasted that the company was 'driving government thinking' regarding the reform of Incapacity Benefit (24) leads to the much more sinister possibility that the DWP are simply administrators of these brutal welfare reforms, and that the perpetrators of the devastation caused to the victims of this UK government funded medical tyranny are, in fact, Unum Insurance. Michael O'Donnell was the author of the 2005 internal Unum report that was written when he was the Chief Medical Officer (CMO) for Unum Insurance. Michael O'Donnell is now the CMO for Atos Healthcare...

The difficulty remains that no-one is asking the relevant questions. Perhaps MPs should be asking the Prime Minister why he's been funded by 'healthcare companies' to the value of £750,000 (27) since he became Prime Minister (25) or why every report produced by the President of the Appeal Tribunals, all of which identified the Atos Healthcare WCA assessments as "failing to coincide with reality", was totally disregarded by the DWP? (12)

Until and unless more significant questions are asked in the House of Commons, victims of this government funded medical nightmare will be forced to turn to the law for help, just as in America.(26) Until and unless the national press demonstrate that the UK really does benefit from a free press, and not a government controlled press, the most vulnerable of all British people will continue to suffer and the British public will continue to be deceived. (12)

The Hidden Agenda [162]

Mo Stewart
March 2013

ResearchGate

epidemic of psychosomatic illnesses. In reality, the modified BPS model of assessment, as used by the DWP to create the '*non-medical*' WCA, has no clinical credibility and was the invention of the private healthcare insurance industry to justify resisting health insurance claims.[166]

Illustration 7:2 Puppeteer ~ exclusively designed by the artist

It seems so wrong that a man who was once the DWP Chief Medical Officer can align himself with a foreign private insurance corporate giant, identified in 2008 as the second worst insurance company in America[166] who, as a consequence of falling profits in America decided to make a beeline for the UK market in 1992 and were welcomed with open arms by John Major's government who were continuing with '*Thatcher's Legacy.*' The WCA is the result of this collusion between Aylward and Unum (Provident) Insurance as interpreted by the DWP. Once he had left the DWP in 2005, Aylward walked straight into his own research department at Cardiff University, funded for five years by Unum (Provident) Insurance, to produce 'academic research' commissioned by the DWP. (Chapter 3)

Aylward has been doing anything he can to support the UK Government's planned welfare cost reduction ever since. He has built quite a career as an *'expert'* helping to convince other nations to introduce the same bogus '*non-medical*' BPS modified assessment model to reduce welfare costs whilst, of course, claiming he knows nothing about the WCA that has caused so much '*preventable harm*'. Disabled people in New Zealand are not happy now that the bogus assessment model has been adopted[167] and Canada, it seems, may be next…

BOX 7:7 *Work tests concern disability organisations*

Disability services group CSS says it has "grave concerns" about plans to introduce work capability assessments, influenced by controvertial tests conducted in Britain.

From July, the invalid's benefit, paid to about 85,000 New Zealanders, will be replaced by the supported living payment, as part of wide-ranging welfare changes.

Social Development Minister Paula Bennett has said this would mean little change, although in a speech to health professionals late last year she signalled a new assessment regime which "echoes" the British process.

CSS Disability Action chief executive David Matthews cited research showing the British Government had spent £42.2million (NZ$80.5m) on appeals against these tests, about 40 per cent of which overturned Atos' findings.

The tests were developed partially on the work of disability expert Professor Sir Mansel Aylward, who has visited New Zealand to advise on health reform, meeting Mrs Bennett. [Emphasis MS]

Mr Matthews said most government policy focused on how society builds barriers for the disabled, whereas a key part of Professor Aylward's work focused on the extent to which a disabled person could overcome barriers.

"The whole philosophy and approach to disability in New Zealand is based on the social model… which looks at barriers to employing people, rather than what's wrong with the individual," he said. "We have grave concerns about basing welfare changes in New Zealand on such a flawed approach."

A work ability test would be an extra requirement for the disabled.

Mrs Bennett's spokeswoman said details of the assessments were being considered by a select committee and had not been finalised.

Work tests concern disability organisations [167]
Hamish Rutherford

Business Day, New Zealand
11th January 2013

Challenged in 2012 by disability activists, Aylward claimed innocence and advised that he no longer supported the BPS model of assessment,[168] then continued travelling the world to help to support this bogus assessment model to terrify countless more chronically sick and disabled people.[169]

BOX 7:8 *Former DWP medical boss makes WCA pledge to protestors*

A former Department for Work and Pensions (DWP) medical director has pledged to speak out about the government's "fitness for work" test if he finds it is "not proper", after he was ambushed by campaigners at a conference…

Sir Mansel is closely associated with the biopsychosocial (BPS) model, which campaigners say puts much of the blame for disability on the disabled person, rather than the social model explanation, which says disability is created by the barriers of attitude and environment disabled people face.

A small group of protesters delivered a copy of a letter written to the Guardian newspaper – signed by 420 disabled people, including many leading activists – to Sir Mansel, outside the hall where he had given his speech. The letter claims the BPS model is "nothing short of a creation of the insurance industry", and is being used to deny disabled people the support they need through the benefits system…

The protesters told Sir Mansel that the much-criticised work capability assessment (WCA) – used to test eligibility for out-of-work disability benefits, and introduced in 2008 – was based on the BPS model and had been heavily influenced by the insurance industry…

He added: "I think I am a man of integrity. If I think the WCA is not proper I will speak out against it."

Sir Mansel said he sympathised with the protesters, and himself now found the BPS model "unsatisfactory" and believed it "no longer addresses the real needs of disabled people and the exclusion of disabled people from society".

He said the "social" element of the BPS model had been "neglected" and that he had a personal "distaste" for the medical model, which focuses on people's impairments as the cause of their disability…

Former DWP medical boss makes WCA pledge to protesters [168]
John Pring

Disability News Service
14th September 2012

For more than twenty years successive UK governments have used the past guidance of Aylward and Unum (Provident) Insurance, one of the most disreputable of all healthcare insurance corporate giants[170], to work towards the planned demolition of the welfare state. The

WCA is a clone of the discredited assessment model used by Unum (Provident) Insurance at the time of its design, and is used to reduce the welfare budget and to convince the British public that most claimants of income replacement benefits are *'malingerers'*. An unofficial moratorium of the national press has prevented the British public from being alerted to the past influence of Unum (Provident) Insurance with UK welfare reforms, as the planned demolition of the welfare state, first suggested by Thatcher and the 1982 Conservative government, moves ever closer to fruition. (Chapter 3)

In 2013 the original Webmaster of MS, known online as *'Mike Bach'* produced his final research report prior to his untimely death in February 2015. Mike had also exposed the influence of Mansel Aylward and his close links with Unum (Provident) Insurance.[170]

As long as the government disregard reported deaths, suicides, suffering, illness, despair and disability and consider all ESA claimants as unemployed malingerers, using discredited official research commissioned by the DWP from a research centre sponsored by Unum (Provident) Insurance, successive UK governments can justify the continued use of a totally bogus assessment model. This will force as many claimants as possible from ESA onto the JSA unemployment benefit; regardless of the predictable human consequences of this identified State funded tyranny.

The United Nations is aware and the UK government is to be officially investigated.[171]

A long time ago, in one of this then novice researcher's first ever reports, MS identified the WCA as guaranteed to cause pain, suffering and death in what was exposed as *'government funded slaughter.'* Certain critics chastised MS at the time as, seemingly, that isn't the *'diplomatic language'* as is required for academic writing. Well, this researcher has never claimed to be an academic. MS is a former healthcare professional who never terrified her patients and, given the recently published DWP mortality statistics, I do believe the first description by MS is demonstrably correct.

REFERENCES:

** **All references accessed and confirmed 5th September 2015**

* *'Money, money, money'* lyrics by Benny Goran Bror Andersson, Bjoern K. Ulvaeus, Marcelo Kotliar

Illustration 7:1
Skeletons ~ courtesy of Dave Lupton of Crippen Cartoons www.daveluptoncartoons.co.uk

Illustration 7:2
Puppeteer ~ exclusively designed for this book by Dave Lupton of Crippen Cartoons

Table 7:1
Source: DWP: Freud and Error in the Benefit System 2011/12 Estimates [147] (p13)

Table 7:2:
Source: DWP Mortality Statistics [157] (p2)

Table 7:3
Source: Combined DWP Mortality Statistics, Jan 2011 to Feb 2014 [157, 160]

144. STEWART M: March 2013: *The Hidden Agenda*
http://www.researchgate.net/publication/263673312_THE_HIDDEN_AGENDA
145. DORLING D: 2012: *Fair Play – A Daniel Dorling reader on social justice*
ISBN: 978 1 84742 879 0 paperback
146. FALSE ECONOMY: July 2012: *Benefit fraud – the levels are very low*
http://falseeconomy.org.uk/blog/repost-benefit-fraud-the-levels-are-very-low
147. DWP: FRAUD & ERROR IN THE BENEFIT SYSTEM 2011/12 Estimates (p13)
https://www.gov.uk/government/uploads/system/uploads/attachment_data/file/244844/fem_1112.pdf
148. PRING J: November 2014: DISABILITY NEWS SERVICE: *No explanation from ministers for soaring ESA sanctions*
http://www.disabilitynewsservice.com/explanation-ministers-soaring-esa-sanctions/
149. STEWART M: 2014: *UK government refuses to accept responsibility for Crimes Against Humanity*
http://blacktrianglecampaign.org/2014/05/08/british-disability-rights-abuses-uk-government-refuses-to-accept-responsibility-for-crimes-against-humanity-a-report-by-mo-stewart/
150. DWP: November 2014: *Jobseeker's Allowance and Employment and Support Allowance Sanctions: decisions made to June 2014.*
https://www.gov.uk/government/statistics/jobseekers-allowance-and-employment-and-support-allowance-sanctions-decisions-made-to-june-2014
151. DWP: November 2013: *Benefit sanctions – ending the 'something for nothing' culture.*
https://www.gov.uk/government/news/benefit-sanctions-ending-the-something-for-nothing-culture
152. RYAN F: 9th September 2014: *David Clapson's awful death was the result of grotesque government policies* The Guardian – Comment is Free
http://www.theguardian.com/commentisfree/2014/sep/09/david-clapson-benefit-sanctions-death-government-policies
153. POULTON S: 20th March 2012: *British people are committing suicide to escape poverty. Is this what the State wants?* Mail online.

http://www.dailymail.co.uk/debate/article-2117718/British-people-committing-suicide-escape-poverty-Is-State-wants.html

154. GREEN PARTY: 6th May 2012: *Green Party Calls On Duncan Smith To Apologise For Misleading Public Over Benefit Claimant Deaths.*
https://www.greenparty.org.uk/news/2015/05/06/green-party-calls-on-duncan-smith-to-apologise-for-misleading-public-over-benefit-claimant-deaths/

155. SIVIER M: 6th May 2015: *Benefit deaths: IDS lies while DWP evades.*
http://voxpoliticalonline.com/2015/05/06/benefit-deaths-ids-lies-while-dwp-evades/

156. WEBSTER D: 10th January 2014: *Independent review of Jobseeker's Allowance (JSA) sanctions for claimants failing to take part in back to work schemes.*
http://www.cpag.org.uk/sites/default/files/uploads/CPAG-Oakley-Review-D-Webster-Evidence-rev%20-13-Jan-2014.pdf

157. DWP: August 2015: *Mortality Statistics: Employment and Support Allowance, Incapacity Benefit or Severe Disablement Allowance* - updated death totals p5
https://www.gov.uk/government/uploads/system/uploads/attachment_data/file/456359/mortality-statistics-esa-ib-sda.pdf

158. PRING J: 6th May 2015: *DWP told to publish ESA deaths report, after two-year delay*
http://www.disabilitynewsservice.com/dwp-told-to-publish-esa-deaths-report-after-two-year-delay/

159. SIVIER M: 27th August 2015: *Known number of deaths while claiming incapacity benefits nears 100,000*
http://voxpoliticalonline.com/2015/08/27/known-number-of-deaths-while-claiming-incapacity-benefits-nears-100000/?subscribe=error#blog_subscription-2

160. DWP: Incapacity Benefits: Deaths of recipients: 9th July 2012 p6
https://www.gov.uk/government/uploads/system/uploads/attachment_data/file/223050/incap_decd_recips_0712.pdf

161. BLOOM D: 19th June 2015: *200,000 join petition demanding Tories reveal how many people died after being found 'fit for work'.* The Mirror
http://www.mirror.co.uk/news/uk-news/200000-join-petition-demanding-tories-5909676

162. STEWART M: March 2013: *The Hidden Agenda*
http://www.researchgate.net/publication/263673312_THE_HIDDEN_AGENDA

163. REFORM: 24th August 2015: *Rt Hon Iain Duncan Smith MP: speech on work, health and disability.*
http://www.reform.uk/publication/rt-hon-iain-duncan-smith-mp-speech-on-work-health-and-disability/

164. STEWART M: 2014: *UK government refuses to accept responsibility for identified Crimes Against Humanity*
http://pf7d7vi404s1dxh27mla5569.wpengine.netdna-cdn.com/files/library/GVT%20refuses%20responsibility%20for%20crimes%20agains t%20humanity%20-%20FINAL%20-%203rd%20May.pdf

165. VARIOUS AUTHORS: CONFERENCE PAPERS: Malingering and Illness Deception ISBN: 0 19 851554 52003: p287-296
http://www.meactionuk.org.uk/Malingering_and_Illness_Deception.pdf

166. STEWART M: 2015: *The influence of the private insurance industry on the UK welfare reforms.*
https://www.researchgate.net/publication/271199429_The_influence_of_the_private_insurance_industry_on_the_UK_welfare_reforms

167. RUTHERFORD H: 11th January 2013: Business Day New Zealand: *Work tests concerndisability organisation*
http://www.stuff.co.nz/business/industries/8165236/Work-tests-concern-disability-organisation

168. PRING J: 3rd September 2012: *Former DWP medical boss makes DWP pledge to protesters.*
http://www.disabilitynewsservice.com/former-dwp-medical-boss-makes-wca-pledge-to-protesters-2/

169. RUTHERFORD H: 11th January 2013: Business Day New Zealand: *Work tests concerndisability organisation*
http://www.stuff.co.nz/business/industries/8165236/Work-tests-concern-disability-organisation

170. BACH M 2012: *Memorandum on Disability Insurance.*
http://www.whywaitforever.com/dwpatosmemodisins.html

171. DOYLE J: 27th August 2015: *Now UN sparks fury after launching human rights investigation into Britain's disability benefit reforms.* Mail Online
http://www.dailymail.co.uk/news/article-2735958/UN-sparks-fury-launching-human-rights-investigation-Britain-s-treatment-disabled.html

CHAPTER 8:
MEMORANDUM ON DISABILITY INSURANCE
~ the Legacy of Mike Bach

The conspicuously wealthy turn up urging the character
building values of the privation of the poor.
John Kenneth Galbraith
1908~2006

Known online as *'Mike Bach'*, my original Webmaster shared his website at *Why Wait Forever* to allow the early research reports of Mo Stewart (MS) to be published to permit public access.[172]

At the time of our first contact, in June 2010, Mike was busy exposing the influence of Unum (Provident) Insurance and Professor Sir Mansel Aylward with the United Kingdom (UK) government's welfare reforms. His research is very valuable and should be widely accessed by anyone with an interest in the influence of corporate America with the UK welfare reforms.[173] Mike's research is *'copyleft'* and may be reproduced.

Mike's research exposed the fact that **UnumProvidentᴛᴍ Insurance were in financial trouble** in America[173] and the (bogus) *'non-medical'* assessment model was introduced to solve the problem as the *'...financial forecast was so dire that minor changes such as time limiting payments, increasing premiums greatly with age and denying disability insurance to many groups (only sell to the employed through their employers) would not be sufficient to bridge the growing gap between premium income and outgoings. It was the 'medical' aspect of the disability insurance that was the problem that needed to be addressed. This was solved at a stroke (no pun intended) by claiming* **a 'non-medical' model should be used**.*'* [173]

Mike also identified McKinsey and Company[174] as the consulting firm representing the interests of major corporate clients and advisors to the Department for Work and Pensions (DWP), offering detailed and influential reports to the DWP as summarised by the National Audit Office in a 2013 report.[175] In his Memorandum[176] submitted to the DWP Work and Pensions Select Committee in 2012, Mike's evidence contains a wealth of information regarding the Work Capability Assessment (WCA), including the flaws in the DWP documents, the breaches of the DWP contract by Atos, the dangers of the WCA, the disturbing reputation of Unum (Provident) Insurance, the challenge to Cardiff University for permitting Aylward to produce bogus research from their campus, the challenge to Derby University for

---

BOX 8:1 *Unum (previously UnumProvident) and Business*

An overview of the business operations of Unum (previously UnumProvident) and how Unum has influenced UK Government policy through the Department for Work and Pensions (DWP) to the detriment of the disabled. The Unum UK website is www.unum.co.uk. Unum has set up a website to sell to employers www.backupplan.com.

Topics include statements made by Unum to the UK Parliament's Work and Pensions Select Committee, financial information and supporters of the Unum "non-medical" model for dealing with medical conditions.

The supporters include Professor Mansel Aylward (previous DWP Chief Medical Officer who left the DWP to direct Cardiff University's UnumProvident Centre for Psychosocial and Disability Research, Dame Carole Black, Lord Freud and Lord Kirkwood of Kirkhope (Chairman of the Unum Customer Advisory Panel when Chair of the UK Parliament's Work and Pensions Select Committee).

If there is a direct relationship between Unum and Atos, its nature is unknown. Unum and Atos were part of the DWP Technical Working Groups that defined the details of the "non-medical" model assessments that were mandatory if a person with a disability was to be eligible to receive benefits. The same private equity funds have interests in both Unum and Atos. Private equity fund managers are not slow to drive companies to maximize profits.

Unum (previously UnumProvident) and Business [173]

Why Wait Forever
Mike Bach
2013

---

offering courses to accredit Atos Healthcare's training in 'disability assessment', the influence of Dame Carole Black and the influence of CAPITA and other corporate giants with the preventable harm created by the welfare reforms. The evidence in this significant body of research should be appreciated and reproduced and we owe a huge debt of gratitude to Mike for his valuable efforts, on behalf of the UK's sick and disabled people. Mike is sadly missed by many, and by this researcher in particular, since he lost his battle for life in February 2015.

Mike's website was the first to expose the DWP contract with Atos Healthcare [177] and highlights the Unum conspirators who support the (bogus) WCA '*non-medical*' assessment model, and who influence the DWP, such as Dame Carole Black and David Freud.[178]

Mike's lasting legacy is summarised in his 2013 **Memorandum on Disability Insurance** and the contents are a warning of what may be still to come.[179] Further research is urgently needed.

BOX 8:2 *Memorandum on disability insurance*

(2) US private healthcare and disability insurance companies are keen to expand into the UK market. (3) The UK market is regarded as a prime area for growth as it is immature and protections for claimants are few and costly. (4) The UK market is regarded as a test market in that if the state near monopoly for disability insurance can be undermined and private disability insurance can grow then this model can be applied elsewhere. (5) In the US there are protections in place for claimants. Claimants in each US state receive protection from the state's Department of Health. The DoH can take action on behalf of claimants to set precedents and fine companies. (6) UK governments have been very welcoming to the McKinsey & Company processes for handling insurance claims (deny, delay, and defend). These processes have been discredited in the US.

Memorandum on Disability Insurance [179]
Mike Bach
2013

*'Areas for Further Research and Summary are of high significance. MS

This is a direct copy from Mike Bach's website used with permission:[179]

Re: Memorandum on Disability Insurance

Findings – Mansel Aylward

39. Mansel Aylward along with many influential people in government attended functions in the UK and elsewhere funded by the private healthcare industry.
40. Mansel Aylward has had a major role in introducing to the UK a 'non medical' model for assessing disability insurance (state or private) claims which was obtained from the USA and has been discredited in the USA.
41. Mansel Aylward has had a major role in the decision to contract out assessing disability claims to private healthcare companies.
42. Mansel Aylward has had a major role in undermining the reputation of the state in carrying out the state's duty to meet disability claims.
43. Mansel Aylward has produced research papers, presented at conferences and used every opportunity to give credibility to the 'non medical' model for assessing disability claims.
44. Mansel Aylward works closely with industry bodies and the major companies to meet their needs to reduce payouts to claimants.
45. Mansel Aylward has supported the Unum suggested name changes of benefits to confuse and misdirect e.g. IB to ESA, DLA to PIP, various to UTC etc.

Rest In Peace Mike

REFERENCES

** **All references accessed and confirmed 6th September 2015**

172. STEWART M: http://www.whywaitforever.com/dwpatosveterans.html
173. BACH M: http://www.whywaitforever.com/dwpatosbusinessunum.html
174. McKINSEY and COMPANY: http://www.mckinsey.com/about_us
175. NAO: 2013: DWP: *Universal Credit: early progress:*
     [HC 621 SESSION 2013-14 5 SEPTEMBER 2013]
     http://www.nao.org.uk/wp-content/uploads/2013/09/10132-001-Universal-credit.pdf
176. BACH M: March 2012: *Memorandum to DWP W&P Select Committee*
     http://www.whywaitforever.com/dwpatosmemowca.html
177. BACH M: *The Contract between the DWP and Atos Healthcare*
     http://www.whywaitforever.com/dwpatoscontract.html
178. BACH M: *Influential People and Unum:*
     http://www.whywaitforever.com/dwpatosbusinessunum.html#product
179. BACH M: 2013: *Memorandum on Disability Insurance*
     http://www.whywaitforever.com/dwpatosmemodisins.html

CHAPTER 9: ACADEMIC EXCELLENCE

The difference between stupidity and genius
is that genius has its limits.
Albert Einstein
1879 ~ 1955

ACADEMIC EXCELLENCE

On 9th September, 2015 Mo Stewart (MS) entered the 7th year of independent research that has confirmed both government tyranny and government stupidity, which presumed that the identified *'preventable harm'* of various welfare reform policies would not be exposed.

Little did MS realise when this epic voyage of research discovery began that evidence from the research would be used during welfare reform debates in both the House of Lords and the House of Commons. Nor did MS know that she would benefit from personal contact with professionals and academics, from a variety of United Kingdom (UK) universities, who were happy to share their published manuscripts and research papers with her. Their kindness, trust, advice and tolerance of her contact often brought a welcome confirmation of human decency during many dark times when MS was convinced that it had all but been abandoned in the UK.

Throughout the text, extracts from academic research has been used wherever possible to support MS research findings, and this chapter will offer the reader a greater understanding of the text, as there is so much detailed evidence contained within it from a variety of experts in their field of study. Additional detailed academic research is referenced in MS published reports, from 2010 – 2015, and in *Appendix* 6 that lists suggested further reading.

MS is duty bound to offer a note of caution. It is expected that some readers may be other sick and disabled people, and their carers, and some may not be too experienced when accessing academic papers. A little warning is therefore needed for the inexperienced reader when it comes to accessing and accepting published 'academic' research.

Not all academic research can be taken at face value as, in my lengthy experience, it does depend on who funded it.(!!) Therefore, when accessing evidence from published research, it is **necessary to identify who funded it** before the content is accepted, as successive UK governments have used unlimited resources in an effort to manipulate the British public, helped by 'academic research' commissioned by the Department for Work and Pensions. (DWP)

Be alert to apparently detailed research evidence[180] awarded critical acclaim by Ministers from the DWP, that tends to make sweeping generalisations and demonstrates that the authors have no comprehension of chronic illness or disability, or the realities of unemployment, other than demonstrating exactly what the DWP want to see given that the DWP commissioned the research. *'There are economic, social and moral arguments that work is the most effective way to improve the well-being of individuals..'[180]* Such texts tend to be very selective in the evidence they reference and claim to have conducted a review *'..in broad general terms'*[180] (p241) and *'..this makes the review difficult to reproduce and requires a measure of trust in the author's judgement.'* [180] (p241) Compare that with the detailed evidence produced by high calibre professionals such as Mary O'Hara in her book *'**Austerity Bites**'[181]* or in the book *'**Injustice**'*[182] by Professor Danny Dorling, both published by Policy Press.

Therefore, when accessing 'academic' research the inexperienced reader is advised to first identify who funded the research and, if *commissioned* by the DWP[183], great caution is needed. Such research may have been critiqued by experts and the exposure of **the bias and inaccuracies in such DWP commissioned research** is well worth the time invested to read the critique.[184]

The lay reader also needs to be alert to the various types of academic research that are possible and common place depending on the research project and, if the reader doesn't know the difference between *Qualitative* versus *Quantitative* research then I suggest it may be very helpful to find out.[185] Enjoy your personal voyage of research discovery.

BOX 9:1 *Mandela on Education*

Education is the most powerful weapon which you can use to change the world.

Nelson Mandela

A very good place to begin listing academic excellence is by quoting one such critique of DWP commissioned research, as provided in 2006 by Emeritus Professor Alison Ravetz.[186]

BOX 9:2 *Green Paper: A New Deal for Welfare:*
empowering people to work. 2006
An independent assessment of the arguments for
proposed Incapacity Benefit reform

The aim is nothing less than a reversal of the common attitude towards sickness, disability and capacity for work – 'a fundamental transformation in the way society deals with sickness and disabilities.' (S/C Basis* p123) In practical terms, it means opting out by the state of responsibility for a large section – estimated at two thirds – of those afflicted by illness and disability. In future, it will be harder to qualify for the benefit, while those already receiving it, in many cases over long periods, will despite assurances have justifiable anxieties about their future benefits status. (p5)…

Most are presented with what looks like exhaustive bibliographies, references, footnotes, tables, graphs, diagrams and statistics, leading readers to suppose that arguments for reform are supported by inexorable logic and swaying them towards conclusions reached, if necessary, by tedious repetitions and platitudes. There is a tendency to 'blind with statistics' that are manipulated towards sometimes dubious conclusions…

On closer examination, it appears that this entire body of work is largely self-referential – that is, it appeals for validation to itself and is all framed within the same political and policy agenda. (p6)

An independent assessment of the arguments for
proposed Incapacity Benefit reform

Alison Ravetz M.A, PhD
March 2006 [186]

*S/C Basis – The Scientific and Conceptual Basis of Incapacity Benefits

---

Much more detailed evidence was to follow.

In her 2012 book, '*Authors of our own misfortune?*'[187] social sciences lecturer Angela Kennedy demonstrated the possible dangerous hypocrisy in medicine, the social exclusion of disadvantaged groups and **the constructions of moral panics**.

From the back cover: '*Authors of Our Own Misfortune? proposes that psychogenic explanations for physical illnesses are subject to a complex mix of confusing concepts, accompanied by certain moralistic and ideological assumptions about people and their illnesses. Most crucially, such explanations are also, almost always, fatally flawed both scientifically and logically. Furthermore, the widespread, uncritical acceptance and use of such explanations has had serious and specific adverse effects on the people upon whom they are used... is essential reading for academics, health professionals, and those directly or indirectly affected by psychogenic explanations of illness.'* [187]

BOX 9:3 *Authors of our own misfortune?*

Medical practitioners have frequently claimed that somatic[1] illnesses are caused by psychological, behavioural and emotional dysfunction. These claims have also often been taken for granted and reiterated by social scientists, humanities scholars, government agencies, various public media and the public at large. The purpose of this book is to explain the problems inherent in these claims. It will be demonstrated how: flaws in logic; prejudicially moralistic belief systems; conceptual ambiguity and confusion; and misinterpretation and misuse of scientific evidence have led to unsound diagnoses of 'mental disorder', and, as I will argue, accompanying assignations of 'deviance', being placed upon people suffering serious physiological impairments. These have led to devastating consequences for those people in terms of physical health, and in resulting material and social inequalities and exclusion... (p1&2)

Wessely et al (1999:936) advocate treating alleged 'functional somatic syndromes' as one, based on alleged similarities of patients in 'sex, outlook and response to treatment', no matter what the actual condition. If the premise of this book is correct, the possibility of misdiagnosis of illnesses as 'psychogenic' is to be found across all medical disciplines... (p2)

Psychogenic explanations for somatic illnesses are therefore extremely unsafe: physically and ethically (for the patient), scientifically and logically. In light of this, any psychogenic explanations of bodily illness should be made, at the very least, with extreme caution. Yet, as will be seen, diagnosis of psychogenic illnesses are made often, within clinical practice and medical, academic and lay 'common-sense' discourses: and they are made, far too often (perhaps almost always), without sufficient caution or critical reflection, with devastating effects on patients. (p3)

Authors of our own misfortune? [187]
The problems with psychogenic explanations
for physical illness.

Angela Kennedy
2012

The Village Digital Press

When it comes to quoting extracts from published academic papers, there are limitations if the information is not to be used for private study. The most important limitation is that academic papers are required to be published in academic journals for the research to receive *'indicators of esteem'*. To be published, the research will have been anonymously 'peer reviewed', which means three other academics will have read the paper and agreed to its publication.

Invariably, academic journals are of interest to a limited number of people in a specific profession or field of study. The general public, for whom the research may be of vital importance, will never know of its content as the research isn't in the public domain and, if evidence of important research is discovered online then, usually, it will be cost prohibitive to many in the disabled community or in the general public as the academic journals make their money by charging for access. There are exceptions and, perhaps depending on the research funding, it is possible to download some academic research papers free of charge, which will be indicated in the specific journal where the research is published. No matter how important, the evidence from detailed academic research isn't usually shared with the national press, so the British public remain in ignorance until someone brings the often essential evidence to their attention.

It is also important to note that there are copyright limitations to the amount of academic research that may be reproduced, which depends on the amount being quoted as to if specific permission from the publisher is required. An unexpected point MS learned was that, when academic papers are offered for publication in an academic journal, the copyright passes to the journal as the identified publisher. There is a process of fair usage that permits limited amounts of research to be quoted without permission, but for anyone wishing to pursue research it is better to learn all about this before reproducing published research for anything other than private study.

In past reports, and in this book, MS has used research extracts from the high calibre team at Durham University, led by Professor Clare Bambra who is the Director of the Wolfson Research Institute. Clare is Professor of Public Health Geography and Director of Durham's Centre for Health and Inequalities Research. She leads a £1million funded Leverhulme Research Leadership Award, which examines local health inequalities in the Age of Austerity.[188] **The research papers from the Durham team are often published using open access and are free of charge to download.**

Assisting Clare are Dr Kayleigh Garthwaite and Dr Jon Warren, who in the past have been kind enough to share their research papers with MS. The research from the Durham team is highly regarded, is always significant and recent research is especially relevant to the chronically sick and disabled community who are totally dependent upon welfare benefits for their survival. In 2014, the Durham team published a paper in the *Disability and Society* academic journal, basically asking if the income replacement Employment and Support Allowance (ESA) benefit was '*fit for purpose*' and if the Work Capability Assessment (WCA) had a future? [189]

BOX 9:4 *After Atos Healthcare: is the Employment and Support Allowance fit for purpose and does the Work Capability Assessment have a future?*

The latest review by David Litchfield (2013), Harrington's successor and former head of occupational health at BT, has also recommended numerous changes to the system... What is staggering is not so much the detail of the recommendations, but the fact that a system which has been in use for over five years should still be in need of this amount of modification...(p1320)

Not only has this system been found essentially unfit for purpose, there is much evidence to suggest that it has been positively harmful, with WCA assessments being linked to, and arguably contributing to, numerous deaths of individuals who had recently undergone or were about to be reassessed by the process... There have been many high-profile cases; in February of this year The Guardian reported the death of Mark Wood. Mark, age 44, was ruled fit for work against the advice of his general practitioner and despite having complex mental health conditions.
As a result, Mark's benefits were suspended and he
died of starvation (The Guardian 2014)... (p1321)

One can argue that all of these models are flawed as they are not really about work capability or helping find individual's appropriate work. Instead, they are concerned with establishing and enforcing a threshold for benefit eligibility via a system of tests dressed up to look in some way scientific and objective... They are in other words a benefit eligibility assessment; there is also an inherent assumption within them that that they are seeking to root out undeserving 'malingerers' and this is arguably the primary purpose rather than enabling and supporting individuals...(p1321)

One should therefore not be surprised that an outsourced marketised version of state welfare is incapable of dealing with problems the market has created...(p1322)

After Atos Healthcare: is the Employment and Support Allowance
fit for purpose and does the Work Capability Assessment
have a future? [189]

Jon Warren, Kayleigh Garthwaite & Clare Bambra

Disability & Society Journal
Vol 29, No 8, p1319-1323

September 2014

Illustration 9:1 Highway to Hell – artwork kindly provided by the artist Kevin Marman

Published by the Journal of Social Policy[190] in April 2014, a very important paper was produced by the Durham team identifying those suffering under the Coalition government as Incapacity Benefit (IB) is migrated to the Employment and Support Allowance. (ESA) The conclusions were not unexpected.

BOX 9:5 *Shifting the goalposts:*

The UK social security safety net for those who are out of work due to ill health or disability has experienced significant change, most notably the abolition of Incapacity Benefit (IB) and the introduction of Employment and Support Allowance (ESA). These changes have been underpinned by the assumption that many recipients are not sufficiently sick or disabled to 'deserve' welfare benefits - claims that have been made in the absence of empirical data on the health of recipients. Employing a unique longitudinal and mixed-methods approach this paper explores the health of a cohort of 229 long-term IB recipients in the North East of England over an 18 month period, during a time of significant changes to the UK welfare state… Contributing to debates surrounding the conceptualisation of work-readiness for sick and disabled people, findings indicate IB recipients had significantly worse health than the general population, with little change in their health state over the 18 month study period. Qualitative data reinforced the constancy of ill health for IB recipients. Finally, the paper discusses the implications for social policy, noting how the changing nature of administrative definitions and redefinitions of illness and capacity to work can impact upon the lives of sick and disabled people…

Taken together, the two data sources show that those in long term receipt of IB experience significant – and constant – ill health and other barriers to labour market participation, and that their lives are difficult and limited by both illness and the stigmatisation of benefit receipt. This is coupled with shifting interpretations of 'work readiness' that are being attached to benefits recipients; what constitutes ill health for benefit recipients – or at least ill health of a sufficient level to receive state support – is a constantly changing and politically determined state, which may bear no relation to the real health or lived experiences of recipients. Adopting a 'health-first', together with a 'life-first', approach could allow for a consideration of the intricacies of the experiences of sick and disabled benefits recipients.

Shifting the goalposts: a longitudinal mixed-methods study [190]
of the health of long-term Incapacity Benefit recipients
during a period of substantial change to the UK
social security system.

K Garthwaite, C Bambra, J Warren, A Kasim & G Greig

Journal of Social Policy
Vol 43, issue 2, p311-330

April 2014

Using evidence based on doctoral research, Dr Kayleigh Garthwaite of Durham University identified the stigma, shame and uncertainty experienced by many claimants of long-term sickness benefit in her powerful 2015 article, published in the Social Policy and Administration Journal.[191]

BOX 9:6 *'Keeping meself to meself'* …

This article focuses upon social networks and their relationship to stigma and identity for long-term sickness benefits recipients in the North East of England. Drawing on empirical qualitative research with long-term sickness benefits recipients, this article demonstrates how the co-construction of stigma is fundamental in shaping how long-term sickness benefits recipients participate in social networks with friends, family and the community. The findings support the idea that the stigma of receiving benefits can be contrasted with nostalgia for the social elements of employment. Utilizing the work of Goffman, the article focuses on how the stigma and shame felt at receiving sickness benefits for an extended period of time interacts with social networks and identity. Reluctance to disclose a claimant identity to friends and family could lead to social isolation and a perceived need to *'keep meself to meself'* which can be linked to a wider rhetoric surrounding benefits recipients that characterizes them as 'scroungers'… (p199)

These extracts suggest that suffering chronic illness can serve to isolate and separate people from their social networks, which could have a damaging effect upon their health; similar sentiments can be found in the work of Gallant *et al*. (2007) on family and friends in relation to chronic illness management… (p204)

Others such as Sandra chose not to fully share their problems with family and friends. Concealing identities and controlling information meant not only deciding who can be given information about their illness, but also how much and what information they would be given, thereby employing a form of stigma management (Goffman 1963). Just as there was an avoidance of accepting the term 'disabled', the stigma of receiving sickness benefits could be so overwhelming that people refused to admit they were receiving it (Garthwaite 2013). In some cases, interviewees refused to reveal their 'claimant identity' to close family and friends, and would avoid social situations to avoid being asked the question. (p204)

'Keeping meself to meself' -
how social networks can influence narratives
of stigma and identity for long-term
sickness benefits recipients [191]

Kayleigh Garthwaite
Social Policy and Administration Journal
Volume 49, No 2, p199-212

March 2015

When it comes to generosity of spirit, and tolerance of this researcher's contact, there are none better than Professor Danny Dorling of the University of Oxford. Yet another decent man who encouraged the efforts of MS, despite the fact that he knew that MS was not an academic by profession and that she refused to adopt the required protocol of 'diplomatic writing' for what was identified long-ago as *'government funded slaughter.'* Danny has been prolific with his writing and his most recent book, **INJUSTICE**[192], continues his mission to warn people as to what happens to society when the top 1% keep getting richer, at the expense of everyone else, as the UK is transformed to replicate the United States.

BOX 9:7 *INJUSTICE*

Private medicine is found to be inefficient by every decent study carried out on it. The UN Research Institute for Social Development (based in Geneva) recently confirmed that it was the spending of a significantly higher proportion of money on state healthcare, rather than private healthcare, which marked out countries where life expectancy was high and infant mortality low. The WHO*, OECD** and numerous other international bodies constantly rank the UK's NHS as the most efficient health service in the affluent world. Spending on private or even charitable health services is counter-productive,[39] and it is even counter-productive for the rich…(p320) It is often suggested in Britain that free-market ideas brought over from the US are increasingly incorporated where they make least sense – in our much better health service, and in 2012, significant sections of the NHS were part-privatised by the UK coalition government. By 2013, it became possible for up to half the beds in an NHS hospital to be private health sector beds. Private health care is more often poor health care… (p321)

Over two centuries ago, among those with power who thought that there was too little to go around to cater for all, it was becoming widely recognised that: '[Slavery] … is attended with too much trouble, violence, and noise, ... whereas hunger is not only a peaceable, silent, unremitted pressure, but as the most natural motive to industry, it calls forth the most powerful exertions.... Hunger will tame the fiercest animals, it will teach decency and civility, obedience and subjugation to the most brutish, the most obstinate, and the most perverse.'[53] …(p324)

'The ideal wage, therefore, must be sufficient to persuade a man to offer his labour, but insufficient to allow him to withdraw it for more than a few days. Capitalism thus replaces the whip of the overseer with the lash of a more terrifying slave-driver – hunger.'[54] (p325)

INJUSTICE [192]
why social inequality still persists

Danny Dorling
2015

*WHO – World Health Organisation
** OECD – Organisation for Economic Co-operation and Development

Courtesy of Policy Press

In his 2013 book *The Double Crisis of the Welfare State and what we can do about it* [193], Professor Peter Taylor-Gooby, Professor of Social Policy at the University of Kent, drew attention to how bad things are with the Coalition government in power, and how the Welfare State could be protected instead of demolished.

BOX 9:8 *The double crisis of the welfare state..*

The NHS, education, social care, local government, employment services, social housing and benefits for the poor face major challenges from a government determined to entrench a radical and divisive liberalism permanently in British public life. This book analyses the immediate challenges from headlong cuts that bear most heavily on women, families and the poor, and from a root-and-branch restructuring which will fragment and privatize the bulk of public services. It sets this in the context of escalating inequalities and the longer-term pressures from population ageing. It demonstrates that a more humane and generous welfare state that will build inclusiveness is possible by combining policies that limit child poverty, promote more equal outcomes from health care and education, introduce a greater contributory element into social benefits, invest in better child and elder care and address low wages and workplace rights. It analyses the political forces that can be marshalled to support these shifts and shows that, with political leadership, the welfare state can attract mass support.

This book address the double crisis of the welfare state with a particular focus on the UK. It shows how the immediate and longer-run pressures interact. The second, slow-burn crisis sets the mass of the population against more vulnerable minorities. The high-spending expensive services, such as health, education and pensions, are top priorities for most people. Spending on the less popular benefits and services that redistribute to the poor is steadily eroded. The government's response to the immediate economic crisis builds on this division, cutting the redistributive benefits to maintain the big-spending mass services. The fact that this is happening in a context of growing inequalities and social divisions makes the task of developing a humane and generous, effective and politically feasible response to the double crisis that much harder.

The double crisis of the welfare state [193]
and what we can do about it.

Peter Taylor-Gooby
2013

Courtesy of Palgrave Macmillan

In his 2014 paper *'The dying of the light'* [194] Rupert Harwood, of the Business School at the University of Greenwich, exposed the impact of the spending cuts, and cuts to employment law protections, on disability adjustments in British local authorities. This offers a warning of the future implications for disabled people and the likely consequences of government cuts.

BOX 9:9 *'The dying of the light'*

The last few years have been difficult for many people with disabilities. Benefits (Cross 2013) and social care support (Lymbery 2012, 788) have been cut; and for those wishing to challenge the cuts that they have suffered, legal aid has also been cut (Byrom 2013). In addition, and perhaps helping to make all this possible, media and political demonisation of disabled people has transformed public attitudes (Briant, Watson, and Philo 2011). Those with disabilities appear to have gone from being 'objects of pity and aid' (Shakespeare 1994, 288) (which is not necessarily great in itself) to often being regarded as fraudsters and legitimate objects of hate (e.g., Sykes, Groom, and Desai 2011).

It also seems that those with disabilities could be among the hardest hit with regards to employment, including for reasons related to reasonable adjustments. This is in part because it would be surprising if negative attitudes towards minority groups did not spill over into the workplace (Lopez, Hodson, and Roscigno 2009), and it seems that negative management attitudes towards disability can reduce willingness to make adjustments (e.g., Jackson, Furnham, and Willen 2000). In addition, cuts to central government grant (HM Treasury and UK National Statistics 2013) are leaving local authorities with smaller budgets from which to fund adjustments. Failure to make adjustments could, in turn, put those with disabilities – long disadvantaged in relation to employment (e.g., Hills et al. 2010) – at greater risk of being among the thousands of public-sector workers being made redundant (e.g., ONS 2013). At the same time, a rolling back of employment protection (e.g., Hepple 2013) is leaving those with disabilities even more vulnerable.

'The dying of the light': the impact of the spending cuts, and cuts to employment law protections, on disability adjustments in British local authorities [194]

Rupert Harwood

Disability & Society Journal
Vol 29, Issue 10, p1511-1523

2014

In her critically acclaimed 2014 research report, supported by MIND and the Centre for Welfare Reform, *'Fulfilling Potential? ESA and the fate of the Work-Related Activity Group'* [195], Catherine Hale exposed the total failure of the key aim of the Employment and Support Allowance (ESA) that was meant to increase the numbers of disabled people in work. The DWP claims of a *'culture of dependency'* of ESA claimants was demonstrated to have no foundation, as confirmed in the detailed testimony of 500 research participants.

BOX 9:10 *Fulfilling Potential? ESA & the fate of the WRAG*

This report examines the journey of more than 500 people placed in the WRAG*. From their initial feelings and expectations about work and the WRAG, we explore their encounter with employment advisers, the activities and interventions they were offered and those they were compelled to undertake, the procedures and impact of compulsion, through to their reflections at time of research in relation to work and wider psycho-social factors, following their engagement with the Work Programme or JCP**.(p5)

Through the introduction of ESA***, it was hoped that two strategies in particular would improve employment rates among disabled people. One was more intensive and personalised support, specifically through the marketisation of employment support services. The other was activation – the introduction of obligations, or conditionality, to engage in work preparation enforced by financial sanctions. In short, more rights in return for more responsibilities.[3] (p5)

Our survey results suggest that, contrary to promises, the experience of participation in the WRAG is neither personalised nor supportive, regardless of whether it is delivered by private contractors paid by results, or by the Government via JCP. Moreover, findings suggest that, far from "activating aspirations"[4], the regime of conditionality and sanctions has left participants in the WRAG fearful, demoralised, and further away from achieving their work-related goals or participating in society than when they started…(p5)

When ESA was introduced, a wealth of evidence existed about the most effective strategies for increasing employment opportunities for disabled people.[6] However, our research found that these evidence-based interventions are not being deployed in work preparation schemes for the WRAG. Instead, activation programmes for the WRAG appear to be underpinned by the "culture of dependency" theory, which presumes that the receipt of benefits itself creates the main barrier to work for people on ESA, and that corrective measures are needed to restore work incentives and instil personal responsibility. We found no evidence to support these assumptions, which seem to be so central to successive governments' policies around disability, benefits and work.(p5)

Fulfilling Potential? [195]
ESA and the fate of the
Work-Related Activity Group

Catherine Hale
2014

*WRAG – Work Related Activity Group   **JCP – Jobcentre Plus
    ***ESA – Employment and Support Allowance

Research supported by MIND & The Centre for Welfare Reform

The Spartacus Network are a group of highly capable sick and disabled people who access the opinion of others via social media and then produce detailed, in depth reports and analysis. Their reports are highly valued and have been referenced and quoted during political debate.

Using the collective skills and talent of chronically sick and disabled people, reports of high value are produced with evidence the government don't want the general public to know. In the 2012 report '*Responsible Reform*',[196] this remarkable team of likeminded chronically sick and disabled people collated evidence from over 500 people to expose the realities, and the bogus government claims, of the need to remove Disability Living Allowance (DLA) and replace it with the Personal Independence Payment. (PIP) Using social media, the report went viral after publication[197] and demonstrated that the opinion of chronically sick and disabled people could not be disregarded or silenced, no matter how hard the government tried to ignore them, and they helped to inflict a hat-trick of welfare reform defeats on the government in the Lords. The government invoked '*financial privilege*' to disregard the decisions of the Lords.

BOX 9:11   *How the Spartacus welfare cuts campaign went viral*

Something extraordinary happened last week in the volatile micro-blogging world of Twitter: a medium normally obsessed by celebrities, football and sex turned its collective attention instead to disability. A handmade campaign against welfare cuts launched by a tiny band of disabled activists took the social media world by storm.

Over the course of Monday 9 January, hundreds of thousands of people tweeted around #spartacusreport. In the jargon, the hashtag "top trended" for most of the day. In other words, of all the topics of the day, a serious report (entitled Responsible Reform) outlining in careful detail the government's alleged multiple lies and evasions over its proposed disability living allowance (DLA) reform had proved, incredibly, hugely popular…

Despite their success, the Spartacus campaigners are already counting the personal cost to their health. Some, already ill, have retired exhausted.

For herself, Franklin feels this is a price she may have to accept as the welfare reform bill debate intensifies: "It's a position of moral conscience. We could not live with ourselves if we did not give everything. Those of us in the core group [of campaigners] have understood that we risk damaging our health by doing this. But some things in life are more important."

How the Spartacus welfare cuts campaign went viral [197]

Patrick Butler
The Guardian
17th January 2012

Courtesy of Guardian News & Media

Not all important evidence is provided by academics in universities and, when it comes to exposing the plight of chronically sick and disabled people, there is none better than disability activist Merry Cross, who used referenced evidence from research by MS, in the Current Issues section of a 2013 article for the Disability and Society Journal[198], which is regularly quoted in academic papers.

BOX 9:12 *Demonised, impoverished and now forced into isolation:*

In the United Kingdom, there has been a series of unprecedented attacks on every source of support and help for disabled people, with the latest to hit us being the scrapping of Disability Living Allowance (DLA) and the introduction of Personal Independence Payment (PIP). Before considering the particular iniquities of this measure it is necessary to put it in the context of all the other attacks on our human rights. Reforms began quietly under the last government, with the introduction of the Work Capability Assessment (or WCA). The introduction of the WCA followed concerted lobbying by disability insurance company Unum as early as 1992…(p719)

The WCA is based on a model of disability called the biopsychosocial model, the development of which they initially funded by setting up what was then the Unum Centre for Psychosocial and Disability Research based at Cardiff University. The main proponent of the model there has been Prof Sir Mansell Aylward who, despite saying it no longer addresses the social issues for disabled people when confronted by activists last year, continues to promote it heavily around the world (Stewart 2013). Needless to say, disabled people have had no part in the development of this model. Equally it probably does not need to be pointed out that the more disabled people lose the security of benefits, the more likely they are to have to turn to insurance companies like Unum (American Association for Justice 2011)…(p720)

All of this can leave us in no doubt, should there have been any, that the intention of this government is not to improve the lives of disabled people; not to find them jobs; not to increase their independence – indeed, they have little interest in us at all.

The clear intention is to destroy the welfare state and push all of us, disabled and non-disabled alike, into the arms of private companies whose sole aim is, of course, the creation of profit for their shareholders.(p722)

Demonised, impoverished and now forced into isolation: the fate of disabled people under austerity.[198]

Merry Cross

Disability & Society Journal
Vol 28, No 5, p719-723

July 2013

When it comes to empowering chronically sick and disabled people, and emphasising the fact that their voice counts, look no further than academic Peter Beresford OBE, Emeritus Professor of Social Policy and the Director of the Centre for Citizen Participation at Brunel University, London. Peter is the Chair of Shaping Our Lives, the national disabled people's and service users' organisation and network, he leads the field in user involvement research and has been instrumental in encouraging the research efforts of MS over a number of years. Peter has published widely in his fields of interest, writes regularly for *The Guardian* and writes a regular column in the Journal of the College of Social Work. In his significant new book, *All Our Welfare*[199], Peter exposes the welfare reforms as moving the United Kingdom back to the past with a replica of the poor laws, and all the cruelties they implied.

BOX 9:13 *All Our Welfare*

Much of my first hand experience of the welfare state has been complicated and problematic. Yet in my work, I have argued and fought determinedly for the welfare state. What explains this apparent contradiction? First, while the welfare state has frequently fallen short in practice, I believe its key principles remain groundbreaking and illuminating. Second, the alternatives offered to it, have frequently seemed backward-looking, unfair and defective. How inadequate, I have come even more to appreciate finding out more about them. They have often just taken us back to the indignities and cruelties associated with the poor law of the past, instead of transcending the limitations of the welfare state.

The aim of this book is not just to try and make sense of past and present struggles over welfare, but more important, to explore a different vision for the future. It draws on personal and other experience, as well as academic evidence, both to explore the inconsistencies of the welfare state and to highlight the possibilities of new participatory ways forward already emerging, to secure our rights and needs as citizens and human beings. It starts from the belief that if we are to learn from the strengths and shortcomings of the original welfare state and what it has become since, then we need to have as good an understanding as possible of its origins and reality. Sadly, much current discussion about welfare is superficial, ahistorical and tendentious.

All Our Welfare: [199]
towards participatory social policy

Peter Beresford
January 2016

Courtesy of Policy Press

The listed research in this chapter is just a very small sample of the detailed evidence that is available. The Internet is the source of a vast amount of very important research just waiting to be discovered and reported to a much wider audience and *Appendix* 6 offers a list of suggested further reading.

REFERENCES

** **All references accessed and confirmed 18th October 2015**

Illustration 9:1
Highway to Hell ~ reproduced by kind permission of the artist Kevin Marman

180. WADDELL G, BURTON AK: 2006: *Is work good for health and well-being?*
https://www.gov.uk/government/uploads/system/uploads/attachment_data/file/214326/hwwb-is-work-good-for-you.pdf
181. O'HARA M: 2015: Policy Press: *Austerity Bites* ISBN: 978-1-4473-1570-4 paperback
182. DORLING D: Policy Press: *Injustice* ISBN: 978-1-4473-2075-3 paperback
183. WADDELL G, AYLWARD M: 2005: *The Scientific and Conceptual Basis of Incapacity Benefits*: ISBN: 0 11 703584 X
184. RAVETZ A: 2006: *Green Paper: A New Deal for Welfare: empowering people to work. 2006.*
http://disability-studies.leeds.ac.uk/files/library/ravetz-Green-Paper-IB-critique.pdf
185. RESEARCH METHODOLOGY: 2010:
http://www.enotes.com/homework-help/what-research-what-various-types-research-explain-137387
186. RAVETZ A: 2006: *Green Paper: A New Deal for Welfare: empowering people to work. 2006.*
http://disability-studies.leeds.ac.uk/files/library/ravetz-Green-Paper-IB-critique.pdf
187. KENNEDY A: 2012: *Authors of our own misfortune?* ISBN: 978-0-85718-101-5
188. BAMBRA C: 2011: Staff Profile Durham University
https://www.dur.ac.uk/geography/staff/geogstaffhidden/?id=2991
189. WARREN J, GARTHWAITE K, BAMBRA C: September 2014: *After Atos Healthcare: is the Employment and Support Allowance fit for purpose and does the Work Capability Assessment have a future?* Disability and Society, 2014 Vol. 29, No. 8, 1319– 1323
http://dx.doi.org/10.1080/09687599.2014.948746
http://www.tandfonline.com/doi/abs/10.1080/09687599.2014.948746
190. GARTHWAITE K, BAMBRA C, WARREN J, KASMIN A, GREIG C: April 2014: *Shifting the goalposts: a longitudinal mixed-methods study of the health of long-term incapacity benefit recipients during a period of substantial change in the UK social security system.* Journal of Social Policy: April 2014, pp311-330, Vol 43, issue 2. doi:10.1017/S0047279413000974 Durham University: http://dro.dur.ac.uk/12797/
http://journals.cambridge.org/action/displayAbstract?fromPage=online&aid=9185002&fileId=S0047279413000974
191. GARTHWAITE K: March 2015: *Keeping meself to meself' – How Social Networks Can Influence Nattatives of Stigma and Identity for long-term Sickness Benefits Recipients* Social Policy & Administration Journal, Vol 49, No 2, March 2015, p199-212.
http://dro.dur.ac.uk/14925/
http://onlinelibrary.wiley.com/doi/10.1111/spol.12119/abstract

192. DORLING D: 2015: Policy Press: *Injustice* ISBN: 978-1-4473-2075-3 paperback

193. TAYLOR-GOOBY P: 2013: Palgrave Pilot: *The Double Crisis of the Welfare State and what we can do about it.* ISBN: 9781137328120

194. HARWOOD R: 2014: *'The dying of the light': the impact of the spending cuts, and cuts to employment law protections, on disability adjustments in British local authorities.* Disability & Society Journal: October 2014. Vol 29, Issue 10, p1511-1523
http://dx.doi.org/10.1080/09687599.2014.958132

195. HALE C: 2014: *Fulfilling Potential? ESA and the fate of the Work-Related Activity Group* http://www.mind.org.uk/media/933438/2014-support-not-sanctions-report.pdf

196. SPARTACUS NETWORK: 2012: *Responsible Reform:*
http://www.ekklesia.co.uk/files/response_to_proposed_dla_reforms.pdf

197. BUTLER P: 2012: *How the Spartacus welfare cuts campaign went viral.* The Guardian
http://www.theguardian.com/society/2012/jan/17/disability-spartacus-welfare-cuts-campaign-viral

198. CROSS M: 2013: *Demonised, impoverished and now forced into isolation: the fate of disabled people under austerity.* Disability & Society Journal, July 2013, Vol 28, No 5, p719-723.
http://www.tandfonline.com/doi/abs/10.1080/09687599.2013.808087?journalCode=cdso20+-+.VSF4RNKBHIU&

199. BERESFORD P: 2016: *All Our Welfare: Towards participatory social policy*, Policy Press
http://www.policypress.co.uk/display.asp?K=9781447328940&sf1=contributor&st1=Peter%20w/2%20Beresford&m=2&dc=4

CHAPTER 10: CONCLUSION ~ FINAL THOUGHTS

Never believe anything until it's officially denied.
John Pilger

Over the last six years this research was conducted on behalf of chronically sick and disabled people who are dependent upon welfare benefits and who, historically, don't have a voice.

They have tolerated an unprecedented political attack against them in recent years, with many paying the ultimate price for what is identified government tyranny (Chapter 3) by successive United Kingdom (UK) governments, who were influenced long-ago by the opinion of a former Department for Work and Pensions (DWP) Chief Medical Officer (CMO) when involved with a notorious American corporate insurance giant who had an alternative agenda.(Chapters 4,5)

Due to one man's influence, the authority of General Practitioners (GP) and their ability to determine if their patients were well enough to consider paid employment or not was removed (Chapter 3) as the new income replacement benefit, known as the Employment and Support Allowance (ESA), was introduced in 2008 to replace Incapacity Benefit.(IB) To access ESA claimants would be subjected to a Work Capability Assessment (WCA) by an unaccountable corporate giant, as recommended by former City Banker David Freud in his 2007 report when adviser to the New Labour government.(Chapter 3) That report was the template for the future demolition of the welfare state, and the unelected Freud was appointed as a Minister in the 2010 Coalition government to permit him to continue to create ways to reduce the deficit, and demolish the welfare state, making the poorest in the land suffer the most. (Chapter 4)

This voyage of research discovery by Mo Stewart (MS) exposed the abuse of power, by various UK governments, used to threaten all long-term chronically sick and disabled benefit claimants because one senior Civil Servant had a hunch that many of them should work. There was no evidence of the presumed mass *'malingering'* of course, but that suggestion was enough to introduce American designed government funded medical tyranny into the UK. (Chapters 3, 5)

The intimidation was dramatically increased by the Coalition government, led by Prime Minister David Cameron who **knowingly misdirected** [N3] the British people in order to remove the psychological security of the welfare state en route to its demolition. It seems that Thatcher's disciple was religiously following her legacy to demolish the welfare state, regardless of the very predictable and inevitable human consequences. (Chapter 6)

125

As long ago as 1992, successive UK governments knowingly accepted President Clinton's American style social security policies for the UK (Chapter 6), **without the mandate of the British people**, when adopting policies that guaranteed that the poor would eventually be sacrificed as the rich increased their wealth and chronically sick and disabled people, dependent upon welfare funding for their very survival, have died in their thousands; sometimes actually **starving to death** in C21st UK. (Chapter 7) Detailed evidence that supports this research, demonstrating the influence of corporate America with the UK government, was conducted by my Webmaster, known online as '*Mike Bach*'. A selection of the evidence from Mike's research is reproduced in Chapter 8, with this book dedicated to Mike who lost his battle for life in February 2015. He is missed by many people and, especially, by this researcher.

This research voyage of discovery would not have been so meaningful had it not been for the ability to highlight mainstream academic research that is valuable and vital, but is always published in academic journals that most of the British public are unlikely to access. Therefore, considerable time has been spent accessing and referencing detailed academic research in MS published reports over the last six years. Chapter 9 is dedicated to a small selection of academic excellence, with *Appendix* 6 listing recommended further reading.

As this research draws to a close it is important to highlight two recent events. At very long last, a London coroner identified the WCA as '*the trigger*' for the suicide of a benefit claimant in a '***Prevention of Future Deaths report***'[200] to the Department for Work and Pensions (DWP). Yet, this January 2014 coroner's report has only just been brought to the attention of the public thanks to John Pring of Disability News Service (DNS)[201], who also highlighted the DWP's inadequate and defensive response to the coroner's report. (*Appendix* 2)

On a related topic, I suggest that it is more than a little sinister that the DWP press office decided in April 2015 not to accept any further enquiries from John Pring, the editor of the UK's only disability news agency.[202] DNS provides detailed information relevant to disabled

---

NOTES

N3: Cameron knowingly misdirected the British people: Debbie Abrahams MP:

"I have previously raised concerns in the House of Commons about Duncan Smith's misuse of statistics as well as other members of the Government including the Prime Minister."
"Misleading statements were made, not in this House, but in relation to Government business. The Government have been rebuked on a number of occasions, for example by the chair of the UK Statistics Authority, for making misleading remarks. It is unparliamentary behaviour. What action can be taken?"
"Yesterday the Secretary of State for Work and Pensions and the Prime Minister made very misleading statements about the impact of welfare reform…"

people and their carers, and this decision suggests that the DWP actually fear the evidence that John has regularly supplied to his readers when the DWP missed his press deadline. If the DWP thought that refusing to answer John's enquiries would reduce the importance of the weekly DNS reports, and the impact they have, they were very much mistaken.*

BOX 10:1 *Coroner's groundbreaking verdict: suicide 'triggered' by 'fit for work' test*

The former orthopaedic surgeon, employed by Atos Healthcare, who carried out the WCA, concluded that Mr A was "at no significant risk by working" and failed to ask him if he had suicidal thoughts.

Following the inquest, the coroner wrote what is known as a regulation 28 report, on the grounds that evidence revealed during her investigation suggested that there was "a risk that future deaths will occur unless action is taken." That report was sent directly to the DWP.

In the report, Hassell said the Atos Healthcare professional had failed to take into account the views of any of Mr A's doctors during a 90-minute assessment, telling him the DWP decision-maker would look at that evidence instead.

But the DWP decision-maker did not request any letters from Mr A's GP (who had assessed him as not being well enough to work), his psychiatrist (who diagnosed him with recurrent depression and panic disorder with agoraphobia), or his clinical psychologist (who had assessed him as "very anxious and showing signs of clinical depression.")

Instead, Mr A was found fit for work. Six months later he killed himself.

The coroner said in her report that she believed that action should be taken "to prevent future deaths" and that the DWP had the power to take such action.

Dr Stephen Carty, medical adviser for Black Triangle and himself a GP, said the case provided "clear and irrefutable evidence of systematic failure"… "The coroner has quite rightly identified some of the dangerous, systemic failings in the WCA that effectively allows diability and harm to occur."

DWP said in its response to the coroner's report: "While the Department is committed to a continuously improving process for this group wherever possible, with such a large number of people involved … there will inevitably be instances where the processes are not conducted in line with stated policy."

It added: "It remains important to retain a balance between the added value of further evidence in any claim for ESA and time demands on GPs and other healthcare professionals."

John Pring[201]
Disability News Service
18th September 2015

In her narrative determination – or verdict – the coroner said: '*The anxiety and depression were long term problems, but the intense anxiety that triggered his suicide was caused by his recent assessment by the Department for Work and Pensions (benefits agency) as being fit for work, and his view of the likely consequences of that.'*

Another recent event involved the former DWP CMO, Professor Sir Mansel Aylward. Three years ago, John Pring of DNS was with activists who spoke with the Professor to invite his comments regarding the WCA and the harm it had created.[203] At the time, the Professor claimed that he had just given a presentation at the International Forum on Disability Management and that the biopsychosocial (BPS) model of assessment, as used in the WCA to resist access to DWP benefit funding, was *'no longer satisfactory'*. Aylward also pledged that he would look into the WCA and that if he felt there was a problem with it he would speak out. However, Aylward didn't speak out against the WCA and instead visited New Zealand, where a similar WCA model was being introduced following his advice.[204]

More recently, Aylward spoke to a group of Welsh activists who were holding a vigil outside the Socialist Health Association[205] to protest against the decision to invite the Professor to speak with them in his capacity as Chair of Public Health Wales. It seems that the Professor now claims that his research was not sponsored at Cardiff University by Unum (Provident) Insurance and that he never supported the BPS model of assessment.

DAN Cymru are the disabled activists' network in Wales who sent out a press release to encourage participation in the vigil against Aylward.[205] They reported back via Facebook:

Tuesday, 8ᵗʰ September 2015, via Facebook:

"So DAN Cymru picketed the Socialist Health Association's meeting this evening. Sir Mansel Aylward came & spoke with us for approx half an hour. He claims he's grievously misunderstood, that he never had anything to do with the Work Capability Assessment, that he never supported the Biopsychosocial model, he insists that the Social model is the only valid model of disability, that he never accepted money from Unum, and that he's merely an academic. I pointed out that there appears to be a rather extensive body of academic literature which seems to indicate otherwise on all these points. He insists he opposes Unum, the WCA and the Biopsychosocial model. He wants to engage with us, to defend his work and to work with DAN Cymru to improve things for disabled people. He strongly urged us to meet with him..."

Oh dear…

Perhaps it may help if the Professor remembered that group academic papers, reports, conference presentations and his own books, speeches and academic papers are all a matter of public record, and MS has referenced most of them over the past six years. The evidence in the chapters of this book has demonstrated that the Professor's recent claims suggest, in the often misquoted words of a very famous playwright, *'methinks thou dost protest too much'*...

It is possible that Aylward knows little about the actual WCA. He left the DWP in 2005 and the WCA was introduced in 2008 with the launch of the ESA income replacement benefit. However, as the former DWP CMO, he was involved with Unum from 1992, when John Lo Cascio became a DWP 'Consultant' and, from 1994, when Unum (Provident) Insurance became official 'advisers' to the UK government. (Chapter 2) Aylward and LoCascio wrote a joint academic paper in 1995 (Chapter 5), and UnumProvident_TM Insurance made reference to the funding of the *'UnumProvident Centre for Psychosocial and Disability Research, Cardiff University'* (the Centre) in memos to the Work and Pensions Select Committee (Chapter 4). So, the Professor can't really claim to be innocent when he co-authored the template for the WCA in the influential 2005 report, co-authored by and exclusively copyrighted to Gordon Waddell: The Scientific and Conceptual Basis of Incapacity Benefits (SCBIB)[206], which disregarded the opinion of family doctors and recommended 'incentives' for non-compliance of claimants. The SCBIB report identifies Aylward as the co-author based at the *'UnumProvident Centre for Psychosocial and Disability Research, Cardiff University'* so, clearly, at the time of the report Unum were sponsoring Aylward at the Centre. As an academic report, it was then up to the DWP to decide how to interpret the content and, following that report, the WCA was introduced in 2008 when the ESA was launched to replace Incapacity Benefit.

As demonstrated in earlier chapters, Aylward insisted for years that the introduction of a *'non~medical'* biopsychosocial (BPS) assessment model, as copied from Unum (Provident) Insurance and guaranteed to cause death and despair by disregarding diagnosis, prognosis and medical history should be used to assess claimants of the long-term sickness and disability benefit, now known as the ESA. It may also help if the Professor remembered his various BPS model presentations that were all available via YOU TUBE, **until recently when they were removed**, and his contribution to the 2001 Malingering and Illness Deception conference[207], as identified in Chapter 5. He should also note well the adverts announcing the UnumProvident_TM Insurance sponsorship of the Centre, at Cardiff University, by various sources, in 2004, which are a matter of record and not all have suddenly disappeared. !!

The endless accusations by the Secretary of State for Work and Pensions and DWP Ministers that vast numbers of chronically sick and disabled people, migrating from Incapacity Benefit to claiming ESA, were *'malingering'* is due entirely to Aylward and colleagues' past published research and reports as *commissioned* by the DWP. With some of Aylward's published research identifying him as representing the *'UnumProvident Centre for Psychosocial and Disability Research, School of Psychology, Cardiff University'*[208], it is surely unwise to now suddenly claim that the research wasn't sponsored by Unum (Provident) Insurance, no matter how much the company, Cardiff University and all others attempt to **remove the evidence** that confirms that the company did indeed sponsor the Centre's research for five years from 2004. **The question remains as to why all this evidence is being removed from the Internet and why all involved are now suddenly attempting to deny that it happened??**

Whilst, historically, a lot of websites **have a tendency to disappear** within days of a research report by MS being published in the public arena, it is almost impossible to remove all evidence of a subject matter from the Internet, and MS usually finds more than mysteriously disappears.[N4] Given Aylward's recent claims, it seems much more likely that the Professor didn't expect to be held to account by victims of an assessment model that his advice and expertise helped to create, when producing academic reports commissioned by the DWP. *'Innocent until proven guilty'* is a legal concept. As demonstrated throughout this book, 'guilty until proven otherwise' is the DWP mantra when 'assessing' chronically ill and/or disabled people using the totally bogus *'non-medical'* BPS assessment model, known as the WCA, created to resist funding disability benefit, regardless of diagnosis or prognosis. It's as if medical opinion doesn't exist as the so called DWP *'Decision Makers'* still totally disregard detailed medical opinion provided by claimants, and accept the findings of the entirely bogus WCA, conducted by an unaccountable corporate giant, as the death totals rise annually when using the dangerous *'non-medical'* assessment model as recommended by Aylward in years gone by. (Chapter 7) Back to reality…

NOTES
N4 Historically, with previous research, significant websites that supported the argument of MS disappeared within days of the research being published in the public arena. Recently, within two days of sending an email to one person, in January 2016, offering websites from 2004 both reporting the new partnership between Cardiff University and UnumProvident Insurance, who funded the 'UnumProvident Centre for Psychosocial and Disability Research, Cardiff University' both websites suddenly disappeared. Both Unum Insurance and Cardiff University used to celebrate the funding of the Centre. Now, attempts are being made to remove all evidence of the past funding and Aylward claims it didn't happen. It is actually very difficult to remove all evidence from the Internet and evidence from 2004 still exists. Screenshots have been used to confirm and to retain the online evidence, which has been shared with others, via Royal Mail, so several people now have access to it.

It should be remembered that it was the Cameron government who promoted and activated in full the findings of the seriously flawed 2007 Freud Report[209] that used 2006 DWP commissioned '*academic research*' from the Centre at Cardiff University[210] to support the Freud Report findings. Since 2010 the Cameron government have been masters at misleading the British public, when using well reported commentry that detracts from the most important issues, negatively impacting on the wellbeing of the sick and disabled public as they attempted and failed to 'incentivise' MS to stop the research with a witnessed telecom from the Cabinet Office.

Witnessed by a third party, the personal telecom from the Cabinet Office attempting to incentivise MS to stop the research in return for War Pensioners being allowed to retain access to Disability Living Allowance (DLA) confirms the Cameron government's attempt to stop this research by using emotional blackmail. MS refused to stop the research, so now approximately 80,000 older disabled veterans are paying the price for the refusal of MS to be silenced, as the Cameron government threaten disabled working-age War Pensioners with the removal of their independence via the DLA reforms.[211] Disabled working-age older veterans now have their Motability cars removed as they fail to achieve the necessary points for the new Personal Independence Payment that replaced the DLA using yet another assessment model from the private sector.

Since David Cameron became Prime Minister in May 2010, and the adoption of the infamous '*austerity measures*' that experts advise were based on ideology and not fiscal necessity (Chapter 3), the UK has seen the return of Rickets – a disease from the Victorian age caused by poor diet[212] as increasing poverty forced many to adopt a dangerously poor diet. In a letter in the British Medical Journal (BMJ), health experts warned of '*a public health emergency that could go unrecognised until it is too late to take preventative action*'[213] as the government resisted all evidence of increasing levels of malnutrition in the UK, and the DWP refused to publish the updated death totals of ESA claimants following a WCA until they were forced to do so. (Chapter 7)

And let's not forget that the UK government, led by David Cameron, were identified by MS in May 2014 as permitting identified crimes against humanity [214] and that the United Nations are now investigating the UK government for breaches of the Human Rights of chronically sick and disabled people.[215] However, as always, Cameron has a 'get-out clause' as it seems that, regardless of evidence provided in any future UN report, and the fact that the UK government is required to accept the findings in any UN report, *'there is no legal obligation for it to act on it.'* [215] Does this not beg the question as to the point of any UN investigation if the host nation can then totally disregard the findings? Raising hopes that atrocities by the UK government will be exposed by a UN investigation is brutal if the UN really don't have any authority to hold the Cameron government responsible for the deaths, despair and the unnecessary human suffering they have created for ideological reasons, regardless of any deficit.

The vast majority of politicians don't know about the history behind the introduction of the WCA. They only know what government and opposition briefings tell them to know, then they all tend to lose their moral code and conscience when the Whips in the House of Commons order them to support a vote, as the UK continues to pretend to be governed by a democracy.

Surely it's time politicians knew the truth, and they should be alerted to the contents of this book so they are much better informed and, one day, they may begin to vote with their conscience more often instead of blindly following the party line.

Perhaps the election of Jeremy Corbyn in September 2015, as the new Leader of the Labour Party, may restore some long lost courage to the opposition benches, may prevent them from colluding with the Tories to introduce welfare bills that were guaranteed to kill people, and may once again offer the ordinary working people of this once great nation a political leader who thinks that they are important and not *'scroungers'*. Time alone will tell.

A little over six years ago MS began this research in September 2009 and the first research report, *Atos Healthcare or Disability Denial Factories*[216] was published online in June 2010, one month after Cameron became Prime Minister, exposing the influence of corporate giants with the assessment of chronically sick and disabled people in the UK and the obvious dangers of the WCA. Six years later, a new report by Dr Benjamin Barr and colleagues was recently published online in November 2015 in an academic journal. *'First do no harm: are disability assessments associated with adverse trends in mental health? A longitudinal ecological study'*[217] has also been published in full under licence by the BMJ.[218]

This very significant, detailed academic research has concluded that the WCA, as used by the government to remove people from disability benefit or resist access to it, was *'…independently associated with an increase in suicides, self-reported mental health problems and antidepressant prescribing.'* **The research conclusion also states that: *'Our study provides evidence that the policy in England of reassessing the eligibility of benefit recipients using the WCA may have unintended but serious consequences for population mental health, and there is a danger that these adverse effects outweigh any benefits that***

***may or may not arise from moving people off disability benefits.*'[218]**

With more disturbing evidence exposed in this chapter, demonstrating that the UK government have routinely disregarded warnings by coroners, about the **<u>risk to life</u>** posed by the WCA in relation to claimants with a serious mental health problem,[218] I rest my case as the conclusion to this lengthy research coincided with the resignation of Iain Duncan Smith (IDS) from his post as Secretary of State for Work and Pensions.[219] It seems quite ironic that my first ever research report was published online in June 2010,[220] one month after IDS was appointed as the Secretary of State, and my research now concludes with his resignation in March 2016…

CASH NOT CARE is now confirmed… which leads automatically to **GREED NOT NEED**.

And finally… Especially for other sick and disabled people who may one day read this book, the biggest lesson MS has learned in the past six years is that mainstream academic research is not some big mystery only available to funded graduates locked away in universities. Academic research is available to anyone who wishes to access it. There is no great mystery. Academics are people who conduct research for a living but they are people first, and I have rarely met a more decent and supportive group of people who have done all they can to encourage my work and to tolerate my contact. This research evidence was made more credible due to their very valuable help (Chapter 9) and all the academics who have helped me over the years have my everlasting thanks.

On a personal note, it hardly seems possible that I have spent over six years conducting this research when on my personal voyage of research discovery. If it has helped chronically sick and disabled people and their carers, and the Disabled Peoples' Organisations, to comprehend why this government imposed tyranny was introduced then I hope and believe that it was time well spent. If it helps future academic research to identify why the UK government adopted American social security policies in a covert move to demolish the UK welfare state, I'm very pleased to have possibly helped with any future mainstream academic research.

In closing, I wish the reader the very best of all possible luck for the future and I regret that it will be needed for the battles still to come, as the welfare state is gradually demolished by the UK government… as all planned a very long time ago in what will be the ultimate '*Thatcher Legacy.*'

Per Ardua Ad Astra
through endeavour to the stars

N3: NOTES:

  1. Debbie Abrahams MP

I have previously raised concerns in the House of Commons about Duncan Smith's misuse of statistics as well as other members of the Government including the Prime Minister. http://www.debbieabrahams.org.uk/2014/dwp-misuse-of-statistics

  2. HANSARD

Point of Order – July 2013 – column 953

Debbie Abrahams: Misleading statements were made, not in this House, but in relation to Government business. The Government have been rebuked on a number of occasions, for example by the chair of the UK Statistics Authority, for making misleading remarks. It is unparliamentary behaviour. What action can be taken?

  3. Point of Order – July 2013 – column 953

Debbie Abrahams (Oldham East and Saddleworth) (Lab): On a point of order, Mr Speaker. Yesterday the Secretary of State for Work and Pensions and the Prime Minister made very misleading statements about the impact of welfare reform…
http://www.debbieabrahams.org.uk/2014/dwp-misuse-of-statistics

N4: NOTES

Historically, with previous research by MS, significant websites that supported the argument of MS disappeared within days of the research being published in the public arena. Recently, within two days of sending an email to one person, in January 2016, offering websites from 2004, both reporting the new partnership between Cardiff University and UnumProvident Insurance, who funded the '*UnumProvident Centre for Psychosocial and Disability Research, Cardiff University*' both websites suddenly disappeared. Both Unum Insurance and Cardiff University used to celebrate the funding of the Centre. Now, attempts are being made to remove all evidence of the past funding and Professor Aylward claims it didn't happen. It is actually very difficult to remove all evidence from the Internet confirming the sponsorship of the Centre at Cardiff University by Unum, and evidence from May 2004 still exists. Screenshots have now been used to confirm and retain the online evidence. **NB: The evidence has been shared with trusted colleagues and will not be made available in the public arena in order to prevent these websites also suddenly disappearing.** MS

REFERENCES

  *This issue between the DWP and DNS was resolved in October 2015.

** **Most references accessed and confirmed 20th October 2015**
     References 217 and 218 accessed and confirmed 3rd December 2015
     References 219 and 220 accessed and confirmed 18th March 2016

200. COURTS AND TRIBUNALS JUDICIARY: 13th January 2014: *Regulation 28: Prevention of Future Deaths report to the Department for Work and Pensions*
      https://www.judiciary.gov.uk/wp-content/uploads/2014/06/OSullivan-2014-0012.pdf

201. PRING J: 18th September 2015: *Coroner's 'ground-breaking' verdict: Suicide was 'triggered by 'fit for work' test* : Disability News Service
      http://www.disabilitynewsservice.com/coroners-ground-breaking-verdict- suicidewastriggered-by-fit-for-work-test/

202. PRING J: 17th April 2015: *DWP carries out threat to ban questions from Disability News Service* : Disability News Service
http://www.disabilitynewsservice.com/dwp-carriesout-threat-to-ban- questions-fromdisability-news-service/

203. PRING J: 3rd September 2012: *Former DWP boss makes WCA pledge to protesters*: Disability News Service
http://www.disabilitynewsservice.com/former-dwp-medicalboss-makes-wca- pledgeto-protesters-2/

204. RUTHERFORD H: 11th January 2013: Business Day New Zealand: *Work tests concern disability organisation*
http://www.stuff.co.nz/business/industries/8165236/Work-tests-concern-disability-organisation

205. DAN CYMRU: 7th September 2015: *Press release*
https://www.facebook.com/DanCymruDisabledActivists/posts/

206. WADDELL & AYLWARD: 2005: *The Scientific and Conceptual Basis of Incapacity Benefits*: UnumProvident Centre for Psychosocial and Disability Research, Cardiff University: TSO : ISBN 0 11 703584 X

207. VARIOUS AUTHORS: CONFERENCE PAPERS: Malingering and Illness Deception ISBN: 0 19 851554 52003:
http://www.meactionuk.org.uk/Malingering_and_Illness_Deception.pdf

208. HALLIGAN AND AYLWARD: 2006: *The Power of Belief*, Edited by Peter W Halligan, School of Psychology, Cardiff University and Mansel Aylward, UnumProvident Centre for Psychosocial and Disability Research, School of Psychology, Cardiff University ISBN: 0-19-853011-0
https://global.oup.com/academic/product/the-power-of-belief- 9780198530114?cc=gb&lang=en&

209. FREUD D: 2007: *Reducing dependency, increasing opportunity: options for the future of welfare to work* ISBN: 907 1 84712 193 6
http://base-uk.org/sites/base-uk.org/files/%5Buser-raw%5D/11-07/welfarereview.pdf

210. WADDELL G & BURTON K: 2006: *Is work good for health and well-being?* ISBN: 0 11 703694 3
https://www.gov.uk/government/uploads/system/uploads/attachment_data/file/214 326/h wwb-is-work-good-for-you.pdf

211 PRING J: 21st November 2014; *History month hears of Cameron's 'broken promise' to disabled veterans.*
http://www.disabilitynewsservice.com/history-month-launch-hears- camerons-brokenpromise-disabled-veterans/

212 McVEIGH T: 30th August 2014: *Rickets returns as poor families find healthy diets unaffordable:* The Guardian
http://www.theguardian.com/society/2014/aug/30/child-poverty-link-malnutritionrickets

213 CHANNEL FOUR NEWS: *Malnutrition a public health emergency, experts warn*
http://www.channel4.com/news/malnutrition-health-emergency-dwp-british-medicaljournal

214 STEWART M: May 2014: *UK Government Refuses to Accept Responsibility for*

identified Crimes Against Humanity
http://disability-studies.leeds.ac.uk/files/library/GVT%20refuses%20responsibility%20for%20crimes%20against%20humanity%20-%20FINAL%20-%203rd%20May.pdf

215 BUTLER P: 20th October 2015: *UN inquiry considers alleged UK disability rights violations.* The Guardian
http://www.theguardian.com/society/2015/oct/20/un-inquiry-uk-disability-rightsviolations-cprd-welfare-cuts

216 STEWART M: June 2010: *Atos Healthcare of Disability Denial Factories*
http://www.whywaitforever.com/dwpatosveteranssummary.html

217 BARR B, TAYLOR-ROBINSON D., STUCKLER D, LOOPSTRA R, REEVES A, WHITEHEAD M: *'First do no harm': are disability assessments associated with adverse trends in mental health? A longitudinal ecological study.* BMJ 16th November 2015
http://jech.bmj.com/content/early/2015/10/26/jech-2015-206209 (Open Access)

218 BARR B, TAYLOR-ROBINSON D., STUCKLER D, LOOPSTRA R, REEVES A, WHITEHEAD M: November 2015: *'First do no harm': are disability assessments associated with adverse trends in mental health? A longitudinal ecological study.*
http://press.psprings.co.uk/jech/november/jech206209.pdf (Open Access)

219 LEWIS H: *Iain Duncan Smith resigns, citing disability cuts – and with a swipe at Osborne.*
http://www.newstatesman.com/politics/uk/2016/03/iain-duncan-smith-resigns-cabinet-over-disability-cuts

220 STEWART M: June 2010: *Atos Healthcare of Disability Denial Factories*
http://www.whywaitforever.com/dwpatosveteranssummary.html

APPENDICES ~ INTRODUCTION

Throughout the text various extracts are included from previously published research by Mo Stewart (MS). Earlier research from 2010 to 2013 is published on the *Why Wait Forever* website, with all later research published at both the Centre for Disability Studies at Leeds University and via ResearchGate, as listed below:

All past published research reports by MS are available via the following websites:

(1)   Why Wait Forever ~ Veterans:

http://www.whywaitforever.com/dwpatosveterans.html

(2)   ResearchGate ~ Mo Stewart

http://www.researchgate.net/profile/Mo_Stewart/publications

(3)   The Centre for Disability Studies, Leeds University ~ Mo Stewart

http://disability-studies.leeds.ac.uk/library/author/stewart.mo

There are six Appendices listed that are most relevant to the text.

Appendix 1 is the research caveat used for the production of the research.

Appendix 2 offers extracts and links to significant articles by the Editor of the Disability News Service, John Pring.

Appendix 3 offers extracts and links to significant articles by the Editor of Vox Political, Mike Sivier.

Appendix 4 offers extracts and links to significant articles by *Private* Eye rescued from obscurity and identifying the influence of Unum (Provident) Insurance with the UK government. *As long ago as 1995, journalist Paul Foot was exposing the influence of the American corporate healthcare insurance giant with future UK welfare reforms. In his memory, *Private Eye* hold an annual Paul Foot Awards ceremony to celebrate investigative journalism.

Appendix 5 offers extracts and links to significant and very relevant commentary by Bernadette Meaden of the *Ekklesia* thinktank.

Appendix 6 concludes the text with a detailed list of recommended further reading, mostly from distinguished academic experts, and a warning is given to alert readers as to the often disturbing evidence to be found in these books and academic papers.

APPENDIX 1

Research Caveat

The evidence identified in this text was available in the public domain at the time of writing. The author is an independent researcher and has carried out this work for no remuneration or other emolument. This referenced research was conducted for the benefit of the greater good, and to collate detailed evidence that may otherwise not be brought to public attention. All referenced websites within the text were live and accessed as listed but there can be no guarantee that listed websites will remain permanently available. Readers are advised that this research is especially written for ease of access by the general public, who may be unfamiliar with mainstream academic texts.

Exceptions to copyright

This research has benefitted from access to and quoted extracts from published research and commentary from third parties that supports the argument of MS. Other extracts have been used to demonstrate the argument of MS. In keeping with mainstream academic manuscripts, this research uses the 2014 UK Government 'Exceptions to copyright guidance' for the use of some third party evidence quoted in the text, which states:

Overview

"Details of the exceptions to copyright that allow limited use of copyright works without the permission of the copyright owner.

As well as owning copyright works yourself, you may wish to make use of someone else's copyright protected works. There are certain very specific situations where you may be permitted to do so without seeking permission from the owner. These can be found in the copyright sections of the Copyright, Designs and Patents Act 1988 (as amended)…

Criticism, review and reporting current events

Fair dealing for criticism, review or quotation is allowed for any type of copyright work. Fair dealing with a work for the purpose of reporting current events is allowed for any type of copyrighted work other than a photograph. In each of these cases, a sufficient acknowledgement will be required…

Fair dealing

Certain exceptions only apply if the use of the work is a 'fair dealing'. For example, the exceptions relating to research and private study, criticism or review, or news reporting.

'Fair dealing' is a legal term used to establish whether a use of copyright material is lawful or whether it infringes copyright. There is **no statutory definition*** of fair dealing - it will always be a matter of fact, degree and impression in each case. The question to be asked is: how would a fair-minded and honest person have dealt with the work?

Factors that have been identified by the courts as relevant in determining whether a particular dealing with a work is fair include:

- does using the work affect the market for the original work? If a use of a work acts as a substitute for it, causing the owner to lose revenue, then it is not likely to be fair

- is the amount of the work taken reasonable and appropriate? Was it necessary to use the amount that was taken? Usually only part of a work may be used."

https://www.gov.uk/guidance/exceptions-to-copyright

* My emphasis. MS.

APPENDIX 2

Disability News Service

John Pring is the disabled Editor of Disability News Service, which is the UK's only disability news agency. John's work is highly valued by the nation's chronically sick and disabled people, he regularly offers a voice to disabled activists who oppose the government's welfare reforms and this list demonstrates some of John's significant work relevant to the book content. I am grateful to John for his kind permission for me to collate extracts from his work.

**This list includes the latest deeply disturbing evidence, exposed by John in November 2015, (11, 12) identifying the fact that Coroners have been warning DWP Ministers since 2010 that the Work Capability Assessment is <u>a risk to the lives </u>of people diagnosed with serious mental health problems and this legally imperative information has been totally <u>disregarded by Ministers and by the DWP.</u>

1. ***Insurance giant denies welfare reform will boost profits: 9th October 2011***

   The UK's largest provider of "income protection insurance" (IPI) has denied that it stands to gain financially from incapacity benefit reforms that campaigners believe it helped to influence.

   Unum launched a major media campaign this year aimed at persuading more working individuals to ask their employers to provide them with IPI, which is intended to pay out if they become disabled or ill and are unable to work.

   But questions have been raised because the start of Unum's campaign coincided with the launch of the government's three-year programme to reassess about 1.5 million claimants of old-style incapacity benefit through a new, stricter test.

   Campaigners believe tougher welfare rules could persuade more people to take out IPI.

   http://www.disabilitynewsservice.com/insurance-giant-denies-welfare-reform-will-boost-its-profits/

2 ***New evidence of corporate giant's influence on welfare reform: 1ˢᵗ November 2011***

New evidence suggests that an insurance giant that could make huge financial gains from government reform of incapacity benefit played a much larger part in influencing those reforms than previously admitted…

But now a detailed memo has emerged, which was submitted to the Commons work and pensions committee in 2002 and was written by Joanne Hindle, Unum's corporate services director.

In the memo, Unum calls for a fundamental reform of the welfare system, while it says the government "must ensure both that work always pays more than benefits, and more importantly that it is clearly seen to do so."

The memo includes proposals with a strong resemblance to reforms introduced several years later by the Labour government, when it replaced IB with ESA.

http://www.disabilitynewsservice.com/new-evidence-of-corporate-giants-influence-on-welfare-reform/

3. ***Politicians and DWP combine to block answers on Unum links: 2ⁿᵈ January 2012***

The Department for Work and Pensions (DWP) and the three main political parties are refusing to say how often ministers have met with an insurance company set to make huge financial gains from incapacity benefit reform…

Anger over IB reform has grown over the last 18 months, with claims that the coalition's changes – which are even harsher than those introduced by the Labour government – are merely a cover for cuts to welfare spending and are plunging tens of thousands of disabled people further into poverty and distress.

The disabled activist who has done most to raise concerns about the suitability of Unum to be advising the government and its influence within the DWP is Mo Stewart, a retired healthcare professional and veteran of the Women's Royal Air Force.

She said: "Given the diabolical reputation of this company in America, it is a huge concern that the UK government would take advice from such a discredited insurance company as Unum, and someone should surely be asking why this corporate giant has had such influence with the DWP since 1994."

http://www.disabilitynewsservice.com/politicians-and-dwp-combine-to-block-answers-on-unum-links/

4. *Government silent over adviser's Unum admission: 2nd February 2012*

A disabled senior government adviser has admitted failing to tell civil servants about freelance work she carried out for an insurance giant that is set to make millions from the coalition's incapacity benefit (IB) reforms.

Dr Rachel Perkins, chair of the government's Equality 2025 high-level advisory body of disabled people, ran a half-day training event in late 2010 for nurses and occupational therapists employed by the US company Unum.

But she has so far failed to declare this paid work in the Equality 2025 register of interests, even though the event took place several months after she was appointed to the body, although before she became its chair in March 2011.

http://www.disabilitynewsservice.com/government-silent-over-advisers-unum-admission/

5. *ODI gives green light to advisors to work secretly for insurance giant: 4th March 2012*

The Office for Disability Issues (ODI) has angered disabled activists after stating that its own disability advisers do not notify civil servants if they work for the company set to make millions from incapacity benefit reform.

In a response provided under the Freedom of Information Act, ODI claimed there was no conflict of interest involved in a member of Equality 2025 – the government's high-level advisory body of disabled people – working for the insurance giant Unum…

She said the ODI – part of the DWP – was aware that Perkins had delivered a training session to Unum staff, but said that the company "has no financial or commercial links" with DWP.'

http://www.disabilitynewsservice.com/odi-gives-green-light-to-advisors-to-work-secretly-for-insurance-giant/

6. *Former DWP medical boss makes WCA pledge to protesters: 14th September 2012*

…Sir Mansel is closely associated with the biopsychosocial (BPS) model, which campaigners say puts much of the blame for disability on the disabled person, rather than the social model explanation, which says disability is created by the barriers of attitude and environment disabled people face.

A small group of protesters delivered a copy of a letter written to the Guardian newspaper – signed by 420 disabled people, including many leading activists – to Sir Mansel, outside the hall where he had given his speech.

The letter claims the BPS model is "nothing short of a creation of the insurance industry", and is being used to deny disabled people the support they need through the benefits system…

He added: "I think I am a man of integrity. If I think the WCA is not proper I will speak out against it."

Sir Mansel said he sympathised with the protesters, and himself now found the BPS model "*unsatisfactory*" and believed it "*no longer addresses the real needs of disabled people and the exclusion of disabled people from society*"…

The issue of which explanatory "model" to use is important partly because the government's welfare reform minister, Lord Freud, has said that the new assessment of disabled people's eligibility for personal independence payment – the replacement for disability living allowance – will be based on a BPS approach and not the social model.

http://www.disabilitynewsservice.com/former-dwp-medical-boss-makes-wca-pledge-to-protesters/

7. ***Concern over DR UK director's links with insurance investigators: 1ˢᵗ February 2013***

The country's most influential disabled people's organisation is facing fresh controversy after it emerged that one of its directors works for a company that carries out secret surveillance on claimants of disability insurance.

John Gillman is a non-executive director of Disability Rights Enterprises (DRE), the trading arm of Disability Rights UK (DR UK), and held a similar post for three years with RADAR, one of the three organisations that merged to form DR UK last year.

But research by disabled activist Mike Bach* has revealed that Gillman is also a consultant, and a former non-executive director, with Health Claims Bureau (HCB), a company which provides "impartial claims inspection services for disability insurers"…

HCB is also controversial because of its links with the US insurance giant Unum, which has been criticised for influencing welfare reform in the UK over the last two decades and then profiting from resulting policies…

Mo Stewart, the disabled activist who has done most to highlight concerns about Unum, said she was concerned to learn that "a professional involved with DR UK is also involved with the Health Claims Bureau, and I would have thought that such a link gives the impression at least of a conflict of interest."

She said: "DR UK leads the country in disability rights publications, whereas any company involved with the 'secret surveillance' of disabled people is clearly working for the best interests of the healthcare insurance industry."

*[Mike Bach was the Webmaster for *Why Wait Forever* who shared his website with MS. Mike died in February 2015.]
http://www.disabilitynewsservice.com/concern-over-dr-uk-directors-links-with-insurance-investigators/

8. *Unum bragged about 'driving government thinking' on incapacity benefit reform: 15th February 2013*

"… DNS has secured a copy of a Unum document on the assessment of "incapacity", which was published in 2005.

The document was written by Dr Michael O'Donnell*, then the company's chief medical officer and now in the same role at Atos Healthcare, which carries out WCAs on behalf of the government. O'Donnell says in the document that Unum has "always been at the leading edge of disability assessment and management".

He adds: "We know that our views and understanding are not yet in the mainstream of doctors' thinking, but Government Policy is moving in the same direction, to a large extent being driven by our thinking and that of our close associates, both in the UK and overseas." …

Mo Stewart, the disabled activist who has done most to highlight concerns about Unum, said the new evidence was "very significant", and called for an independent inquiry into the role of the company in influencing UK welfare reform, particularly when it had such a "disturbing past history." …

She added: "The WCA is a replica of the assessment system used by Unum to resist funding insurance claimants.

"It is a bogus, dangerous assessment and, with this evidence, it is now time that this DWP medical tyranny was ended."

*[O'Donnell is now working as the medical director for Health Management Ltd, a subsidiary of Maximus, who replaced Atos and have carried out the WCA since March 2015. MS]
http://www.disabilitynewsservice.com/unum-bragged-about-driving-government-thinking-on-incapacity-benefit-reform/

9. *Anger over user-led charity's links with insurance industry: 7th November 2014*

…Disability News Service (DNS) reported last week that Disability Rights UK (DR UK) was under fire for agreeing to work with the US outsourcing giant Maximus, which the government has selected to take over the controversial "fitness for work" contract from Atos Healthcare…

The new Seven Families initiative will see seven disabled people who have been forced to quit their jobs being handed the same amount of money - every month, for one year – that they would have received if they had taken out an income protection insurance *(IPI) policy…

Activists believe that the outsourcing company Atos has made IPI look more attractive by ensuring that the process of applying for ESA – through the work capability assessment (WCA) – has been harsh and stressful.

Linda Burnip, a member of the steering group of Disabled People Against Cuts, said that the organisations DR UK was working with were intent on undermining the welfare state. She said: "I can see, given the state of their finances, that if they want to continue in existence they are going to have to take anything they can get, but I don't think they are representing disabled people." …

Burnip added: "The problem is that the more this idea of private healthcare and private welfare is pushed… the more the welfare state is going to be dismantled bit by bit." One of the companies supporting Seven Families is the US insurance giant Unum, the UK's largest provider of IPI, which was once described by a senior US official as an "outlaw company."

[*Unum Insurance removed their IPI policies from the open market in 2012 due to claimed "*relentless negative publicity*". MS]

http://www.disabilitynewsservice.com/anger-user-led-charitys-links-insurance-industry/

10. *History month launch hears of Cameron's 'broken promise' to disabled veterans: 21st November 2014*

…David Cameron made headlines in July 2012 when he pledged in a speech at Camp Bastion in Afghanistan that seriously wounded veterans would be exempt from controversial reforms to replace working-age disability living allowance (DLA) with the new personal independence payment (PIP)…

Cameron was reported as saying that "the military are going to have a special set of circumstances so they get a special deal. I intervened to make sure that happens and I think that is one of the many ways we should respect our armed services for what they do for us."

But researcher and campaigner Mo Stewart told this week's launch event of UK Disability History Month – which this year has a theme of "war and impairment" – that war pensioners had assumed that all disabled veterans would be exempt and retain access to DLA.

But she said it had now been confirmed that Cameron's promise only applied to "modern veterans" – all those given an award under the armed forces compensation scheme, which replaced the war pension scheme in 2005.

This means that about 80,000 working-age war pensioners currently claiming disability living allowance will eventually have to be reassessed for PIP, and will risk losing some or all of their benefits…

She said: "All disabled veterans were disabled serving this nation and all war pensioners should be treated the same, regardless of age, and be allowed to retain the promised access to DLA for life." …

http://www.disabilitynewsservice.com/history-month-launch-hears-camerons-broken-promise-disabled-veterans/

11. *WCA death scandal: Grayling ordered assessment roll-out, despite coroner's warning. 9th November 2015*

…an investigation by Disability News Service (DNS) suggests that Duncan Smith and Grayling – who is now leader of the House of Commons – should have been aware of a legal letter written by coroner Tom Osborne in the wake of the suicide of a disabled man, Stephen Carre, in January 2010.

The letter – written under Rule 43 of the Coroner's Rules, which were updated in 2013 – said Carre's death was triggered by being found "fit for work", and it called for a review of the policy not to seek medical evidence from a GP or psychiatrist if the claimant has a mental health condition...

Grayling and Duncan Smith made the decision that they would go ahead with the roll-out of the WCA in the spring of 2011, even though Osborne had written directly to the Department for Work and Pensions (DWP), just before the 2010 election, with his warning about the assessment...

Under the Coroner's Rules, DWP had just 56 days to respond to the coroner – taking the deadline for a response to late May 2010 – which Osborne pointed out in his Rule 43 letter.

But despite a legal obligation to respond, and explain what action they planned to take – or explain why they were not taking any action – ministers appear never to have replied to the letter.

That summer, Grayling appointed Professor Malcolm Harrington to carry out an independent review of the "fairness and effectiveness" of the WCA, and later told him that he wanted to go ahead with plans to roll out the WCA, despite Harrington suggesting that the roll-out <u>should be delayed by a year</u>...

<u>http://www.disabilitynewsservice.com/wca-death-scandal-grayling-ordered-assessment-roll-out-despite-coroners-warning/</u>

12. *WCA death scandal: Ministers 'failed to pass 2010 suicide report to Harrington'. 9ᵗʰ November 2015*

Ministers appear to have failed to hand a crucial report about the work capability assessment – warning it put at risk the lives of thousands of people with mental health conditions – to the expert they commissioned to review the test...

It is the second letter uncovered by DNS to have been written by a coroner to warn about the failure to seek further medical evidence when assessing the fitness for work of someone with a mental health condition, and was written more than three years before a similar report into the death of Michael O'Sullivan, from north London...

And the letter does not appear to have been passed by ministers to Professor Malcolm Harrington, who was appointed by Grayling to review the "fairness and effectiveness" of the WCA for the government in late June 2010...

The office of the coroner who wrote the report, Tom Osborne, has not yet been able to confirm whether he received a response, because the relevant files are being retrieved from the archives…

Osborne's Rule 43 letter emerged through a freedom of information request by DNS to the Ministry of Justice.

The request was submitted after DNS uncovered a coroner's report written in January 2014, following the death of Michael O'Sullivan, a father-of-two from north London, which said that the decision to take his own life had been triggered by being found fit for work.

http://www.disabilitynewsservice.com/wca-death-scandal-ministers-failed-to-pass-2010-suicide-report-to-harrington/

APPENDIX 3

Vox Political by Mike Sivier

Mike Sivier is a professional freelance journalist, the carer for his disabled wife and the Editor of Vox Political, which is a leading light in the efforts to expose the ongoing government tyranny as it manipulates the general public via the national press.

Mike had the courage to expose the influence of Unum Insurance with the UK government, to publish the research of MS to bring the evidence to a wider audience and, especially, to offer his able bodied readers an alternative to the government propaganda against sick and disabled people. It's good to know we still have journalists in the UK who will expose reality, and not the government's latest script, and I thank Mike for his kind permission for me to collate extracts from his work.

1. *Here's why Labour needs to go a lot further to win back our trust: 22nd Sept 2013*

Only days after Ed Miliband announced a Labour government would sack Atos, the party's conference is hosting an event part-funded by the architects of the 'work capability assessment' administered by that company – the criminal American insurance giant Unum.

'*New thinking on the welfare state*' is a fringe event taking place at the Labour conference on Monday, September 23, organised by the *right-wing* thinktank Reform (which has Unum as one of its funders) and sponsored by the Association of British Insurers (which includes Unum amongst its members). Does anybody doubt that it has been arranged in order to give Unum a chance to influence high-ranking party members? No?

Then consider: This is a *private* round-table policy seminar, staged by Anne McGuire MP. Rank and file Labour members aren't invited – attendance is by invitation only. Can you smell a rat? Still no?

The event has already been staged at the Liberal Democrat conference, and will also be a feature of the Conservative Party conference… It shouldn't take a genius to work out that Unum wants to ensure that all three parties have the same social security/welfare policy, going into the next election – and that Unum continues to figure prominently in the formulation of that policy…

It is the policy itself that must change…

149

That's why Mo Stewart, the retired healthcare professional and disability researcher who has spent four years examining the relationship between Unum and the UK government, has contacted Ms McGuire, demanding to know why she is having anything to do with the firm. She wrote: "Given the amount of evidence against the practice of the dangerous corporate giant, Unum Insurance, and the fact that Labour MPs have exposed their influence with government during debate, the British disabled community are wondering why you would chose to host a fringe meeting by Unum at the conference on Monday?

"New Thinking on the Welfare State" it seems is the title of the meeting, and they should know since Unum have been helping to systematically destroy the welfare state, as welcomed by various governments, since 1994.

"If you were planning to cause offence, you couldn't have done a better job.

"Keep betraying the British disabled people and you'll be waiting in the wings for a lot longer before Labour ever return to Government. I have spent the past 4 years exposing the links between the DWP, Atos Healthcare and UNUM Insurance. Some of your colleagues are very familiar with my work, which is to be considered by the UN within weeks, and I suggest that if you wish to be taken seriously as the Shadow Minister for Disabled People then you need to be familiar with that evidence." …

https://mikesivier.wordpress.com/2013/09/22/heres-why-labour-needs-to-go-a-lot-further-to-win-back-our-trust/

2. *UK government refuses to accept responsibility for identified crimes against humanity: 9th April 2014*

A guest report by Mo Stewart

Following the bogus Work Capability Assessment (WCA) conducted by Atos Healthcare, as contracted by the Department for Work and Pensions (DWP), the United Kingdom (UK) Government admitted that it was wrong to cut the disability benefits of Mark Wood, the vulnerable disabled man **who starved to death** following the removal of his benefits, in the 21st century UK, when weighing only 5st 8lbs.

Regardless of this tragedy, the UK Conservative led Coalition Government **still refuses to accept any responsibility.**

Despite the fact that the WCA was introduced by the Labour Government in 2008, it was originally designed by previous Conservative governments, in consultation with the notorious American corporate giant now known as Unum Insurance, identified in 2008 by the American Association for Justice as **the second most discredited insurance company in America.**

Without a welfare state, sick and disabled people in America are required to use private healthcare insurance. The tyranny now imposed on the sick and disabled people in the UK, using the WCA, was designed in consultation with Unum Insurance to oblige the general public to purchase private healthcare insurance policies once it was made very clear that chronically sick and disabled people could no longer rely on the British State for adequate financial support.

Due to the similarities of the negative and damaging experiences of claimants, American sick and disabled people are periodically informed about the struggle in the UK by the high calibre and relentless work of Linda Nee, who tries to encourage claimants to publicly protest as witnessed in the UK, which it seems disabled Americans still don't dare to do – such is the intimidation of Unum Insurance & the American authorities.

The new report by The Mental Health Welfare Commission for Scotland, regarding a woman's suicide after being 'stripped of disability benefits', was reported by John Pring at the Disability News Service (DNS) and by many others. The Coalition Government knew this carnage would happen."…

https://mikesivier.wordpress.com/2014/04/09/uk-government-refuses-to-accept-responsibility-for-crimes-against-humanity/

3. *'It's cheaper to help people die rather than support them to live': 13th July 2014*

A "change of heart" by a former Archbishop of Canterbury over 'assisted dying' has dismayed at least one campaigner for the rights of people with disabilities.

Mo Stewart has been researching and reporting what she describes as the "atrocities" against the chronically sick and disabled [people] in the UK for the last four years. She said Lord Carey's decision to support legislation that would make it legal for people in England and Wales to receive help to end their lives would "play right into the hands of this very, very dangerous government".

Justifying his change in position, Lord Carey said: "Today we face a central paradox. In strictly observing the sanctity of life, the Church could now actually be promoting anguish and pain, the very opposite of a Christian message of hope.

"The old philosophical certainties have collapsed in the face of the reality of needless suffering."

The Assisted Dying Bill, tabled by Labour's Lord Falconer, would apply to people with less than six months to live. Two doctors would have to independently confirm the patient was terminally ill and had reached their own, informed decision to die.

But Mo Stewart warned that the proposed legislation, to be debated in the House of Lords on Friday, would be subject to unscrupulous authorities taking advantage of people with depression in order to relieve themselves of the financial burden of paying for their care.

"If this law is granted, what will be deemed a possibility for the few will, very quickly I fear, become the expected for the many," she wrote in a letter to Lord Carey which she has kindly provided for *Vox Political…*.

She pointed out that medicine is an inexact science and policy changes such as this could have an enormous detrimental impact: "My own Webmaster, who is now desperately ill with possibly only weeks to live, was advised he had less than six months to live over four years ago.

"Until very recently, he still enjoyed a high quality of life with his wife, family and friends; a life that could have been removed four years ago" had the Assisted Dying Bill been law at that time…

Mo Stewart's letter concludes: "In the real world, this Bill – if passed – would, I have no doubt, lead to abuses where some were actively persuaded to self-terminate for the convenience, and possibly the inheritance, of others.

"It's really not a very long way away from an assisted dying bill to an assisted suicide bill."

https://mikesivier.wordpress.com/2014/07/13/it-is-cheaper-to-help-people-die-rather-than-support-them-to-live/

APPENDIX 4

Private Eye

Whilst the entire national press resisted all attempts to expose the realities behind the planned future welfare reforms, and the influence of a notorious American healthcare insurance giant with the UK government, *Private Eye* was the one publication, since 1995, who kept exposing what was to come. *Private Eye* should be congratulated and thanked and I am grateful to the *Eye* for their kind permission for me to collate some of their articles.

1. ***Private Eye: Mutual Benefits: Issue 1301, p28,* November 2011**

    Tricky questions are again being asked about the profits American insurance giant Unum stands to make from its massive media push on income protection cover, promoted as the answer to the latest tough welfare reforms.

    Pulling stunts like persuading six bloggers to live for a week on the current average benefit of £95 and then write about it, Jack McGarry, chief executive at Unum UK, earlier this year warned: "The government's welfare reform bill will seek to tighten the gateway to benefits for those people unable to work due to sickness or injury. Each year up to 1m people in the UK become disabled and the reforms mean that working people will be able to rely less on state benefits to maintain the standard of living they were used to prior to their illness."

    Well, Unum should know. Behind the scenes it has been helping Tory and Labour governments slash the benefits of disabled and sick people for years – going right back to Peter Lilley's social security "Incapacity for Work" reforms of 1994. Lilley hired John LoCascio, then vice-president of Unum, to advise on "claims management". Lo Cascio also sat on the "medical evaluation group", which – according to Professor Jonathan Rutherford in the academic journal Soundings – was set up to design and enforce more stringent medical tests.

    At the same time, the UK wing of Unum was launching what it boasted was "a concerted effort to harness the potential" from predicted cuts in benefits, urging people to protect themselves with a "long-term disability policy from Unum..."

    Reproduced by kind permission of Private Eye magazine

    http://www.private-eye.co.uk/sections.php?section_link=in_the_back&issue=1301&article=450

2. ***Private Eye: Disabled Veterans Atossed Aside: Issue 1302, p31*** **November 2011**

While ministers deny leaks that wounded and injured soldiers are about to be sacked as part of the defence cuts, it's worth recalling the thousands cut down in their prime who are already "War Pensioners"...

They're also at the mercy of the Department for Work and Pensions' latest tick-box assessment scheme. The process – operated by French outsourcing company Atos – has been condemned by MPs, charities and others for getting it wrong in up to 40 percent of cases and causing "fear, anxiety and distress" to many.

They include people like Mo Stewart, a retired healthcare professional and WRAF "pensioner"... She became a disabled rights activist after what she understood to be a review of her deteriorating condition was carried out by Atos, instead of her former military medical colleagues.

"I was a lone, disabled woman and this Atos doctor actually refused to offer any form of ID, resisted eye contact, treated me with contempt and then provided a totally bogus medical report, claiming to have examined me when no examination was undertaken", she says. "I decided that I had to expose this nightmare to protect other disabled veterans."...

The former airwoman has now compiled an impressive dossier documenting both Atos and American Insurance giant Unum's involvement in welfare reform (see last *Eye*), set out on her *"Why Wait Forever"* website. Last week she sent the *Eye* a lengthy Unum memo, which revealed how it had cosied up to Labour ahead of its controversial reforms to reduce incapacity benefit with the introduction of the far more stringent work capability assessment. It said its experience was that most disabled people are capable of some work, labelling them "unemployed inactives"...

Reproduced by kind permission of Private Eye magazine

http://blacktrianglecampaign.org/2011/11/23/private-eye-atossed-aside/

3. ***Private Eye: Unum Ad Nauseam: Issue 1300, p13*** **October 2011**

With its "Back-up Plan" currently airing during Downtown Abbey ad breaks and in other peak viewing slots on ITV and Channel 4, insurer Unum is pushing its income protection insurance hard.

This push is also helped by The Guardian whose ongoing Work Life UK feature is produced "in association with Unum" with plenty of scare stories about employees stricken by injury or illness that prevent them from working. There is even an official @unumGDN Twitter feed.

There is no mention in all the Guardian coverage, however, of a 2009 report by the American Association of Justice, (the huge US association of trial lawyers), which rated Tennessee based Unum the second worse insurance company in the US, based on a history of claims handling abuses that have "consistently been the subject of regulator and media investigation."

After Unum turned down nearly a quarter of all claims in California, the state's department of insurance investigated in 2005, finding that the firm "systematically violated state insurance regulations and fraudulently denied or low balled claims using phony medical reports, policy misrepresentation and biased investigations". California insurance commissioner John Garamendi has described Unum as an "outlaw company."

Reproduced by kind permission of Private Eye magazine

http://blacktrianglecampaign.org/2011/10/28/private-eye-again-unum-ad-nauseam/

4. *Private Eye: Fit-For-Work-Tests : Issue 1306, p29* **2012**

IN THE *Eye*'s growing post-bag of appalling decisions made by French service company Atos in assessing sick and disabled people as being "fit for work", one of the most shocking concerns Keith Tilbury.

Mr Tilbury spent 13 days in a coma fighting for his life after he was accidentally shot in the stomach by a police firearms officer...

Since that disaster in 2007, Mr Tilbury has suffered two heart attacks, two while undergoing surgery, a quadruple coronary bypass, two transient ischemic attacks (mini-strokes), one full-blown stroke resulting in reduced vision in his eyes, post-operative complications – and post-traumatic stress disorder...

Given his well-documented health records, Mr Tilbury, who had been an emergency call centre operator, is trying to establish how on earth an Atos nurse or doctor – he's not sure which – could decide that he is fit to work without *"dropping down dead"* when there has been no improvement in his health since his last assessment.

Like thousands of others, Mr Tilbury is having to go through the ordeal of appealing against the decision. He sees the box-ticking Atos test – drawn up with the help of US insurance giant Unum, which was fined millions in the US for cheating its clients – as no more than a government tool to slash the benefits of people who through no fault of their own can no longer work.

As the *Eye* has extensively reported (see issues 874, 1300, 1301 and 1302) Unum has been helping both Tory and Labour governments with so-called welfare reform, going right back to Peter Lilley's 1994 social security "Incapacity for Work" shake-up.

Atos, which boasts that its contract with the current government is worth "approximately £100m a year", happened to be the only other private company sitting alongside Unum on the then Labour government's panel which reviewed and came up with the hated "work capability test" which is now failing Mr Tilbury and thousands like him…

There is no point in subjecting people with permanent disability to regular assessments and those whose conditions do improve would welcome reform – and indeed assessments – if they were simplified and considered robust, fair and transparent. But as Mr Tilbury and so many like him have found, the government's work and capability tests, delivered by Atos, is none of those things…"

Reproduced by kind permission of Private Eye magazine

https://beastrabban.wordpress.com/2015/01/20/from-2012-private-eye-on-bad-atos-decisions-and-flawed-government-reports/

5. ***Private Eye: Paul Foot on the insurance company Unum and cuts to disability benefit as reported in Private Eye in 1995: Issue 874, p26* 1995**

… Founded in Portland, Maine, in 1848, the Unum Corporation describes itself as "the world's leading light in disability insurance." Unum Ltd, its British arm, is based in Dorking, Surrey. It issued its annual report last September, when chairman Ward E. Graffam enthused about "exciting developments" in Britain.

He explained: "the impending changes to the State ill-health benefits system heralded in the November 1993 Budget will create unique sales opportunities across the entire disability market and we will be launching a concerted effort to harness the potential in these". In January, the full extent of Lilley's plans to replace invalidity benefit with incapacity benefit was revealed to the Commons. Estimated "savings" for the year

1995-1996 were £410 million; for 1996-97 £1.2 billion; and for 1997-98 an astonishing £1.7billion... One Unum ad warned: "April 13, unlucky for some. Because tomorrow the new rules on state incapacity benefit announced in the 1993 autumn budget come into effect. Which means that if you fall ill and have to rely on state incapacity benefit, you could be in serious trouble". Lurid tables estimating weekly outgoings for an average family at £276, and benefit under the new rules at £100, urged people to "protect yourself with a Long Term Disability policy from Unum"...

The most famous of the [incapacity benefit medical valuation group] group is John Lo Cascio, second vice-president of the Unum Corporation, who has recently been seconded by the company's British arm. Dr LoCascio was also invited last year by Lilley's department to help in the extensive training of doctors in the new techniques of testing. The DSS stresses that "the doctors don't decide the incapacity benefit – that is done by the Adjudicating officer". No doubt, but the officer makes a decision on the expert medical information provided by the tests. No press release was issued about Dr LoCascio's appointment. No one told taxpayers that the DSS is shelling out £40,000 to Unum Ltd for Dr LoCascio's services in the year from October 1994 to September this year. A DSS spokeswoman explained: "this comes down basically to a daily rate of £440 a day. That's cheap for a consultancy actually"...

The use by the government of a private company, in this case Unum that stands to profit from cuts to the welfare system and the recruitment of a new corps of professionals by BAMS to make the tests more difficult. The only difference is that BAMS has now gone and been replaced by ATOS. It's another example of the way Blair merely inherited and developed a system that was put forward by the Tories."

Reproduced by kind permission of Private Eye magazine

https://beastrabban.wordpress.com/2013/08/12/paul-foot-on-the-insurance-company-unum-and-cuts-to-disability-benefit-in-private-eye-from-1995/

APPENDIX 5

The Ekklesia blog by Bernadette Meaden

Bernadette Meaden is an Associate of the Ekklesia think-tank and an author of significant commentary on the social security policies of the UK government, and their consequences on the most vulnerable citizens of this once great nation. I thank Ekklesia for their kind permission for me to collate extracts from Bernadette's commentary.

1. *Suicides and the WCA: How much more evidence does the government want?*: **17th November 2015**

   … **'In total, across England as a whole, the WCA disability reassessment process during this period was associated with an additional 590 suicides.'**

   An academic study of the impact of the Work Capability Assessment published today (17th November) confirms what people and campaigners have been saying for years. It is associated with many deaths, and has had a catastrophic impact on the mental health of disabled people.

   The report, published in the Journal of Epidemiology and Community Health, makes grim reading. It states: 'The programme of reassessing people on disability benefits using the Work Capability Assessment was independently associated with an increase in suicides, self-reported mental health problems and antidepressant prescribing. This policy may have had serious adverse consequences for mental health in England, which could outweigh any benefits that arise from moving people off disability benefits.' And as if that wasn't enough; 'The reassessment process was associated with the greatest increase in these adverse mental health outcomes in the most deprived areas of the country, widening health inequalities.'

   During the General Election campaign, in a live television debate, Iain Duncan Smith was challenged about the number of deaths and suicides linked to welfare reform. The Secretary of State denied any such link, and called the suggestion 'scurrilous', warning the Green Party's Jonathan Bartley to 'be very careful' about making such 'cast off allegations.'…

   This report has grave implications for the government, but also, as the report points out, for the healthcare professionals who are recruited on very good salaries to carry out the assessments; 'Given that doctors and other health professionals have professional and statutory duties to promote the health of patients and the public, our evidence that this process is potentially harming the recipients of these assessments raises major ethical issues for those involved.'…   http://www.ekklesia.co.uk/node/22321

*[NB: **The academics have made reasonable but incorrect assumptions.** Regardless of damning evidence, the government will continue to disregard all evidence against the WCA. According to the General Medical Council, the company (previously Atos and now Maximus) '…have total immunity from all medical regulation' and the company insists that doctors working for the company are 'trained in disability.' As established in my earlier research, the protocol for the WCA insist that the healthcare professionals conducting the WCA are conducting a 'functional assessment' and are 'not making a diagnosis.' Claimants are referred to as 'customers' not patients. QED regardless of increasing numbers of deaths directly related to the WCA, neither the company nor the doctors conducting the (totally bogus) WCA 'assessment' are directly accountable for the preventable harm it has created. MS.]*

2. ***Malingering, illness deception and disability benefit reforms* : 1ˢᵗ June 2015**

   To understand the thinking behind the reform of disability benefits, we need to look at a Conference held in 2001, called 'Malingering and illness deception'. The Conference papers were later published as a book, in which 'the enthusiastic support of Professor Mansel Aylward [then Chief Medical Officer at the DWP] and funding from the Department for Work and Pensions' was acknowledged.

   The book 'Malingering and illness deception' gives a revealing insight into the thinking which eventually led to the Work Capability Assessment, and the reform of Incapacity Benefit.

   One chapter asks, 'Can monkeys malinger? And, from observations of 'genuinely disabled' great apes whose hands have been maimed, notes that, with no help from their able-bodied fellows, (perhaps because they get no help) they overcome their impairments to a great extent. They conclude that for both apes and humans, it is possible to be disabled without being handicapped**.**

The authors go on to suggest that, in human society, it may be better not to even try to decide who is guilty of intentional malingering and deception, but to 'simply change the pay-off matrix' to discourage malingering.

So in other words, if we make being sick or disabled more difficult, if we provide less assistance or support, it will have a deterrent effect. When there is less to be gained by being sick or disabled, malingering will be a much less attractive option. Treat the genuine and the malingerers in the same way. That may strike a chord with many disabled people who now live in fear of a brown envelope from the DWP.

This concern about malingering arose because the DWP seemed to believe that, as medicine had advanced and people were living longer, rising numbers of claims for incapacity benefit indicated that "inappropriate illness behaviours" must be a significant problem…

Because the DWP ignored such evidence and pursued its own agenda, Griffiths says, "The health needs of people who are the subject of huge investment by the Department of Health have been treated counterproductively as invisible, or worse, as malingering, by the DWP and successive Work and Pensions ministers driven by a compulsion to judge and to privatise." He sees this as "a failure of compassion, unacknowledged incompetence and injustice on a massive scale: a social policy tragedy."

I am indebted to disability researcher Mo Stewart for alerting me to the two publications quoted. http://www.ekklesia.co.uk/node/2171

3. ***The truth about spending on disability benefits – it's halved:*** **27th May 2015**
When the ongoing process of cutting and restricting access to disability benefits began, we were told it was necessary because spending on them was out of control. A new report from the Institute of Fiscal Studies (IFS) shows that, in fact, the exact opposite is the case.

The report says that spending on disability benefits last year was 0.8 per cent of national income, and say, "this is half the level of disability benefit when at its peak in 1995-96."

So the peak for spending on disability benefits occurred under the Conservative government of John Major. The narrative that the Labour government allowed such spending to get out of control is false – as a percentage of our national income it actually fell during those years.

The report makes another point which disproves the rhetoric about large numbers of scroungers and malingerers who could work, but prefer to claim disability benefits.

Whilst the overall number of individuals receiving disability benefits has fallen only slightly since the mid-1990s, *"...this is in the presence of underlying demographic change that would have tended to push up the numbers receiving considerably – both overall population growth and the baby boomer generation reaching older working ages. The proportion of older men receiving disability benefits has actually fallen sharply since the mid-1990s... Disability benefit receipt among men increases much less steeply with age than it used to."* http://www.ekklesia.co.uk/node/21740

4. ***People with disabilities, the DWP and the struggle ahead.*** **17th May 2015**

In the last Parliament, people with disabilities who challenged government cuts were labelled extremists. Political opposition was weakened by a fear of being seen as on the side of 'scroungers'. But with more cuts coming, perhaps that is about to change. As more and more lives are affected, awareness of just how bad these policies are is growing.

Jane Hawking, ex-wife of Stephen Hawking, now fears for the future of her autistic grandson. She has said, "Being Stephen's carer was such a struggle… Thinking back, I honestly wonder how I got through it. But what you hope is that the years since have brought improvements to the lives of disabled people and their carers, and I think for a while it was like that. But now the clock is turning back, and we can't let that happen."

The way the Department for Work and Pensions (DWP) treats sick and disabled people is increasingly cruel, perverse and contradictory. It talks about getting disabled people into work. Even people who are currently deemed too ill or disabled to work face benefit sanctions if the DWP deems they are not trying hard enough to get themselves closer to the jobs market. http://www.ekklesia.co.uk/node/21711

5. ***Far from rethinking sanctions, IDS plans to extend them.*** **24th March 2015**

By publishing today's report on benefit sanctions it feels as if the Department for Work and Pensions Select Committee has caught up with what the churches, campaign organisations and benefit claimants have been saying for a long time.

The current sanctions regime is punitive, unfair, and in some tragic cases, lethal. But far from rethinking sanctions, Iain Duncan Smith has plans to extend them to the working poor.

One report after another has shown how sanctions do very little to increase chances of getting a job (though they may remove them from the unemployment figures). Drive up the need for foodbanks and often target the most disadvantaged claimants.

The words 'inhumane' and 'un-Christian' have been used, and it is difficult to see any reason why sanctions should not be scrapped altogether, rather than having further enquiries whilst people continue to suffer.

Officially, the DWP expects sanctions to cause a deterioration in the health of the claimant. This is surely a violation of human rights? One hopes that in the UK we would not consider it acceptable if convicted criminals were starved as a punishment, so why should we accept it as punishment for being late for a Jobcentre appointment?

Now that the truth about sanctions is so clear, there's an urgent needed to make the public aware that, far from rethinking sanctions, as the churches and others have asked, under Universal Credit, sanctions will be applied not only to the unemployed, sick and disabled, but also to the working poor.

As Welfare Weekly reported last November, "Iain Duncan Smith told the Work and Pensions Select Committee that trials were being carried out in parts of the North-West of England, on removing benefits from part-time workers who refuse to take on extra hours." …

"However, the Department for Work and Pensions has confirmed to Inside Housing that under the government's flagship welfare reform, where a tenant is working less than 35 hours a week at minimum wage and is not eligible for JSA or ESA, the housing element can be sanctioned instead."

So we will have scenarios where a part time worker, who may be combining a job with caring responsibilities, will come under pressure from the DWP to increase their hours, or get another job, and face sanctions if they fail to do so.

This expansion of the sanctions system clearly has the potential to cause hardship and disruption on an even bigger scale than we have hitherto seen. It needs to be challenged before it gets that far. http://www.ekklesia.co.uk/node/21533

APPENDIX 6

Recommended further reading and academic video presentations

Below is a list of recommended further reading together with relevant and highly recommended academic video presentations.

Inexperienced readers of mainstream academic texts are advised that academic books are often expensive, such as 'The Power of Belief' which costs £59 and 'Work, Worklessness and the Political Economy of Health' costs £29 whilst, due to their funding mandate, many academics are able to offer important academic papers with free open access via academic journals and websites.

Not all relevant evidence is provided by academics. Some is offered by distinguished, trusted journalists or by talented chronically sick and disabled people themselves, who collate group evidence via social media and then create very significant, detailed and critically acclaimed research reports. Their evidence is always important. ** See below.

NB: Readers are alerted to the fact that some evidence and information discovered in these listed texts may cause distress to those who are unfamiliar in any great detail with the subject matter. I have, therefore, alerted readers to certain titles of particular note.

RECOMMENDED BOOKS:

*Treat with caution. Commissioned or co-sponsored by the DWP.
*Books and research of special significance.

1. **NB: If readers want to learn how bad things can be for those without a voice, I refer you to this very powerful book by John Pring, but offer caution as this book is deeply disturbing and demonstrates the horrors possible in a 'care home':**

   *LONGCARE SURVIVORS – The Biography of a Care Scandal by John Pring
   Published in 2011 by Disability News Service ISBN: 978-0-9568922-0-1 (pbk)
   http://www.disabilitynewsservice.com/longcare-survivors-the-biography-of-a-care-scandal/

2. **NB: Caution is needed when accessing this significant book as more deeply disturbing evidence is exposed by distinguished journalist Katharine Quarmby about the subject that is never discussed in polite society: disability hate crime:**

   *SCAPEGOAT – Why We Are Failing Disabled People by Katharine Quarmby
   Published in 2011 by Portobello books ISBN: 978 1 84627 321 6 (pbk)
   http://www.amazon.co.uk/Scapegoat-Why-Failing-Disabled-People/dp/1846273226

3. *HOW POLITICS MAKES US SICK: Neoliberal Epidemics by Ted Schrecker and Clare Bambra, Durham University.** Published in 2015 by Palgrave Macmillan ISBN: 9781137463098 (pbk)
   (NB: *The first elected 'neoliberal' politician was Margaret Thatcher. MS.*)
   https://www.waterstones.com/book/how-politics-makes-us-sick/ted-schrecker/clare-bambra/9781137463098

4. *INJUSTICE: Why Social Inequality Still Persists by Danny Dorling.**
   Revised edition. Published in 2015 by Policy Press ISBN: 978-1-4473-2075-3 (pbk)
   http://www.dannydorling.org/books/injustice/

5. *AUSTERITY BITES: a journey to the sharp end of the cuts in the UK by Mary O'Hara.** Published in April 2015 by Policy Press ISBN: 9781447315704 (pbk)
   http://www.amazon.co.uk/Austerity-bites-Journey-Sharp-Cuts/dp/144731560X

6. *GETTING BY - estates, class and culture in austerity Britain by Lisa Mckenzie.**
   Published by Policy Press in January 2015. ISBN: 9781447309956 (pbk)
   http://www.amazon.co.uk/Getting-By-Estates-Austerity/dp/1447309952

7. *WHY WE'RE NOT BENEFIT SCROUNGERS – Life with chronic illness or disability in modern Britain by Stef Benstead.** Published in 2012 by Aleksia Publishing ISBN: 978-0-9574597-0-0 (pbk)
   http://www.amazon.co.uk/Why-Were-Not-Benefit-Scroungers/dp/095745970X

8. *FAIR PLAY. A Daniel Dorling reader on social justice.**
   Published in 2012 by Policy Press ISBN: 978-1-84742-879-0 (pbk)
   http://www.dannydorling.org/books/fairplay/Homepage.html

9. *IT'S OUR LIVES by Peter Beresford**
   First published in 2003 by OSP for Citizen Press in association with Shaping Our Lives.
   ISBN: 0-9517554-2-0 Freely available online:
   http://www.shapingourlives.org.uk/documents/ItsOurLives.pdf

10. *THE SPIRIT LEVEL: Why Equality is Better for Everyone by Kate Pickett and Richard Wilkinson** Revised edition published by Penguin Books in 2010
    ISBN: 978-0-141-03236-8 (pbk)
    http://www.amazon.co.uk/The-Spirit-Level-Equality-Everyone/dp/0241954290

11. *$2 a Day: LIVING ON ALMOST NOTHING IN AMERICA by Kathryn J Edin and H Luke Shaefer** Published in September 2015 by Houghton Mifflin Harcourt ISBN-13: 978-0544303188 (Hardback) Readers are alerted to the fact that this is a **powerful and disturbing read**. MS * ***This nightmare is happening now the UK.*** MS
    http://www.amazon.co.uk/2-00-Day-Living-Nothing-America/dp/0544303180

12. *ALL OUR WELFARE towards participatory social policy by Peter Beresford**
    "..if we are to learn from the strengths and shortcomings of the original welfare state and what it has become since, then we need to have as good an understanding as possible of its origins and reality. Sadly, much current discussion about welfare is superficial, ahistorical and tendentious." Published by Policy Press in January 2016
    ISBN: 978 1 44732 894 0 (pbk)
    http://www.amazon.co.uk/All-Our-Welfare-Towards-Participatory/dp/1447328949

13. ***RETHINKING THE WORK CAPABILITY ASSESSMENT** *"Incapacity needs to be assessed in the real world..."* **by Ben Baumberg, Jon Warren, Kayleigh Garthwaite and Clare Bambra** Freely available online – a Demos report: Published by Demos in 2015. ISBN: 978 1 909037 80 9 (pbk) http://www.demos.co.uk/files/Rethinking_-_web_1_.pdf?1426175121

14. * **HOW TO MAKE A DISEASE DISAPPEAR by Professor Malcolm Hooper and Margaret Williams.** Published online in February 2010 Freely available. http://www.investinme.org/Article400%20Magical%20Medicine.htm

15. * **WHY WE CAN'T AFFORD THE RICH by Professor Andrew Sayer** Published by Policy Press, November 2015. ISBN: 978-1-4473-2086-9 (pbk) http://www.policypress.co.uk/display.asp?K=9781447320791

16. ***DEMOCRACY UNDER ATTACK – How the media distort policy and politics by Malcolm Dean.** *NB: This book demonstrates the corruption of the national press.* Published in 2013 by Policy Press ISBN: 978 184742 849 3 (pbk) http://www.amazon.co.uk/Democracy-Under-Attack-Distort-Politics/dp/1847428495

17. **THE RISE AND FALL OF THE BIOPSYCHOSOCIAL MODEL by S Nassir Ghaemi.** Published in 2010 by Johns Hopkins University Press US ISBN: 978-1421407753 (pbk) http://www.amazon.co.uk/The-Rise-Fall-Biopsychosocial-Model/dp/1421407752

18. ***THE NEW POLITICS OF DISABLEMENT by Michael Oliver and Colin Barnes** Published in 2012 by Palgrave Macmillan ISBN: 978-0-333-94567-4 (pbk) http://www.amazon.co.uk/The-Politics-Disablement-Michael-Oliver/dp/0333945670

19. ***MALINGERING AND ILLNESS DECEPTION** – 2001 conference papers by various authors, published in 2003 by Oxford University Press. ISBN: 0 19 851554 5 (pbk) *This conference created the **'malingering'** theory. MS Freely available online: http://www.meactionuk.org.uk/Malingering_and_Illness_Deception.pdf

20. ***THE SCIENTIFIC AND CONCEPTUAL BASIS OF INCAPACITY BENEFITS - a report by Gordon Waddell and *Mansel Aylward,** *UnumProvident Centre for Psychosocial and Disability Research, Cardiff University.* Published in 2005 by The Stationary Office (TSO) ISBN: 9780117035843 (pbk) *This 2005 report **was commissioned by the DWP, removed the authority of GPs,** would lead to the introduction of the Work Capability Assessment in 2008 and **recommended incentives** to encourage compliance. http://orca.cf.ac.uk/3257/

21. ***THE POWER OF BELIEF - psychosocial influences on illness, disability and medicine based on 2003 conference papers.** Edited by Peter Halligan, School of Psychology, Cardiff University and *Mansel Aylward, *UnumProvident Centre for Psychosocial and Disability Research, School of Psychology, Cardiff University.* *Conference co-sponsored by the Department for Work and Pensions.** Published in 2006 by Oxford University Press. ISBN: 0-19-853011-0 (pbk) http://www.amazon.co.uk/The-Power-Belief-Psychological-Psychosocial/dp/0198530110

22. **THE DOUBLE CRISIS OF THE WELFARE STATE and what we can do about it by Peter Taylor-Gooby.** Published in 2013 by Palgrave Macmillan ISBN: 978-1-137-32811 (pbk) Draft manuscript freely available online: http://www.open.ac.uk/ccig/files/ccig/The%20Double%20Crisis%20paper.pdf

23. ***WORK, WORKLESSNESS AND THE POLITICAL ECONOMY OF HEALTH** by Clare Bambra.** Published in 2011 by the Oxford University Press. ISBN-13: 9780199588299
   http://www.amazon.co.uk/Work-Worklessness-Political-Economy-Health/dp/0199588295

24. **DELAY, DENY, DEFEND**: **Why Insurance Companies Don't Pay Claims and What You Can Do About It by Jay M Feinman**. Published in 2010 in the US by Portfolio Hardcovers. ISBN-13: 978-1591843153
   http://www.amazon.co.uk/Delay-Deny-Defend-Insurance-Companies/dp/1591843154

RECOMMENDED ACADEMIC PAPERS, REPORTS AND ARTICLES:

** Detailed, acclaimed research reports created by chronically sick and disabled people.
* Research papers and reports of special significance. * Treat with caution.

25. * *'First do no harm': are disability assessments associated with adverse trends in mental health? A longitudinal ecological study* **by Ben Barr, D Taylor-Robinson, D Stuckler, R Loopstra, A Reeves and M Whitehead.** Published online in the BMJ with free open access, 16th November 2015. **Disturbing academic research results.**
   http://jech.bmj.com/content/early/2015/10/26/jech-2015-206209 Freely available

26. * *W&P 2014: Work and Pensions Committee – First Report: The ESA and WCA full report.* **July 2014 A damning report by the select committee was totally disregarded by the DWP.** Freely available
   http://www.publications.parliament.uk/pa/cm201415/cmselect/cmworpen/302/30202.htm

27. * *In 2014 Samuel Miller, Disability Studies specialist in Canada, kept a list of welfare related deaths in the UK.* **It makes harrowing reading:** Freely available
   http://twishort.com/0x9gc

28. * *New Labour, the market state, and the end of welfare by Professor Jonathan Rutherford, 2007.* **Jon was one of the first to draw attention to the influence of Unum Provident Insurance with the UK government and Mansel Aylward of the DWP.** http://www.midmoors.co.uk/Unum/unum_in_uk.pdf Freely available

29. * *'Unum's Game Plan' is accessed via the Black Triangle Campaign website from 2011, is published 'in the public interest' and was never meant to be available to the public.* **It offers information produced for financial advisers of the company and relates to the expected company benefits following the introduction of the ESA.**
   http://blacktrianglecampaign.org/2011/09/15/unums-game-plan/ Freely available

30. * *Welfare Reform, the dread of things to come.* **Edited by Jonathan Rutherford and Sally Davison – a short eBook written 'in the moment of political campaigning'.**
   http://www.lwbooks.co.uk/sites/default/files/free-book/WelfareReform.pdf
   Freely available

31. * *Getting Away With Murder – Disabled people's experience of hate crime in the UK* **by Katherine Quarmby.** Published by SCOPE August 2008 ISBN: 0946828989
   A detailed, **deeply disturbing** report offering graphic details of disability hate crimes.
   Freely available online.

http://www.scope.org.uk/Scope/media/Images/Publication%20Directory/Getting-away-with-murder.pdf?ext=.pdf

32. ** **DIGNITY AND OPPORTUNITY FOR ALL: Securing the rights of disabled people in the austerity era by Jane Young, London, Just Fair, 2014.** Freely available http://www.centreforwelfarereform.org/uploads/attachment/438/dignity-and-opportunity-for-all.pdf

33. ** *FULFILLING POTENTIAL? ESA and the fate of the Work-Related Activity Group* **by Catherine Hale, 2014** supported by MIND and the Centre for Welfare Reform. Freely available online:
https://www.mind.org.uk/media/933438/2014-support-not-sanctions-report.pdf

34. ** *The People's Review of the Work Capability Assessment* **by the Spartacus Network of chronically sick and disabled people.** Published in November 2012 by the Centre for Welfare Reform. Freely available online: http://www.centreforwelfarereform.org/library/type/pdfs/the-peoples-review-of-the-wca.html

35. ** *The People's Review of the Work Capability Assessment* - **Further Evidence by the Spartacus Network** Published by *Ekklesia* December 2013 Freely available online:http://www.ekklesia.co.uk/files/peoples_review_of_the_wca_-_further_evidence_december_2013.pdf

36. ** *BEYOND THE BARRIERS A Spartacus Network report regarding the ESA, the Work Programme and recommendations for a new system of support.* Published in 2014 by the Spartacus team. Freely available online: http://www.spartacusnetwork.org.uk/images/reports/BBReportAndAppendices.pdf

37. * *Why are old people in Britain dying before their time?*
    An article by Professor Danny Dorling in the New Statesman, February 2014:
    "Between 2008 and 2013, cuts led to some 483,000 old and disabled people in the UK either losing their care support or becoming no longer eligible to claim it.
    According to the Personal Social Services Research Unit, the "reductions... are particularly acute for older people." There are now millions fewer social care visits a year to the elderly than took place five years ago..." Freely available online http://www.newstatesman.com/politics/2014/02/why-are-old-people-britain-dying-their-time

38. * *Thatcherism's lethal legacy and the politics of reporting research*
    An article by Professor Clare Bambra in The Conversation, February 2014 *"Our study, which looked at material from existing research and data from the Office for National Statistics, concludes that Thatcherism resulted in the unnecessary and **unjust premature deaths** of British citizens, together with a substantial and continuing burden of suffering and a widespread degradation of well-being."*
    Caution – this is disturbing. Freely available online
    https://www.dur.ac.uk/research/news/thoughtleadership/?itemno=20180

39. * *The assault on universalism: how to destroy the welfare state* **by Martin McKee and David Stuckler.** Freely available online Published by the BMJ December 2011.
    http://www.bmj.com/content/343/bmj.d7973

RECOMMENDED ACADEMIC VIDEO PRESENTATIONS:

The video lecture series from the Durham University website is at:
https://www.dur.ac.uk/wolfson.institute/events/?eventno=24904

1. **Work, Worklessness and the Political Economy of Health – Clare Bambra**
   Inaugural Lecture by Professor Clare Bambra, 25th November 2011 given at Durham University: 43 minutes with one of the UK's top academics - includes commentary on the impact of the ESA on the health of the working poor and the *'psychosocial work environment'* in the workplace. MS
   https://www.dur.ac.uk/wolfson.institute/events/?eventno=24904

2. **Health Inequalities and the 1% - Danny Dorling**
   The Wolfson Annual Lecture by Professor Danny Dorling, 19th November 2014, Queen's Campus, Durham University: a fascinating, **often disturbing** and at times entertaining 51 minutes with the leading academic expert on social injustice.

   "Everything is connected to everything else…" "High and rising income inequalities result in rising inequalities in wealth, health and many opportunities (social mobility falls, education outcomes are poor, housing conditions decline, jobs become less fulfilling, mental illness rises…)"

   NB: Danny mentions the greatest inequality is when society changes. The UK society changed in the mid-80's due to the *"no such thing as society"* influence of the then Conservative government, led by Margaret Thatcher. MS
   https://www.youtube.com/watch?v=yfvCL-c1swk#t=48

3. **It Ain't What You Know, It's Who Knows It: User involvement and the secret of knowledge - Peter Beresford OBE**
   The Institute for Public Policy and Professional Practice anniversary lecture at Edge Hill University, by Professor Peter Beresford, held on 4th February 2015 on the first anniversary of the I4P Lecture Series. A *"significant event"* for issues around public policy, which offers 60 minutes of **significant debate regarding service users possible involvement with policy**, using their 'knowledge' of their own disabilities and service limitations. Referring to the book Austerity Bites by Mary O'Hara which exposed: *"..the risks and threats that have been imposed on some of the most disadvantaged people in society…."*

   Peter emphasises the need for *'empowerment'* and argues against conventional assumptions by traditional academic research, demonstrating the significance of *'experiential'* knowledge of ordinary people and service users in academic research. He also acknowledges independent research conducted by people using their own lived experiences. MS

   Peter is the leading academic expert in the UK regarding the empowerment of chronically sick and disabled service-users. By his involvement with Shaping Our Lives as Co-Chair, as well as via his significant work as an academic, Peter encourages and emphasises the importance of disabled people being the experts regarding their own lives, their needs and the policies created for them. He has encouraged the research of MS for years and it is largely due to Peter's insistance that my work was of value that this book was attempted. Peter is an inspiration to the disabled community, and to this researcher in particular, and he was the natural

choice to invite to write the Foreword for the book. MS
https://www.youtube.com/watch?v=U7I-mIxAMN8

4. **Austerity, a Failed Experiment on the People by Martin McKee**
A brilliant and entertaining 44 minute presentation given to health professionals in New Zealand in August 2014 by Professor Martin McKee, exposing the fact that 'austerity' as introduced in the UK is *"a complete bluff"* and *"is a political choice, not a financial necessity'* introduced *"without any ethical approval."* MS
https://www.youtube.com/watch?v=G7Fd-uBRPqY

NOTES AND REFERENCES

NOTES

N1: **Epitaph for the eighties? "there is no such thing as society"**

This famous quote was taken from an interview with Prime Minister Margaret Thatcher in the Women's Own Magazine on October 31 1987, reprinted in the Sunday Times and redistributed via the Internet by award winning journalist Brian Deer. (Chapter 2)
http://briandeer.com/social/thatcher-society.htm

N2: **Updated mortality totals were finally published by the DWP in August 2015:**

DWP: August 2015: *Mortality Statistics: Employment and Support Allowance, Incapacity Benefit or Severe Disablement Allowance* - updated death totals (Chapters 3, 4 and 5)
https://www.gov.uk/government/uploads/system/uploads/attachment_data/file/456359/mortality-statistics-esa-ib-sda.pdf

N3: **Cameron knowingly misdirected the British people: Debbie Abrahams MP:**

"I have previously raised concerns in the House of Commons about Duncan Smith's misuse of statistics as well as other members of the Government including the Prime Minister."
http://www.debbieabrahams.org.uk/2014/dwp-misuse-of-statistics (Chapter 10)
"Misleading statements were made, not in this House, but in relation to Government business. The Government have been rebuked on a number of occasions, for example by the chair of the UK Statistics Authority, for making misleading remarks. It is unparliamentary behaviour. What action can be taken?"
"Yesterday the Secretary of State for Work and Pensions and the Prime Minister made very misleading statements about the impact of welfare reform…" (Chapter 10)
http://www.debbieabrahams.org.uk/2014/dwp-misuse-of-statistics

N4: **Cardiff University and UnumProvident announce new partnership.**

Historically, with previous research, significant websites that supported the argument of MS disappeared within days of the research being published in the public arena. Recently, within two days of sending an email to one person, in January 2016, offering links to websites from 2004, both reporting the new partnership between Cardiff University and UnumProvident Insurance, who funded the *'UnumProvident Centre for Psychosocial and Disability Research, Cardiff University'*, both websites also suddenly disappeared. Both Unum Insurance and Cardiff University used to celebrate the funding of the Centre. Now, attempts are being made to remove all evidence of the past funding from the Internet and Professor Aylward claims it didn't happen. It is very difficult to remove all evidence from the Internet and evidence from May 2004 still exists. **Screenshots are now used to confirm the existance of the information, the evidence has been shared with trusted colleagues and the websites will not be published in the public arena to prevent them from also disappearing.** (Chapter 10)

REFERENCES

CHAPTER 2

**All references accessed 19th September 2015

3.   MEADEN B: 27th May 2015: *The truth about spending on disability benefits – its halved*: http://www.ekklesia.co.uk/node/21740

4.   AYLWARD M: 2003: *Malingering and Illness Deception* p290
     Conference papers: ISBN: 0 19 851554 52003:

5.   BERESFORD P: 2003: *It's Our Lives – A short theory of knowledge, distance and experience* ISBN No 0-9517554-2-0

CHAPTER 3

** All references accessed 15th May 2015

Illustration 3:1   *Fish In A Barrel* courtesy of Dave Lupton of Crippen Cartoons: http://www.crippencartoons.co.uk/

Table 3:1: Incapacity Benefits: deaths of recipients 2011
https://www.gov.uk/government/uploads/system/uploads/attachment_data/file/223050/incap_decd_recips_0712.pdf

6.   TRAVIS ALAN: 2012: *Margaret Thatcher's role in plan to dismantle welfare state revealed.*
     The Guardian: 28th December 2012 : courtesy of Guardian News & Media Ltd
     http://www.theguardian.com/politics/2012/dec/28/margaret-thatcher-role-plan-to-dismantle-welfare-state-revealed

7.   SCOTT-SAMUEL et al: 2014: *The impact of Thatcherism on health and well-being in Britain* : Alex Scott-Samuel, Clare Bambra, Chik Collins, David J Hunter, Gerry McCartney, Kat Smith. International Journal of Health Services, Volume 44, Number 1, Pages 53-71, 2014   http://pcwww.liv.ac.uk/~alexss/thatcherism.pdf

8.   BBC NEWS 2008: 13th October: *UK banks receive £37bn bail-out*
     http://news.bbc.co.uk/1/hi/business/7666570.stm

9.   PAC 2010: Support to IB claimants through Pathways to Work Public Accounts Committee: 13th Sept 2010
     http://www.publications.parliament.uk/pa/cm201011/cmselect/cmpubacc/404/40405.htm

10. FREUD DAVID: 2007 March: The Freud Report: *Reducing dependancy, increasing opportunity:options for the future of welfare to work.* An independent report by David Freud. Commissioned and published by the DWP. ISBN: 978 1 84712 193 6
      http://base-uk.org/sites/base-uk.org/files/%5Buser-raw%5D/11-07/welfarereview.pdf

11. WHO IS ATOS? https://www.whatdotheyknow.com/request/who_is_atos

12. 9 WADDELL & BURTON: 2006: DWP: *Is work good for your health and well-being?* ISBN 0 11 703694 3: 13 digit ISBN 978 0 11 703694
     https://www.gov.uk/government/uploads/system/uploads/attachment_data/file/214326/hwwb-is-work-good- for-you.pdf

13. AMERICAN ASSOCIATION OF JUSTICE: 2008: *The Ten Worst Insurance Companies in America*
http://www.bulmanlaw.com/wp-content/uploads/2013/03/TenWorstInsuranceCompanies.pdf

14. WADDELL G and AYLWARD M: 2005: DWP: *The Scientific and Conceptual Basis of Incapacity Benefits*: ISBN: 9780117035843

15. STEWART M: 2015: *The influence of the private insurance industry on the UK welfare reforms* http://disability-studies.leeds.ac.uk/library/author/stewart.mo

16. EXELL R: February 2012: *New figures show low level of benefit freud.*
http://liberalconspiracy.org/2012/02/26/new-figures-show-low-level-of-benefit-fraud/

17. STEWART M: 2010: Item 10: *Atos Healthcare or Disability Denial Factories?*
http://www.whywaitforever.com/dwpatosveteransprint.html

18. HARRINGTON M: November 2010: *An independent review of the work capability assessment*, year 1. ISBN: 9780108509476
https://www.gov.uk/government/uploads/system/uploads/attachment_data/file/70071/wca-review-2010.pdf :

19. DWP: 9th July 2012: Incapacity Benefits: Deaths of recipients
https://www.gov.uk/government/uploads/system/uploads/attachment_data/file/223050/incap_decd_recips_0712.pdf

20. ME ASSOCIATION: 2011: item 2: *ESA – changes to the Working Capability Assessment* descriptors
http://www.meassociation.org.uk/2011/02/esa-%e2%80%93-changes-to-the-working-capability-assessment-descriptors/orking

21. MILLER S: 2014: *Recent recorded deaths related to UK welfare reforms*
http://blacktrianglecampaign.org/2014/10/21/uk-welfare-reform-deaths-updated-list-october-21st-2014/

22. SOMMERLAD NICK: 2012: *32 die a week after failing test for new incapacity benefit.* The Mirror: 4th April 2012
http://blogs.mirror.co.uk/investigations/2012/04/32-die-a-week-after-failing-in.html

23. GENTLEMAN AMELIA: 2014: *Vulnerable man starved to death after benefits were cut.* The Guardian: 28th February 2014
http://www.theguardian.com/society/2014/feb/28/man-starved-to-death-after-benefits-cut

24. TRAVIS ALAN: 2012: *Margaret Thatcher's role in plan to dismantle welfare state revealed.* The Guardian: 28th December 2012
http://www.theguardian.com/politics/2012/dec/28/margaret-thatcher-role-plan-to-dismantle-welfare- state- revealed

25. BBC NEWS 2008: 13th October: *UK banks receive £37bn bail-out*
http://news.bbc.co.uk/1/hi/business/7666570.stm

26. SCOTT-SAMUEL A et al: 2014: *The Impact of Thatcherism On Health And Well-being In Britain*: International Journal of Health Services, Volume 44, Number 1, Pages 53-71 Alex Scott-Samuel, Clare Bambra, Chik Collins, David J Hunter, Gerry McCartney and Kat Smith http://pcwww.liv.ac.uk/~alexss/thatcherism.pdf (Free access)

27. McKEE M: 29th August 2014: *Austerity, A Failed Experiment on the People* – a presentation to health professionals at Ko Awatea, Auckland, New Zealand:
https://www.youtube.com/watch?v=G7Fd-uBRPqY

27b. McKEE M, KARANIKOLOS M, BELCHER P, STUCKLER D: 2012: *Austerity: a failed experiement on the people of Europe*: Clinical Medicine 2012, Vol 12, No4: 346-50
https://www.rcplondon.ac.uk/sites/default/files/documents/clinmed-124-p346-350-mckee.pdf

28.   YOUNG H: 2003: *Margaret Thatcher's Legacy*. The Guardian: 11th April 2013
Courtesy of Guardian News & Media Ltd
http://www.theguardian.com/politics/interactive/2013/apr/11/margaret-thatcher-legacy-best-writing

28b.   TOYNBEE P: *Thatcher's reckless acolytes don't know when to stop.* The Guardian 9th
April 2003   Courtesy of Guardian News & Media Ltd.
http://www.theguardian.com/politics/interactive/2013/apr/11/margaret-thatcher-legacy-best-writing

29   DAGURRE A & ETHERINGTON D: 30th June 2014
Welfare reform in the UK under the Conservative-led Coalition government: ruptures and continuities
http://workfare.org.uk/images/uploads/docs/Welfare_Reform_in_the_UK_PubReady.pdf

CHAPTER 4

** **All websites accessed 18th July 2015**

Illustration 4:1:
Hit Men courtesy of Dave Lupton of *Crippen* Cartoons: http://www.crippencartoons.co.uk/

Illustration 4:2
Spin courtesy of Dave Lupton of *Crippen* Cartoons: http://www.crippencartoons.co.uk/

30.   BBC NEWS: 10th April 2015: *Liberal Democrats cry foul in election race*
http://www.bbc.co.uk/news/uk-england-32248326
31.   Conservative manifesto: 14th April 2015:
http://www.bbc.co.uk/news/election-2015-32295970
32.   THE DAY: 15th April 2015: *Cameron revives 'home-owning democracy' dream*
http://theday.co.uk/politics/cameron-revives-home-owning-democracy-dream
33.   MAY B: Common Decency, colour blind politics: www.commondecency.org.uk
34.   BBC NEWS: Labour manifesto: 14th April 2015:
http://www.bbc.co.uk/news/election-2015-32284159
35.   SCOTT-SAMUEL A et al: 2014: *The Impact of Thatcherism On Health And Wellbeing In Britain* : International Journal of Health Services, Volume 44, Number 1, Pages 53-71Alex Scott-Samuel, Clare Bambra, Chik Collins, David J Hunter, Gerry McCartney and Kat Smith   http://pcwww.liv.ac.uk/~alexss/thatcherism.pdf
36.   BBC NEWS: 15th April 2015: Nick Clegg: The choice is me, Salmond or Farage
http://www.bbc.co.uk/news/election-2015-32311736
37.   MILLER S: October 2014: UK Welfare Refom Deaths – updated list
http://blacktrianglecampaign.org/2014/10/21/uk-welfare-reform-deaths-updated-list-october-21st-2014/
38.   DWP: 9th   July   2012:   Incapacity   Benefits: Deaths   of   Recipients
https://www.gov.uk/government/uploads/system/uploads/attachment_data/file/223050/incap_decd_recips_0712.pdf
39.   GOV.UK: 30th October 2014: Maximus appointed to carry out health assessments for the DWP
https://www.gov.uk/government/news/maximus-appointed-to-carry-out-health-assessments-for-the-department-for-work-and-pensions

40. PRIDE T: September 2014: *Meet MAXIMUS (the new ATOS) and its list of scandals in the US*
https://tompride.wordpress.com/2014/09/13/meet-maximus-the-new-atos-but-even-worse/

41. BLACK TRIANGLE CAMPAIGN: 4th October 2012: *10,600 sick and disabled people died last year…*
http://blacktrianglecampaign.org/2012/10/04/10600-sick-disabled-people-died-last-year-within-six-weeks-of-their-claim-ending/

42. BMA: June 2012: *Scrap work capability assessment, doctors demand*
http://bma.org.uk/news-views-analysis/news/2012/june/scrap-work-capability-assessment-doctors-demand

43. STEWART M: June 2010: *Atos Healthcare or Disability Denial Factories*
http://www.whywaitforever.com/dwpatosveteranssummary.html

44. STEWART M: January 2015: *The influence of the private insurance industry on the UK welfare reforms.*
http://disability-studies.leeds.ac.uk/files/library/The%20influence%20of%20the%20private%20insurance%20industry%20%20-%20FINAL%20-%20Jan%202015.pdf

45. LANGBEIN J: Yale School of Law: The Unum Provident Scandal & Judicial Review of benefit denials under ERISA: 2007
http://papers.ssrn.com/sol3/papers.cfm?abstract_id=917610 – abstract
– full paper may be downloaded as a PDF.

46. BBC 10PM NEWS: 6th November 2007: VIDEO: Mark Daly.
http://www.meactionuk.org.uk/UNUM_on_BBC_News_061107.wmv

47. ADVISER – CORPORATE: September 2011: *Income protection ads in Downtown Abbey as Unum launches £15m TV campaign*
http://www.corporate-adviser.com/home/income-protection-ads-in-downton-abbey-as-unum-launches-15m-tv- campaign/1038714.article

48. BENEFITS AND WORK: 15th March 2012: *Unum withdraws from individual income protection*
http://www.benefitsandwork.co.uk/news/1805-unum-withdraws-from-individual-income-protection166

49. UNUM Back-Up plan: 29th September 2011: You Tube
https://www.youtube.com/watch?v=v8zPl6rHRJw

50. STEWART M: January 2015: *The influence of the private insurance industry on the UK Welfare reforms*
http://www.researchgate.net/publication/271199429_The_influence_of_the_private_insurance_industry_on_the_UK_welfare_reforms

51. BMA: June 2012: *Scrap work capability assessment, doctors demand*
http://bma.org.uk/news-views-analysis/news/2012/june/scrap-work-capability-assessment-doctors-demand

52. RCN: April 2013: *Congress resolved that the disability assessments in the UK were unfit for purpose.*
http://www.rcn.org.uk/newsevents/congress/2013/agenda/1-disability-assessments

53. PARLIAMENT UK: APPENDIX 2: FINANCIAL PRIVILEDGE:
http://www.publications.parliament.uk/pa/ld201011/ldselect/ldconst/97/9705.htm

54. GREY-Thompson T: HOL: Welfare Reform Bill Second Reading: 13th September 2011: column 701
http://www.publications.parliament.uk/pa/ld201011/ldhansrd/text/110913-0002.htm

55. CALUM'S LIST: http://calumslist.org/

56. AAJ: 2008: *The Ten Worst Insurance Companies in America*
The American Association of Justice
http://www.bulmanlaw.com/wp-content/uploads/2013/03/TenWorstInsuranceCompanies.pdf

57. STEWART M: 10th June 2013: *From the British Welfare State to Another American State*
http://blacktrianglecampaign.org/2013/06/10/final-report-from-the-british-welfare-state-to-another-american-state-by-mo-stewart

58. W&P 2014: July: *ESA needs fundamental redesign, says MPs:*
Work & Pensions Select Committee: 23rd July 2014: News Release
http://www.parliament.uk/business/committees/committeesaz/

59. W&P 2014: July: Report: *Employment and Support Allowance and Work Capability Assessments*
http://www.publications.parliament.uk/pa/cm201415/cmselect/cmworpen/302/302.pdf

60. DNS: John Pring: 28th November 2014: *Concern over government's 'dreadful' response to MPs' fitness for work report.*
http://www.disabilitynewsservice.com/concern-governments-dreadful-response-mps-fitness-work-report/

61. MILLER S: October 2014: UK Welfare Refom Deaths – updated list
http://blacktrianglecampaign.org/2014/10/21/uk-welfare-reform-deaths-updated-list-october-21st-2014/

62. DNS: John Pring: 15th February 2013: *Unum bragged about 'driving government thinking' on incapacity benefit reform'*
http://disabilitynewsservice.com/2013/02/unum-bragged-about-driving-government-thinking-on-incapacity-benefit-reform/

63. STEWART M: 10th June 2013: *From the British Welfare State to Another American State*
http://blacktrianglecampaign.org/2013/06/10/final-report-from-the-british-welfare-state-to-another-american-state- by-mo-stewart/

64. CHORLEY M: Mail on Line: 23rd October 2012: *More than half of people who have been claiming incapacity benefit are 'fit for work.'*
http://www.dailymail.co.uk/news/article-2221954/More-half-people-claiming-incapacity-benefit-fit-work.html

65. PEEV G: 26th January 2011: Daily Mail: *400,000 'were trying it on' to get sickness benefits: 94% of incapacity claimants CAN work.*
http://www.dailymail.co.uk/news/article-1350359/400-000-sickness-benefits-cheats-94-incapacity-claimants-CAN-work.html

66. BACH M: 2012: *Why does the Government allow such a company to operate in the UK?* http://www.whywaitforever.com/dwpatosbusinessunum.html#performance

67. RUTHERFORD J: 17th March 2008: *E pluribus Unum*
http://www.theguardian.com/commentisfree/2008/mar/17/epluribusunum

68. RUTHERFORD J: Summer 2007: *New Labour, the market state and the end of welfare*
http://blacktrianglecampaign.org/2011/09/07/new-labour-the-market-state-and-the-end-of-welfare/

69. BBC NEWS: 13th October 2008: *Banking crisis*
http://news.bbc.co.uk/1/hi/business/7666570.stm

70. TRAVIS ALAN: 2012: *Margaret Thatcher's role in plan to dismantle welfare state revealed.* The Guardian: 28th December 2012 Courtesy of Guardian News & Media Ltd http://www.theguardian.com/politics/2012/dec/28/margaret-thatcher-role-plan-to-dismantle-welfare- state-revealed

71. FREUD D: 2007 March: The Freud Report: *Reducing dependancy, increasing opportunity:options for the future of welfare to work.* An independent report by David Freud. http://5.79.19.119/sites/default/files/policy_downloads/freud_review.pdf

72. BROWN C: 2014 January: *Freud: Bedroom tax loophole 'to be closed in March.'* http://www.insidehousing.co.uk/freud-bedroom-tax-loophole-to-be-closed-in-march/7001634.article

73. FREUD D: 2007 March: The Freud Report: *Reducing dependancy, increasing opportunity:options for the future of welfare to work.* An independent report by David Freud. http://5.79.19.119/sites/default/files/policy_downloads/freud_review.pdf

74. WADDELL G & BURTON K: 2006: *Is work good for your health and well-being?* https://www.gov.uk/government/uploads/system/uploads/attachment_data/file/214326/hwwb-is-work-good-for-you.pdf

75. DWP: GREEN PAPER: Jan 2006: *A new deal for welfare: Empowering people to work* https://www.gov.uk/government/uploads/system/uploads/attachment_data/file/272235/6730.pdf

76. RAVETZ A: 2006: *An independent assessment of the argument for proposed Incapacity Benefit reform* Re: Green Paper: A New Deal for Welfare: Empowering People to Work http://disability-studies.leeds.ac.uk/library/author/ravetz.alison

77. WADDELL G and AYLWARD M: 11th October 2005: *The Scientific and Conceptual Basis of Incapacity Benefits* ISBN: 9780117035843

78. RAVETZ A: 2006: *An independent assessment of the argument Incapacity Benefit reform for proposed* Re: Green Paper: A New Deal for Welfare: Empowering People to Work http://disability-studies.leeds.ac.uk/library/author/ravetz.alison

79. ONLINE LAWYER SOURCE: Unum Complaints: _ http://www.onlinelawyersource.com/unum/complaints/

80. ATTORNEY PAGES: *Insurance Group Reverses 42% Of Previously Denied Disability Claims*: http://attorneypages.com/hot/unum-group-reverses-denied-disability-claim.htm

81. WILLIAMS WALSH M: 23rd October 2008: New York Times: *Disability Insurer Found Guilty of Social Security Freud*: http://www.onlinelawyersource.com/unum/complaints/

82. WADDELL G and AYLWARD M: 11th October 2005: *The Scientific and Conceptual Basis of Incapacity Benefits* ISBN: 9780117035843

83. HARRINGTON M: November 2010: *An independent review of the work capability assessment*, year 1. ISBN: 9780108509476 http://www.nationalarchives.gov.uk/doc/open-government-licence/version/3/

84. PRING J: DNS: 14th September 2012: *Former DWP medical boss Sir Mansel Aylward makes WCA pledge to protesters.* http://blacktrianglecampaign.org/2012/09/14/former-dwp-medical-boss-sir-mansel-aylward-makes-wca-pledge-to-protesters-disability-news-service/

85. INTERNATIONAL JOURNAL OF DISABILITY MANAGEMENT 2012: *Abstracts for the International Forum on Disability Management (IFDM), London, England, Sept 10 – 12, 2012*
http://connection.ebscohost.com/c/abstracts/98801873/abstracts-international-forum-disability-management-ifdm-london-england-september-10-12-2012

86. JOLLY D: March 2012: *A Tale of Two Models: Disabled People vs Unum, Atos, Government and disability charities.*:
http://disability-studies.leeds.ac.uk/files/library/A-Tale-of-two-Models-Leeds1.pdf

87. KENNEDY A: 19th September 2012: *Academic responds to Professor Sir Mansel Aylward's statements to Black Triangle and DPAC*
http://blacktrianglecampaign.org/2012/09/19/academic-angela-kennedy-responds-to-professor-sir-manselaylwards-statement-to-black-triangle-and-dpac

88. THORBURN G: 18th September 2012: *Academic response to Aylward's claims*
https://dl.dropboxusercontent.com/u/32109159/Aylward/ResponseToAylward.pdf

89. PRING J: DNS: 14th September 2012: *Former DWP medical boss Sir Mansel Aylward makes WCA pledge to protesters.*
http://blacktrianglecampaign.org/2012/09/14/former-dwp-medical-boss-sir-mansel-aylward-makes-wca-pledge-to- protesters-disability-news-service/

90. RUTHERFORD H: 11th January 2013: Business Day New Zealand: *Work tests concern disability organisation*
http://www.stuff.co.nz/business/industries/8165236/Work-tests-concern-disability-organisation

91. NZ SOCIAL JUSTICE BLOG 2013: Medical and Work Capability Assessments – based on the controvertial bio-psychosocial model.
https://nzsocialjusticeblog2013.wordpress.com/2013/09/02/medical-and-work-capability-assessments-based-on-the-controversial-bio-psycho-social-model/

92. ACC FORUM: NEW ZEALAND:
http://accforum.org/forums/index.php?/topic/15188-medical-and-work-capability-assessments-based-on-the-bps-model-aimed-at-disentiteling-affected-from-welfare-benefits-and-acc-compo/page__st__20

CHAPTER 5

** **All websites accessed 5th August 2015**

Illustration 5:1
Banner headlines ~ courtesy of Express Newspapers/N&S syndication

Illustration 5:2
DWP Death totals ~ courtesy of Dave Lupton of Crippen Cartoons:
http://www.crippencartoons.co.uk/

93. A LATENT EXISTENCE blog: press headlines: 26th July 2011: *Twisting the facts, printing lies. How the DWP and tabloids are wrong about fit for work stats.*
http://www.latentexistence.me.uk/government-launch-new-attacks-even-as-select-committee-condemns-propaganda/

94. STEWART M: January 2015: *The influence of the private insurance industry on the UK welfare reforms.*
http://www.researchgate.net/pu
blication/271199429_The_influence_of_the_private_insurance_industry_on_the_UK_
welfare_reforms

95. MILLER S: October 2014: UK Welfare Reform Deaths – updated list
http://blacktrianglecampaign.org/2014/10/21/uk-welfare-reform-deaths-updated-list-
october-21st-2014/

96. DWP: 9th July 2012: Incapacity Benefits: Deaths of Recipients
www.gov.uk/government/uploads/system/uploads/attachment_data/file/223050/incap_
decd_recips_0712.pdf

97. AAJ: 2008: *The Ten Worst Insurance Companies in America*: The American Association of Justice
http://www.bulmanlaw.com/wp-
content/uploads/2013/03/TenWorstInsuranceCompanies.pdf

98. RILEY-SMITH BEN: 19th June 2012: *Hate crimes against disabled soar to record level:* The Independent:
http://www.independent.co.uk/news/uk/crime/hate-crimes-against-disabled-people-
soar-to-a-record-level-7858841.html

99. HOC WORK & PENSION COMMITTEE Report: 13th July 2011: *The role of incapacity benefit reassessment in helping claimants into employment.*
http://www.publications.parliament.uk/pa/cm201012/cmselect/cmworpen/1015/1015.p
df

100. HOC WORK & PENSION COMMITTEE Report: 13th July 2011: *The role of incapacity benefit reassessment in helping claimants into employment.*
http://www.publications.parliament.uk/pa/cm201012/cmselect/cmworpen/1015/1015.p
df

101. STEWART M: November 2011: *The truth behind the welfare reforms*
http://www.whywaitforever.com/dwpatosveteransreport20111120.html

102. BRIANT E, WATSON N: PHILO G: November 2011: *Bad News for Disabled People:How the newspapers are reporting disability.* Glasgow University
http://eprints.gla.ac.uk/57499/1/57499.pdf

103. AYLWARD M DSS & LO CASCIO J Unum Ltd: August 1995
Problems in the assessment of psychosomatic conditions in social security benefits
and related commercial schemes. Journal of Psychosomatic Research 1995, Vol 39,
No 6, pp755-765
http://www.sciencedirect.com/science/article/pii/002239999500037J

104. STEWART M: August 2010: *Atos Healthcare or Disability Denial Factories –* research summary
http://blacktrianglecampaign.org/2011/08/23/important-read-circulate/

105. MCKEE M and STUCKLER D: December 2011: BMJ: *The assault on universalism: how to destroy the welfare state*: BMJ2011;343:d7973:
http://users.ox.ac.uk/~chri3110/Details/Universalism%20McKee%20Stuckler.pdf

106. HOC 1999: *Permanent Health Insurance debate; Westminster Hall, 21st December 1999.* Unum Provident Insurance exposed during debate.
http://www.publications.parliament.uk/pa/cm199900/cmhansrd/vo991221/halltext/912
21h01.htm#91221h01_head0

107. GIBSON PARLIAMENTARY INQUIRY: Dec 2005: Evidence
http://www.meactionuk.org.uk/HOOPER_CONCERNS_ABOUT_A_COMMERCIAL_CONFLICT_OF_INTEREST.htm

108. MILLER S: October 2014: *UK Welfare Reform Deaths* – updated list
http://blacktrianglecampaign.org/2014/10/21/uk-welfare-reform-deaths-updated-list-october-21st-2014/

109. DWP: 9th July 2012: Incapacity Benefits: Deaths of Recipients ___
ww.gov.uk/government/uploads/system/uploads/attachment_data/file/223050/incap_decd_recips_0712.pdf

110. GRIFFITHS S: October 2010: *Dark Times for Those Who Cannot Work.*
http://www.compassonline.org.uk/wp-content/uploads/2013/06/Dark-Times-Benefit-Reform-Thinkpiece-67.pdf

111. NAO: DWP May 2010: Support to incapacity benefits claimants through Pathways to Work: page 9
http://www.nao.org.uk/wp-content/uploads/2010/05/101121es.pdf

112. VARIOUS AUTHORS: CONFERENCE PAPERS: Malingering and Illness Deception
ISBN: 0 19 851554 52003:
http://www.meactionuk.org.uk/Malingering_and_Illness_Deception.pdf

112. NEE LINDA: Disability Claims Solutions Inc:Licensed Disability Claims Consultant   http://www.disabilityclaimssolutions.com

113. BBC NEWS: UNUM INSURANCE: 7th November 2007 – 6 minutes - VIDEO
http://www.meactionuk.org.uk/UNUM_on_BBC_News_061107.wmv

CHAPTER 6

**All references confirmed and accessed 15th August 2015

Illustration 6:1

Cameron's message ~ courtesy of Dave Lupton of Crippen Cartoons:
www.daveluptoncartoons.co.uk

114. WELFARE definition: http://www.collinsdictionary.com/dictionary/english/welfare

115. STEWART M: 22nd January 2015: *The influence of the private insurance industry on the UK welfare reforms*: Centre for Disability Studies, Leeds University
http://disability-studies.leeds.ac.uk/files/library/The%20influence%20of%20the%20private%20insurance%20industry%20%20-%20FINAL%20-%20Jan%202015.pdf

116. WELFARE REFORM ACT 2012:
http://www.legislation.gov.uk/ukpga/2012/5/contents/enacted

117. SCOTT-SAMUEL BAMBRA C, COLLINS C, HUNTER D, McCARTNEY G, SMITH K: 2014: *The impact of Thatcherism on health and well-being in Britain*
http://pcwww.liv.ac.uk/~alexss/thatcherism.pdf

118. HUDSON T: 15th April 2013: *Of prime ministers and presidents*
http://www.politics.co.uk/comment-analysis/2013/04/15/of-prime-ministers-and-presidents-thatchers-forgotten-legacy

119. STAFF: THE TIMES: 10th August 2013: *Thatcher funeral cost the taxpayer £3.6m*
http://www.thetimes.co.uk/tto/news/uk/article3749333.ece

120. DORLING D: 2015: An introduction to *Injustice~why social injustice still persists*
http://www.dannydorling.org/books/injustice/injustice-anintroduction.pdf

121. DAGUERRE A: August 2008: *The Second Phase of US Welfare Reform, 2000-2006: Blaming the Poor Again?*
http://onlinelibrary.wiley.com/doi/10.1111/j.1467-9515.2008.00609.x/abstract?userIsAuthenticated=false&deniedAccessCustomisedMessage

122. MIDDLESEX UNIVERSITY: one day conference: 20th March 2015: *Assessing 20 years of welfare reform in the US and the UK*
http://www.mdx.ac.uk/events/2015/03/assessing-20-years-of-welfare-reform-in-the-us-and-the-uk

123. DAGUERRE A, ETHERINGTON D: November 2014: *Welfare in 21st century Britain – The erosion of rights to social assistance*
http://workfare.org.uk/images/uploads/docs/workfarein21stcenturybritain.pdf

124. STEWART M: 22nd January 2015: *The influence of the private insurance industry on the UK welfare reforms*: ResearchGate
http://www.researchgate.net/publication/271199429_The_influence_of_the_private_insurance_industry_on_the_UK_welfare_reforms

125. DAGUERRE A: August 2008: *The Second Phase of US Welfare Reform, 2000-2006: Blaming the Poor Again?*
http://onlinelibrary.wiley.com/doi/10.1111/j.1467-9515.2008.00609.x/abstract?userIsAuthenticated=false&deniedAccessCustomisedMessage

126. BRIANT E, WATSON N: PHILO G: November 2011: *Bad News for Disabled People:How the newspapers are reporting disability.* Glasgow University
http://eprints.gla.ac.uk/57499/1/57499.pdf

127. FREUD D: 2007: *Reducing dependency, increasing opportunity: options for the future of welfare to work* ISBN: 978 1 84712 193 6

128. DORLING D: May 2007: *The Real Mental Health Bill*
http://www.dannydorling.org/wp-content/files/dannydorling_publication_id0514.pdf

129. SYLVESTER AND THOMSON: 2nd February 2008: *Welfare is a mess, says adviser David Freud.* Daily Telegraph
http://www.telegraph.co.uk/news/politics/1577313/Welfare-is-a-mess-says-adviser-David-Freud.html

130. O'HARA M: 2015: *Austerity Bites:* Policy Press: ISBN 978-1-4473-1570-4 Reproduced courtesy of Policy Press

131. FLETCHER R: 3rd July 2015: Memo to David Cameron: I have all the incentives I need to stop being ill. It's called "being ill". Reproduced courtesy of New Statesman.
New Statesman – The Staggers ~ The New Statesman's rolling politics blog
http://www.newstatesman.com/politics/2015/07/memo-david-cameron-i-have-all-incentives-i-need-stop-being-ill-its-called-being-ill

132. STEWART M: May 2014: *UK Government refuses to accept responsibility for identified crimes against humanity*
http://www.researchgate.net/publication/263673446_UK_GOVERNMENT_REFUSES_TO_ACCEPT_RESPONSIBILITY_FOR_IDENTIFIED_CRIMES_AGAINST_HUMANITY_-a_report

133. INTERNATIONAL CRIMINAL COURT: CRIMES AGAINST HUMANITY: Definition:
http://www.icc-cpi.int/en_menus/icc/about%20the%20court/frequently%20asked%20questions/Pages/12.aspx

134. GARTHWAITE K, BAMBRA C, WARREN J, KASIM A, GREIG G: February 2014: *Shifting the Goalposts: A Longitudinal Mixed-Methods Study of the Health of Long-Term Incapacity Benefit Recipients during a period of Substantial Change to the UK Social Security System*: The Journal of Social Policy, 43, pp 311-330: Abstract
DOI: http://dx.doi.org/10.1017/S0047279413000974
http://journals.cambridge.org/abstract_S0047279413000974

135. MEADEN B: 12th March 2015: *New Report:* http://www.ekklesia.co.uk/node/21505

136. McGRATH L, GRIFFIN V, MUNDY E: March 2015: *The Psychological Impact of Austerity – a briefing paper:* Psychologists Against Cuts
https://psychagainstausterity.files.wordpress.com/2015/03/paa-briefing-paper.pdf

137. POULTON S: 20th March 2012: *British people are committing suicide to escape poverty. Is this what the State wants?* Mail online. Courtesy of Solo Syndication
http://www.dailymail.co.uk/debate/article-2117718/British-people-committing-suicide-escape-poverty-Is-State-wants.html

138. WHEELER C: 11th January 2015: EXCLUSIVE: *Hate crimes on disabled up 213%*
http://www.express.co.uk/news/uk/551327/EXCLUSIVE-Hate-crimes-on-disabled-rise-by-213

139. WELFARE REFORM ACT 2012:
http://www.legislation.gov.uk/ukpga/2012/5/contents/enacted

140. MALIK S and BUTLER P: 20th February 2014: The Guardian: *People stripped of benefits could be charged for challenging decision*
http://www.theguardian.com/politics/2014/feb/20/people-stripped-benefits-charged-decision

141. QUARMBY K: August 2008: *Getting Away With Murder*: ISBN: 0946828989
http://www.scope.org.uk/Scope/media/Images/Publication%20Directory/Getting-away-with-murder.pdf?ext=.pdf

142. WELFARE WEEKLY: 12th January 2015: *213% Rise in Disability Hate Crimes 'fuelled' by benefits propaganda, say campaigners*
http://www.welfareweekly.com/disability-hate-crime-fuelled-by-propaganda/

143. WHEELER C: 11th January 2015: EXCLUSIVE: *Hate crimes on disabled up 213%*
http://www.express.co.uk/news/uk/551327/EXCLUSIVE-Hate-crimes-on-disabled-rise-by-213

CHAPTER 7

** **All references accessed and confirmed 5th September 2015**

* '*Money, money, money*' lyrics by Benny Goran Bror Andersson, Bjoern K. Ulvaeus, Marcelo Kotliar

Illustration 7:1
Skeletons ~ courtesy of Dave Lupton of Crippen Cartoons www.daveluptoncartoons.co.uk

Illustration 7:2
Puppeteer ~ exclusively designed for this book by Dave Lupton of Crippen Cartoons

Table 7:1
Source: DWP: Freud and Error in the Benefit System 2011/12 Estimates [147] (p13)

Table 7:2:
Source: DWP Mortality Statistics [157] (p2)

Table 7:3
Source: Combined DWP Mortality Statistics, Jan 2011 to Feb 2014 [157, 160]

144. STEWART M: March 2013: *The Hidden Agenda*
http://www.researchgate.net/publication/263673312_THE_HIDDEN_AGENDA

145. DORLING D: 2012: *Fair Play – A Daniel Dorling reader on social justice*
ISBN: 978 1 84742 879 0 paperback

146. FALSE ECONOMY: July 2012: *Benefit fraud – the levels are very low*
http://falseeconomy.org.uk/blog/repost-benefit-fraud-the-levels-are-very-low

147. DWP: FRAUD & ERROR IN THE BENEFIT SYSTEM 2011/12 Estimates (p13)
https://www.gov.uk/government/uploads/system/uploads/attachment_data/file/244844/fem_1112.pdf

148. PRING J: November 2014: DISABILITY NEWS SERVICE: *No explanation from ministers for soaring ESA sanctions*
http://www.disabilitynewsservice.com/explanation-ministers-soaring-esa-sanctions/

149. STEWART M: 2014: *UK government refuses to accept responsibility for Crimes Against Humanity*
http://blacktrianglecampaign.org/2014/05/08/british-disability-rights-abuses-uk-government-refuses-to-accept-responsibility-for-crimes-against-humanity-a-report-by-mo-stewart/

150. DWP: November 2014: *Jobseeker's Allowance and Employment and Support Allowance Sanctions: decisions made to June 2014.*
https://www.gov.uk/government/statistics/jobseekers-allowance-and-employment-and-support-allowance-sanctions-decisions-made-to-june-2014

151. DWP: November 2013: *Benefit sanctions – ending the 'something for nothing' culture.*
https://www.gov.uk/government/news/benefit-sanctions-ending-the-something-for-nothing-culture

152. RYAN F: 9th September 2014: *David Clapson's awful death was the result of grotesque government policies* The Guardian – Comment is Free
http://www.theguardian.com/commentisfree/2014/sep/09/david-clapson-benefit-sanctions-death-government-policies

153. POULTON S: 20th March 2012: *British people are committing suicide to escape poverty. Is this what the State wants?* Mail online.
http://www.dailymail.co.uk/debate/article-2117718/British-people-committing-suicide-escape-poverty-Is-State-wants.html

154. GREEN PARTY: 6th May 2012: *Green Party Calls On Duncan Smith To Apologise For Misleading Public Over Benefit Claimant Deaths.*
https://www.greenparty.org.uk/news/2015/05/06/green-party-calls-on-duncan-smith-to-apologise-for-misleading-public-over-benefit-claimant-deaths/

155. SIVIER M: 6th May 2015: *Benefit deaths: IDS lies while DWP evades.*
http://voxpoliticalonline.com/2015/05/06/benefit-deaths-ids-lies-while-dwp-evades/

156. WEBSTER D: 10th January 2014: *Independent review of Jobseeker's Allowance (JSA) sanctions for claimants failing to take part in back to work schemes.*
http://www.cpag.org.uk/sites/default/files/uploads/CPAG-Oakley-Review-D-Webster-Evidence-rev%20-13-Jan-2014.pdf

157. DWP: August 2015: *Mortality Statistics: Employment and Support Allowance, Incapacity Benefit or Severe Disablement Allowance* - updated death totals p5
https://www.gov.uk/government/uploads/system/uploads/attachment_data/file/456359/mortality-statistics-esa-ib-sda.pdf

158. PRING J: 6th May 2015: *DWP told to publish ESA deaths report, after two-year delay*
http://www.disabilitynewsservice.com/dwp-told-to-publish-esa-deaths-report-after-two-year-delay/

159. SIVIER M: 27th August 2015: *Known number of deaths while claiming incapacity benefits nears 100,000* _
http://voxpoliticalonline.com/2015/08/27/known-number-of-deaths-while-claiming-incapacity-benefits-nears-100000/?subscribe=error#blog_subscription-2

160. DWP: Incapacity Benefits: Deaths of recipients: 9th July 2012 p6
https://www.gov.uk/government/uploads/system/uploads/attachment_data/file/223050/incap_decd_recips_0712.pdf

161. BLOOM D: 19th June 2015: *200,000 join petition demanding Tories reveal how many people died after being found 'fit for work'.* The Mirror
http://www.mirror.co.uk/news/uk-news/200000-join-petition-demanding-tories-5909676

162. STEWART M: March 2013: *The Hidden Agenda*
http://www.researchgate.net/publication/263673312_THE_HIDDEN_AGENDA

163. REFORM: 24th August 2015: *Rt Hon Iain Duncan Smith MP: speech on work, health and disability.*
http://www.reform.uk/publication/rt-hon-iain-duncan-smith-mp-speech-on-work-health-and-disability/

164. STEWART M: 2014: *UK government refuses to accept responsibility for identified Crimes Against Humanity*
http://pf7d7vi404s1dxh27mla5569.wpengine.netdna-dn.com/files/library/GVT%20 refuses%20responsibility%20for%20crimes%20against%20humanity%20-%20FINAL%20-%203rd%20May.pdf

165. VARIOUS AUTHORS: CONFERENCE PAPERS: Malingering and Illness Deception ISBN: 0 19 851554 52003: p287-296
http://www.meactionuk.org.uk/Malingering_and_Illness_Deception.pdf

166. STEWART M: 2015: *The influence of the private insurance industry on the UK welfare reforms.*
https://www.researchgate.net/publication/271199429_The_influence_of_the_private_insurance_industry_on_the_UK_welfare_reforms

167. RUTHERFORD H: 11th January 2013: Business Day New Zealand: *Work tests concern disability organisation*
http://www.stuff.co.nz/business/industries/8165236/Work-tests-concern-disability-organisation

168. PRING J: 3rd September 2012: *Former DWP medical boss makes DWP pledge to protesters.*
http://www.disabilitynewsservice.com/former-dwp-medical-boss-makes-wca-pledge-to-protesters-2/

169. RUTHERFORD H: 11th January 2013: Business Day New Zealand: *Work tests concern disability organisation*
http://www.stuff.co.nz/business/industries/8165236/Work-tests-concern-disability-organisation

170. BACH M 2012: *Memorandum on Disability Insurance.*
http://www.whywaitforever.com/dwpatosmemodisins.html

171. DOYLE J: 27th August 2015: *Now UN sparks fury after launching human rights investigation into Britain's disability benefit reforms.* Mail Online
http://www.dailymail.co.uk/news/article-2735958/UN-sparks-fury-launching-human-rights-investigation-Britain-s-treatment-disabled.html

CHAPTER 8

** All references accessed and confirmed 6th September 2015

172. STEWART M: http://www.whywaitforever.com/dwpatosveterans.html

173. BACH M: http://www.whywaitforever.com/dwpatosbusinessunum.html

174. McKINSEY and COMPANY: http://www.mckinsey.com/about_us

175. NAO: 2013: DWP: *Universal Credit: early progress:*
[HC 621 SESSION 2013-14 5 SEPTEMBER 2013]
http://www.nao.org.uk/wp-content/uploads/2013/09/10132-001-Universal-credit.pdf

176. BACH M: March 2012: *Memorandum to DWP W&P Select Committee*
http://www.whywaitforever.com/dwpatosmemowca.html

177. BACH M: *The Contract between the DWP and Atos Healthcare*
http://www.whywaitforever.com/dwpatoscontract.html

178. BACH M: *Influential People and Unum:*
http://www.whywaitforever.com/dwpatosbusinessunum.html#product

179. BACH M: 2013: *Memorandum on Disability Insurance*
http://www.whywaitforever.com/dwpatosmemodisins.html

CHAPTER 9

** All references accessed and confirmed 18th October 2015

Illustration 9:1
Highway to Hell ~ reproduced by kind permission of the artist Kevin Marman

180. WADDELL G, BURTON AK: 2006: *Is work good for health and well-being?*
https://www.gov.uk/government/uploads/system/uploads/attachment_data/file/214326/hwwb-is-work-good-for-you.pdf

181. O'HARA M: 2015: Policy Press: *Austerity Bites* ISBN: 978-1-4473-1570-4 paperback

182. DORLING D: Policy Press: *Injustice* ISBN: 978-1-4473-2075-3 paperback

183. WADDELL G, AYLWARD M: 2005: *The Scientific and Conceptual Basis of Incapacity Benefits*: ISBN: 0 11 703584 X

184. RAVETZ A: 2006: *Green Paper: A New Deal for Welfare: empowering people to work. 2006.*
http://disability-studies.leeds.ac.uk/files/library/ravetz-Green-Paper-IB-critique.pdf

185. RESEARCH METHODOLOGY: 2010:
http://www.enotes.com/homework-help/what-research-what-various-types-research-explain-137387

186. RAVETZ A: 2006: *Green Paper: A New Deal for Welfare: empowering people to work. 2006.*
http://disability-studies.leeds.ac.uk/files/library/ravetz-Green-Paper-IB-critique.pdf

187. KENNEDY A: 2012: *Authors of our own misfortune?* ISBN: 978-0-85718-101-5

188. BAMBRA C: 2011: Staff Profile Durham University
https://www.dur.ac.uk/geography/staff/geogstaffhidden/?id=2991

189. WARREN J, GARTHWAITE K, BAMBRA C: September 2014: *After Atos Healthcare: is the Employment and Support Allowance fit for purpose and does the Work Capability Assessment have a future?* Disability and Society, 2014 Vol. 29, No. 8, 1319– 1323
http://dx.doi.org/10.1080/09687599.2014.948746
http://www.tandfonline.com/doi/abs/10.1080/09687599.2014.948746

190. GARTHWAITE K, BAMBRA C, WARREN J, KASMIN A, GREIG C: April 2014: *Shifting the goalposts: a longitudinal mixed-methods study of the health of long-term incapacity benefit recipients during a period of substantial change in the UK social security system.* Journal of Social Policy: April 2014, pp311-330, Vol 43, issue 2. doi:10.1017/S0047279413000974 Durham University: http://dro.dur.ac.uk/12797/
http://journals.cambridge.org/action/displayAbstract?fromPage=online&aid=9185002&fileId=S0047279413000974

191. GARTHWAITE K: March 2015: *Keeping meself to meself' – How Social Networks Can Influence Nattatives of Stigma and Identity for long-term Sickness Benefits Recipients* Social Policy & Administration Journal, Vol 49, No 2, March 2015, p199-212.
http://dro.dur.ac.uk/14925/
http://onlinelibrary.wiley.com/doi/10.1111/spol.12119/abstract

192   DORLING D: 2015: Policy Press: *Injustice* ISBN: 978-1-4473-2075-3 paperback

193. TAYLOR-GOOBY P: 2013: Palgrave Pilot: *The Double Crisis of the Welfare State and what we can do about it.* ISBN: 9781137328120

194. HARWOOD R: 2014: *'The dying of the light': the impact of the spending cuts, and cuts to employment law protections, on disability adjustments in British local authorities.* Disability & Society Journal: October 2014. Vol 29, Issue 10, p1511-1523
http://dx.doi.org/10.1080/09687599.2014.958132

195. HALE C: 2014: *Fulfilling Potential? ESA and the fate of the Work-Related Activity Group* http://www.mind.org.uk/media/933438/2014-support-not-sanctions-report.pdf

196. SPARTACUS NETWORK: 2012: *Responsible Reform:*
http://www.ekklesia.co.uk/files/response_to_proposed_dla_reforms.pdf

197. BUTLER P: 2012: *How the Spartacus welfare cuts campaign went viral.* The Guardian
http://www.theguardian.com/society/2012/jan/17/disability-spartacus-welfare-cuts-campaign-viral

198. CROSS M: 2013: *Demonised, impoverished and now forced into isolation: the fate of disabled people under austerity.* Disability & Society Journal, July 2013, Vol 28, No 5, p719-723.
http://www.tandfonline.com/doi/abs/10.1080/09687599.2013.808087?journalCode=cdso20+-+.VSF4RNKBHIU&

199. BERESFORD P: 2016 forthcoming: *All Our Welfare: Towards participatory social policy*, Bristol, Policy Press.

CHAPTER 10

*This issue between the DWP and DNS was resolved in October 2015.

** **Most references accessed and confirmed 20th October 2015**
References 217 and 218 accessed and confirmed 3rd December 2015

200. COURTS AND TRIBUNALS JUDICIARY: 13th January 2014: *Regulation 28: Prevention of Future Deaths report to the Department for Work and Pensions* https://www.judiciary.gov.uk/wp-content/uploads/2014/06/OSullivan-2014-0012.pdf

201. PRING J: 18th September 2015: *Coroner's 'ground-breaking' verdict: Suicide was 'triggered by 'fit for work' test* : Disability News Service http://www.disabilitynewsservice.com/coroners-ground-breaking-verdict-suicidewastriggered-by-fit-for-work-test/

202. PRING J: 17th April 2015: *DWP carries out threat to ban questions from Disability News Service* : Disability News Service http://www.disabilitynewsservice.com/dwp-carriesout-threat-to-ban-questions-fromdisability-news-service/

203. PRING J: 3rd September 2012: *Former DWP boss makes WCA pledge to protesters*: Disability News Service http://www.disabilitynewsservice.com/former-dwp-medicalboss-makes-wca-pledgeto- protesters-2/

204. RUTHERFORD H: 11th January 2013: Business Day New Zealand: *Work tests concern disability organisation* http://www.stuff.co.nz/business/industries/8165236/Work-tests-concern-disability-organisation

205. DAN CYMRU: 7th September 2015 : *Press release* https://www.facebook.com/DanCymruDisabledActivists/posts/

206. WADDELL & AYLWARD: 2005: *The Scientific and Conceptual Basis of Incapacity Benefits*: UnumProvident Centre for Psychosocial and Disability Research, Cardiff University: TSO : ISBN 0 11 703584 X

207. VARIOUS AUTHORS: CONFERENCE PAPERS: Malingering and Illness Deception ISBN: 0 19 851554 52003: http://www.meactionuk.org.uk/Malingering_and_Illness_Deception.pdf

208. HALLIGAN AND AYLWARD: 2006: *The Power of Belief*, Edited by Peter W Halligan, School of Psychology, Cardiff University and Mansel Aylward, UnumProvident Centre for Psychosocial and Disability Research, School of Psychology, Cardiff University ISBN: 0-19-853011-0 https://global.oup.com/academic/product/the-power-of-belief-9780198530114?cc=gb&lang=en&

209. FREUD D: 2007: *Reducing dependency, increasing opportunity: options for the future of welfare to work* ISBN: 907 1 84712 193 6 http://base-uk.org/sites/base-uk.org/files/%5Buser-raw%5D/11-07/welfarereview.pdf

210. WADDELL G & BURTON K: 2006: *Is work good for health and well-being?* ISBN: 0 11 703694 3
https://www.gov.uk/government/uploads/system/uploads/attachment_data/file/214326/h wwb-is-work-good-for-you.pdf

211. PRING J: 21st November 2014; *History month hears of Cameron's 'broken promise' to disabled veterans.*
http://www.disabilitynewsservice.com/history-month-launch-hears-camerons-brokenpromise-disabled-veterans/

212. McVEIGH T: 30th August 2014: *Rickets returns as poor families find healthy diets unaffordable:* The Guardian
http://www.theguardian.com/society/2014/aug/30/child-poverty-link-malnutritionrickets

213. CHANNEL FOUR NEWS: *Malnutrition a public health emergency, experts warn*
http://www.channel4.com/news/malnutrition-health-emergency-dwp-british-medicaljournal

214. STEWART M: May 2014: *UK Government Refuses to Accept Responsibility for identified Crimes Against Humanity*
http://disability-studies.leeds.ac.uk/files/library/GVT%20refuses%20responsibility%20for%20crimes%20against%20humanity%20-%20FINAL%20-%203rd%20May.pdf

215. BUTLER P: 20th October 2015: *UN inquiry considers alleged UK disability rights violations.* The Guardian
http://www.theguardian.com/society/2015/oct/20/un-inquiry-uk-disability-rightsviolations-cprd-welfare-cuts

216. STEWART M: June 2010: *Atos Healthcare or Disability Denial Factories*
http://www.whywaitforever.com/dwpatosveteranssummary.html

217. BARR B, TAYLOR-ROBINSON D., STUCKLER D, LOOPSTRA R, REEVES A, WHITEHEAD M: *'First do no harm': are disability assessments associated with adverse trends in mental health? A longitudinal ecological study.* BMJ 16th November 2015
http://jech.bmj.com/content/early/2015/10/26/jech-2015-206209 (Open Access)

218. BARR B, TAYLOR-ROBINSON D., STUCKLER D, LOOPSTRA R, REEVES A, WHITEHEAD M: *'First do no harm': are disability assessments associated with adverse trends in mental health? A longitudinal ecological study.* 16th November 2015
http://press.psprings.co.uk/jech/november/jech206209.pdf (Open Access)

219. LEWIS H: *Iain Duncan Smith resigns, citing disability cuts – and with a swipe at Osborne.* New Statesman 18th March 2016
http://www.newstatesman.com/politics/uk/2016/03/iain-duncan-smith-resigns-cabinet-over-disability-cuts

220. STEWART M: June 2010: *Atos Healthcare or Disability Denial Factories*
http://www.whywaitforever.com/dwpatosveteranssummary.html

CASH NOT CARE:
the planned demolition of the UK welfare state

MO STEWART

Foreword by Professor Peter Beresford
Illustrations by Dave Lupton of *Crippen* Cartoons